ISLAM

Text by
UMBERTO SCERRATO

Foreword by
RICHARD ETTINGHAUSEN

MONUMENTS OF CIVILIZATION

ISLAM

CASSELL
LONDON

CASSELL & COMPANY LIMITED
35 Red Lion Square, London WC1R 4SG
and at Sydney, Auckland, Toronto, Johannesburg
an affiliate of
Macmillan Publishing Co., Inc.,
New York

AUG 1976

English translation copyright © 1976 by
Mondadori, Milano-Kodansha, Tokyo; originally
published in Italian under the title *Grandi
Monumenti:* ISLAM: copyright © 1972 by
Mondadori, Milano-Kodansha, Tokyo; copyright ©
1972 by Kodansha Ltd., Tokyo, for the illustrations;
copyright ©1972 by Mondadori, Milano-Kodansha,
Tokyo, for the text.

First published in Great Britain 1976

ISBN 0 304 29695 3
Printed and bound in Italy by Mondadori, Verona

Editorial Director
GIULIANA NANNICINI

American Supervisor
JOHN BOWMAN

Graphics Editor
MAURIZIO TURAZZI

Frontispiece:
**Samarra (Iraq): A view of the ninth-century (A.D.) minaret that rises just outside the Great Mosque
of al-Mutawakkil and that has provided the other name for this mosque, al-Malwiya, "the spiral."**

CONTENTS

FOREWORD

In ancient times it took weeks and months to travel from one region of the Moslem world to another; the automobile reduced these long distances to days, and the jet plane does it in a few hours. In olden times, at the end of a long voyage by ship or caravan, the excitement of seeing new lands was further heightened by the sight of unfamiliar buildings decorated in a different manner. Today, however, when a tourist can visit within a few days such places as Istanbul, Cairo, and Isfahan, and be confronted with varied forms of architecture, the loss of the space-time element in travel is apt to leave the foreigner disoriented. A leafing through the following pages echoes this bewilderment. One senses that there must be some underlying themes; unable to grasp them, one is left amazed by the prevailing differences. The key, then, to an understanding and aesthetic enjoyment of Islamic art is to establish an awareness of its characteristic features.

There are two major categories of Islamic architecture: the religious and the secular. The group devoted to sacred purposes is by far the larger, not only because there were more mosques, but because respectful piety preserved them better. Outwardly nearly all mosques have as a distinctive element one or more tall towers, the minarets, from the top of which the faithful are called to prayer. Minarets take many shapes — square, cylindrical, polygonal, spiral, or a combination of several — with each region developing its specific type. In some cases the towers served exclusively to announce Islam's presence; in others, a pair of towers flanked decoratively the gates of religious buildings or the entrances to sanctuaries.

Another almost universal element of mosques was in the interior, the small niche, or *mihrab*, that marked the direction of Mecca, toward which the faithful had to face in prayer. What the *mihrab* lacked in size and structural significance it made up by its decoration; the various techniques included modeled and painted stucco, carved stone, marble incrustations, tiles, or mosaics formed by tesserae or cut faience. In all the major mosques, a pulpit stood next to the prayer niche. This pulpit consisted of several steps leading to a small platform crowned by a canopy. Its main decoration is the carving of the wooden or stone panels that cover the sides of the steps.

Although less universal, two other features characterize many mosques. One is that, unlike Christian churches, most mosques are wider than they are deep. This spatial orientation gives more worshipers a chance to be close to the wall with the *mihrab* — and thus "nearer" Mecca. Secondly, the covered prayer area of the mosque is usually preceded by an open courtyard; this is surrounded by arcades and also offers facilities for ritual washing before prayer.

In their main architectural forms, the majority of the large-scale mosques can be grouped into several types. The most numerous type nearly became adopted throughout the Moslem world; it was generally accepted in the first four to five centuries of Islamic domination, but later its plan became primarily restricted to the Arab-speaking world. This type consists of a hypostyle hall, essentially a hall where the roof is carried by columns or pillars set in parallel alignment with the walls. In those Mediterranean countries where Islam took root, the supports for the ceiling were slender marble columns from older buildings; in Iran and Iraq, the columns or pillars were built of brick and were therefore heavier. In large buildings these supports are numerous and offer spectacular vistas when viewed at an oblique angle.

To stress the importance and sanctity of the *mihrab* in the main mosques of the major cities, a small dome was placed over the square area in front of it. The nave leading to the *mihrab* and the aisle closest to the niche's wall were also widened. But whatever the form the interiors took, the Arab-type mosque gives the impression of accented uniformity — making for what one might call an egalitarian appearance. As to the exteriors, from the early tenth century on there was an endeavor to articulate the facade by means of porches, various types of niches, and real or blind arcades.

Another basic type of mosque appeared in Iran early in the twelfth century. The centers of the interior sides of the courtyard in the Iranian mosques were stressed by incorporating in them an *iwan*, a high, vaulted hall open to the courtyard. One of these halls forms the entrance to the building; the one opposite that leads to the square sanctuary chamber, covered by a dome, before the *mihrab*. The lateral wings of the main prayer area continue to be treated as hypostyle halls. The vaults of many *iwans* later were decorated with a series of small half-niches, the distinctive *muqarnas*, or stalactite device. Although the Iranian mosque might well be called the most dramatic of the various mosque types that evolved throughout the Islamic world, numerically and geographically it is the most limited type. Its layout, however, was also used throughout the Moslem world for religious seminaries, called *madrasas*; the *iwans* served as lecture halls, and the rest of the side walls were subdivided into rooms for students. The Iranian mosque form was also employed for hospitals in Syria and Anatolia and as caravanserais in Iran.

Yet another group of mosques were those made by the Turks during the fourteenth and fifteenth centuries and reaching their apogee in the sixteenth century. These cannot be reduced to a standard type, as the architects were constantly experimenting with and regrouping the constituent architectural features. The dominant element of the Turkish mosque was the dome. The designers first used domes in numbers, then singly and of an ever-increasing size and combined with two or four supporting half-domes. It is this huge, earth-hugging cupola with its dependent range of coordinated secondary features and its juxtaposed slender minarets pointing dartlike toward heaven that has established the image of the Turkish mosque in so many Westerners' minds.

India, meanwhile, under the Moslem Mogul emperors, developed by the seventeenth century a mosque type that was a hybrid of the other major types. The hypostyle hall (often with beautiful marble pillars) was combined with three large onion-shaped domes over the sanctuary (as it was done in some Turkish mosques), while the Iranian entrance *iwan* was developed into a large gateway.

Probably the second largest group of noteworthy religious buildings throughout the Moslem world are the mausoleums, constructed as burial places for rulers, holy men, and such personages. Unlike the mosques, they are usually found outside the towns. Many are of modest size, while others are monumental in scope. Architecturally they fall into two groups: tower-like buildings with conical or globular roofs; or large domed structures of round, square, or octagonal shape.

As for the other major category of Moslem buildings, the secular, the most obviously appealing are the palaces. Yet comparatively few palaces have been preserved, and those only from the twelfth century on, with the majority being much later. All of them, including the older and excavated ones, show the standard two-part organization of a Near Eastern house: the public part for official receptions, meetings, and public prayer, all mainly limited to the male members of this society; and the private sector of the house, reserved for the family life centering around the women and children. Airily built and extremely ornate, Moslem palaces are composed of individual units that are of a varied nature. But from the fourteenth century on, there is a preference for isolated pavilions with courtyards surrounded by greenery and with a central body of water. The setting of these palace pavilions, their interior organization, and the elaborate ornamentation provide ever-changing, enchanting vistas, so that these buildings have become an image, even in our culture, of constant delight.

The remaining secular structures of the Moslem world fall into two groups. The first is military, including those for the protection of the medieval cities or of the places of government within them. Hence we find extensive ramparts, mighty gates, and imposing citadels, all built strongly and beautifully functional. The other major group serves the purpose of a highly mobile trading society and includes bazaars, warehouses, fortified caravanserais, bridges, and even fountains where a weary porter might find refreshment. In addition, there are individual constructions that have been almost miraculously preserved, such as a cistern or a flood gauge, where again a high degree of civil engineering and an innate sense of beauty present remarkable ensembles.

There are many more aspects to Islamic architecture, of course, but here we have space only to single out the all-important decorative elements. In some early buildings, colorful mosaics decorated walls or floors, but these have now mostly disappeared. Likewise, the painting on carved or molded stucco paneling has bleached out. What decorations survive from structures built before the twelfth century, therefore, are carvings in stone or stucco or artfully set bricks or terra-cotta pieces in which the artistic effect results from the play of light over the uneven monochrome surfaces. Starting in the eleventh century, materials with more durable colors came into use, even on the exteriors of buildings. One encounters incrustations of stones of different colors, mosaics made of bricks covered with different glazes or composed of cut faience pieces, and painted tiles. With this flood of color there is suddenly a new aesthetic dimension to Islamic buildings (or in their later restorations or remodelings). These touches of color greatly enliven the cities and landscapes where duller hues of brown, gray, and red otherwise predominate.

It is this vital and stimulating aspect of Moslem architecture that makes the exclusive use of color plates in Professor Scerrato's book such a significant factor. And with this as an aesthetic attraction, and now with some sense of the underlying themes, the reader should be prepared to proceed through this marvelous world of Islamic monuments.

Richard Ettinghausen

INTRODUCTION

The true origins of the monuments and culture portrayed in this volume would have to be sought back in those distant millenniums when Bedouin tribes periodically broke through into the strip of land that was serving as the cradle of ancient civilization. Forming a great arch known as the Fertile Crescent, bordered on the east by the Tigris and Euphrates Rivers, and on the west by the Mediterranean, this strip of arable land hemmed in the great Syrian-Mesopotamian desert that, to the south, merged with the desert of the Arabian peninsula. To stave off the pressures generated by sharp population increases among the Bedouins in this peninsula and by the lure of booty offered by the rich sedentary societies, the inhabitants of the Fertile Crescent made the most of their own close-knit organization, creating a dynamic civilization supported by the land reclaimed from semi-arid territory. Their aim was to protect the more urbanized areas by effecting a kind of social "promotion" of the local tribes, allotting them a role in the intense commercial traffic through the area, which was virtually a mandatory route for a great part of the ancient world.

This balance of forces held for many centuries, until toward the end of the seventh century A.D. the phenomenon assumed a convulsive form that turned out to be irreversible. It was no longer a question of a number of scattered, disorganized tribes often fighting among themselves and which, having given vent to their potential furor locally, either returned to their bases or allowed themselves to be drawn into the orbit of the great empires holding sway in the Fertile Crescent. Rather, this time all the tribes united in their efforts and inexorably pressed forward onto these lands of ancient civilizations — at first, those controlled by the Byzantine and Sassanid empires. In only a few years, the former was stripped of the bulk of its Asian possessions — which in fact had been reduced to Anatolia — as well as of its holdings in Africa; meanwhile, the Sassanid empire, based in Iran, was completely wiped out. The explanation of these shattering developments is but one part of one of history's great epics: the rise of Islam.

The Arab tribes had found cohesion which enabled them, at least for a moment, to set aside their age-old antagonisms in a new religion with an egalitarian tinge. This religion, affecting the totality of the lives of individuals, involving them on the social and political as well as spiritual level, paved the way to the molding of a theocratic type of state. This was Islam, the last of the great historical religions, preached by Muhammad — "the Messenger of God," "the Seal of the Prophets" — to whom over a period of twenty years, from about 612 to Muhammad's death in 632, God revealed His Word, His Law. As set down in the *Koran* ("recitation"), the sacred book of Islam is dogmatically held to be the uncreated attribute of God, coexistent with Him. Islam is a totally monotheistic religion, well summed up in the formula of the profession of faith, the *shahada*: "There is no God but Allah, and Muhammad is His prophet." Islam means "submission to God," and hence regulates the entire life of the Moslem — "one who surrenders" to the faith. (The Arabic for Moslem also gave rise, through the Persian and Turkish languages, to another name for an adherent to Islam, a Mussulman.) The source of Islam's law, the *sharia*, ("the right path," "the beaten path"), is first and foremost the *Koran*. There is also *sunna*, which means "the way to conduct oneself," like our idea of custom or practice; but *sunna* is specifically based on the sayings and decisions attributed to the Prophet Muhammad and handed down in the *hadith* ("tradition"), which in turn becomes the source of doctrine according to the principle of *imitatio Muhammadis* affirmed in the *Koran*. And since Muhammad is so patently crucial to any understanding of Islam, we must take a moment to review his life.

Muhammad was born into a not especially prosperous family of the Quraysh tribe in Mecca, a town in (Saudi) Arabia. It was in Mecca that he began his preaching, collecting a ragged community primarily among the humble, a community that ran up against extremely harsh opposition from Mecca's ruling aristocracy, to the point that Muhammad was forced to abandon his native town and emigrate to Yatrib. This was later called Medina an-Nabi, "the city of the Prophet." The date was 622, and marked the beginning of the Moslem era, the Hegira, which means "flight," or "migration." Showing great political ability as well as religious insight, Muhammad managed to set up in Medina a community governed by a constitution, or charter, under which the various components of the population found themselves united, thus breaking in a revolutionary manner the age-old tribal customs based on consanguinity.

In year two of the Hegira, Muhammad decreed that the direction of prayer, the *qibla*, was no longer to be Jerusalem but the Kaaba in Mecca, a cubelike shrine that had long served as a center of worship for the Arab tribes. Tradition claimed that worship at the Kaaba had been established by Abraham, the patriarch of the Semitic peoples, who was also credited with being a monotheist, but that in time the shrine had been taken over by idolaters. The reconsecration of

Praise be to God, the Lord of all creatures, the
most merciful, the King of the day of judgment. Thee do we worship, and of Thee do we
beg assistance. Direct us in the right way, in the
way of those to whom Thou hast been gra-
cious, not of those with whom Thou art angry,
nor of those who go astray.

Koran (I:1–7)

THE SURA OF TRUE FAITH

In the name of God, the merciful one, say:
"God is one God, the eternal God; He beget-
teth not, neither is He begotten; and there is
not any one like unto Him."

Koran (CXII:1–3)

the Kaaba to Allah has rightly been considered one of Muhammad's most inspired and revolutionary acts, for by this the Prophet brought into Islam the
sanctuary of the forefathers and also absorbed the ritual pilgrimage to Mecca,
both major aspects of pre-Islamic Arab religiosity. This enabled Muhammad to
present himself no longer as a rebel but as a reformer sent by God to purify the
common place of worship of all the Arab peoples. He made his victorious return
into Mecca in 630, winning over to his cause ever more numerous throngs of
followers throughout Arabia. His credo, strong in its simplicity and egalitarian
message, was easily accepted.

The core of Islam is based on "five pillars": the profession of faith (*shahada*);
the ritual prayer (*salat*); the obligatory payment of alms (*zakat*); fasting in the
month of Ramadhan (*sawm*); and the pilgrimage to Mecca (*hajj*). To these must
be added the religious duty of the holy war (*jihad*) against infidels, frequently
urged in the *Koran*. The world was divided into two parts, "the seat of Islam" (*dar
al-Islam*) and "the seat of war" (*dar al-harb*); to this latter belonged the pagans and
"book people," Jews and Christians (and Zoroastrians would be added later), so
called because they belonged to religions that Islam recognized as revealed but
considered surpassed by the teachings of Muhammad. Pagans were given the
choice of either becoming converts or being slain. The Jews, Christians, and
Zoroastrians were to be fought as political entities until they submitted to Moslem rule, under which they were to be allowed to practice their own religions in
exchange for the payment of a tax (*jizya*). They would always have an inferior
social status, but would be protected (*dhimmi*) with a personal statute.

Upon the death of Muhammad in 632, the small state he had founded which,
in addition to Mecca and Medina in the Hijaz district of Arabia, included a large
part of the neighboring Bedouin tribes, was threatened with collapse. The death
of the leader sparked a new flare-up of old tribal disputes; this was the famous
ridda, "secession." In dying, Muhammad had named no successors, but the
community had elected a leader, a Caliph — that is, a vicar, or deputy, of the
Prophet — guardian and executor of the law and temporal head of the community. The first Caliph was Abu Bakr, Muhammad's father-in-law; he was
succeeded in 634 by Omar. During the decade in which Omar was head of the
Moslem community, he laid the groundwork for the Islamic state of the early
centuries. Once he had the situation in hand, Omar directed the turbulent
energies of the Bedouin tribes outside Arabia toward a universalization of the
dar al-Islam, spurred by the religious ideal of the *jihad* and the mirage of rich
booty. In a relatively short time, the Byzantine empire was thrown into disastrous
disarray; Syria and Palestine were swiftly occupied; in 635 Damascus was taken;
in 636, at the battle of the Yarmuk River, a tributary of the Jordan, the army of
the Byzantine emperor Heraclius was defeated; Jerusalem was occupied in 638,
Caesarea in 640. Also, in 640–41, Egypt was captured and the Arabs established
their center at Fostat (actually, al-Fustat, after the name of a rampart, *fossatum*,
on the site), near where modern Cairo would later rise. In 642 it was the turn of
Alexandria to fall. Meanwhile, the Moslems attacked Persia, and with the victory
of Qadisiyya, near Hira, in 636–37, the Sassanid army was put to flight and the
Arab armies rushed into the Babylon area and occupied Ctesiphon. In 641–42,
the battle of Ninavand, near Hamadan, decided the destiny of the Persian
empire, and the Iranian highlands were open to Islamic conquest.

It seems prodigious that only a handful of Bedouins, poorly armed and
knowing little about the crafts of war, should get the better of such colossuses.
But in fact the ancient world had long been in disarray, and Byzantium and
Persia had been prostrated by long wars between themselves and by other wars
along their endless frontiers. Their armies, moreover, made up chiefly of
mercenaries, were devoid of ideals that could hold them together. The two
empires were taken by surprise along borders not equipped to oppose an enemy
that had heretofore been kept at bay by mere "policing" operations or by del-
egating the job of containing Bedouin infiltrations to vassal Arab states such as
the Ghassanids, tributaries of the Byzantines, or the Lakhmids, tributaries of the
Sassanids. The populations of the territories affected, weary of oppressive
regimes, accepted with indifference, if not enthusiasm, their new masters. The
bulk of the populations in the Syrian-Mesopotamian region, furthermore, were
Semitic like the Bedouins, and as a result felt more akin to the Arabs than to their
Greek or Persian overlords.

With political realism — but also because they had no choice, lacking as they
did the necessary cadres — the Arabs left intact as much as they could of the
structures of preceding administrations. Virtually none of the entire Christian
and Jewish populations of the Fertile Crescent was forced to change faith. Instead, the new Islamic rulers accepted their mere submission and the payment of
the *jizya*; this tax, along with any war booty, guaranteed a far from negligible
revenue for the coffers of the new Islamic state. Yet even these elements alone

9

Piety lieth not in turning one's face to East or West, but true piety is his that believeth in God and in the Last Day, and in His Angels and in the Book and in the Prophets, and that giveth of what he hath, for the love of God, to his relations and to orphans and to the poor and to travelers and to beggars and for the ransom of prisoners; his it is that prayeth and payeth the tithe, who keepeth the promises he hath made, who is patient in pain and suffering and in time of famine; these are the sincere, these fear God!

Koran (II:177)

And whosoever desireth a religion that is not that of Islam, shall not be accepted by God, and in the Other Life shall be one of those who have lost.

Koran (II:85)

would not explain the quick success and lasting nature of the conquest. One must further recognize that Islam drew its strength from the fact that it was sinking its roots into a territory, the ancient Near East, where across the millenniums a unified culture and a common religious disposition had come into being.

Conversions in Islam were generally spontaneous, although the motive was often an economic one, particularly the desire to pay lower taxes — it was not by chance that the first among the elite to convert were the great landowners — or for reasons of social promotion. As a rule, the spread of Islam was from the cities to the countryside; Islam was, in fact, essentially an urban religion. It came into being in an urban environment — that of commercial Mecca — to which the Prophet belonged, and it needed the city to realize its religious and social programs. The Prophet saw a threat in the life of the peasant or the nomad. Some of his *hadiths* that throw a light on this fear of his have become famous. This also explains why the peasant was to be at the very bottom of Islam's social scale; indeed, Moslem law was to favor especially the merchant class.

We have noted that the virtual "explosion" of Islam as an imperial force occurred under the second Caliph, Omar. After Omar was knifed to death in 644 by a Persian slave, Othman was elected to the caliphate. Son-in-law of the Prophet, Othman belonged to the Umayyads, a wealthy Meccan merchant family, also of the Quraysh tribe. He himself had been one of the Prophet's first disciples, and his high-ranking position no doubt contributed a great deal to the success of the new religion. A pious man of sincere faith, but weak in character, he was never to stand out as a great personality. His election generated much discontent, particularly because it meant that power had returned to the hands of the Meccan aristocracy, the very people who had originally opposed Muhammad and who had accepted Islamism with a strong dose of opportunism. The discontent was accentuated by Othman's nepotism. Grave dissatisfaction was also sparked by the violation of the principle promulgated by Caliph Omar that forbade individual Arabs to own lands outside of Arabia itself: The conquered territories, often abandoned by their former owners who had belonged to the Byzantine or Sassanid social structure, were supposed to become the common property of the Moslem state. This principle was circumvented by the system of concessions, which allowed individual families to amass great properties and fortunes to the detriment of the community at large. The financial difficulties were now coming to the fore, particularly since the steady flow of booty had dwindled to a trickle because of the decline in conquests; problems had also arisen in connection with the distribution of tax revenues, which some wanted deposited in the central treasury and others wanted spent where collected. These economic, financial, and social reasons for discontent, which in the Islamic framework could not but take on ethical–religious overtones as well, led in the end to the assassination of Othman in 656. This was followed by a series of civil struggles that were to plague Islam for a long time to come.

The next Caliph to be elected was Ali, Muhammad's cousin and son-in-law — he had married the Prophet's daughter, Fatima — as well as the father of male children directly descended from Muhammad. Not having wanted to or not having been able to prosecute those responsible for the murder of Othman, Ali's election was contested by Othman's family, the Umayyads, who demanded satisfaction for the affront to the dignity of the caliphate and wanted the murder to be paid for in blood. Ali was renowned as a brave man, a faithful and expert interpreter of the correct customs (*sunna*) of the Prophet, and a capable speaker; but he was hardly a great politician, hemmed in by rigid patterns as he was. And if this were not enough, he was compelled to operate in highly unfavorable circumstances. Muawiya, nephew of Othman and the powerful governor of Syria, rose up against Ali. The dispute was resolved in favor of Muawiya and the Umayyads, and he was elected Caliph by his troops in 658, thus founding the Umayyad dynasty. Ali was assassinated at Kufa in 661, the third of the first four caliphs to die this way.

Such violent episodes were of crucial importance for the early phase of Islam in that they revealed the schisms dividing the Moslem world. On the one hand there was the majority called the Sunnites (based on *sunna*, the proper way, orthodox), and they recognized the legitimacy of Muawiya. They also recognized the first four caliphs, whom they called "the rightly guided ones," and whose authority came from the principle established at the time of the election of Abu Bakr — specifically, the caliphate was the appanage of the Quraysh tribe, the tribe of the Prophet, from among whose members the man with the sturdiest faith and the most outstanding ability should be elected. And then there were the partisans of Ali who were called Shiites (from *shiat Ali,* "the party of Ali"), who denied the legitimacy of the three preceding caliphs and contended that the only one with the right to be elected was Ali and that the caliphate should remain in the direct line of descent of the Prophet's family.

In addition to the political aspect, this split assumed a religious dimension. In

Sunnism, the caliph is the vicar of the Prophet as defender of the law and material leader of the community; religious authority rests wholly on the *Koran* and on an interpretation based on the consensus of the community, the *ijma*. Shiism does not recognize this consensus interpretation of the *Koran* or other traditions. It recognizes instead the *imam,* "the leader," as the authority for the imparting of lessons, and holds that Muhammad had named Ali as the interpreter of doctrine and that Ali was to name his own successor, who would in turn name his own. These successors were believed by the Shiites to possess a degree of "divinity," an idea that seemed blasphemous to Sunnite Islam. Meanwhile, rising in opposition to both of these two major groupings were the Kharijites ("the seceders," "the rebels"), strict conformists who denied that the Quraysh tribe had any special rights, and asserted that the caliph could be any Moslem — irrespective of his race, "even an Abyssinian slave" — so long as he had the necessary qualifications. This, namely, was the purity needed to make him "the finest of all Moslems." But their fanatical strictness was to condemn the Kharijites to playing an ever narrower role, as compared to the Sunnites and Shiites, in the Islamic world.

But while it is useful and often necessary to make the various distinctions that enable us to speak of not one but many Islams — that of the origins, the classical variety, the modern, the Sunnite, the Shiite, the Kharijite, that of the city, the desert, the villages, the plurilingual, the polyethical, and now pluri-national varieties — one must not lose sight of the fact that, as the noted authority on Islam, André Miquel, has put it, "Islam remains what the Moslems themselves consider it: one and indivisible."

The fundamental contribution, indispensable to this Islamic culture, was made by the Arabs with the vehicles of the religion — the language and writing, which played such a decisive role as a unifying superstructure. Nor should one lose sight of the Arabs' great poetry and taste for oratory. Islam, a legalistic religion that regulated every moment of the everyday life of its faithful, could not but condition all its manifestations and forms of expression, the visual arts in particular. And in the face of considerable regional variations, Islamic culture has a basic aesthetic unity that, as was made clear by the Islamist Louis Massignon, is to be sought in the unities of the Islamic religion, with its fundamental metaphysical principle — contradicting the classical Western one of man as the measure of all things — that God alone is immutable and eternal. Time, according to this principle, is nothing more than a succession of instants that are not connected one with the other and that are even reversible. Everything is changeable and unstable, transient and accidental; forms are unreal, they do not exist in themselves; they are creative acts of the one sole God, the uncorporeal, non-locatable, the all-powerful.

One result of this was a vigorous rejection of an art that imitates nature, for it is seen as a blasphemous bid to mimic the inimitable work of God (although, as we shall shortly see, this rejection was not as absolute as is sometimes claimed). In Islamic art, an abstract, allusive means of expression was developed. Natural forms were conventionalized and rendered unreal, repetitious, fragmentary references to the transitoriness of terrestial life as compared to the infinite, the changeable compared to eternity. This attitude is reflected in the frequent use of poor materials in architecture, such as stucco, unbaked brick, even mud, as well as by the tendency to render the structure of things "disorganic," whether they be objects or edifices. Surfaces are covered with abstract decorations in keeping with a principle tending to ignore the actual structure being covered. In some cases, the structure itself, particularly in architecture, is given an abstract decorative treatment, with a tendency toward splitting up or "atomizing" the various elements. This theological–aesthetic explains the outstanding role played in Islamic art by the arabesque — an abstract reduction of floral or foliage forms — by geometric interlacings, and by calligraphy. Under Islam, in fact, calligraphy was considered an art form par excellence, since writing was the instrument that made it possible to set down the word of God in the *Koran* and spread it through the world. Arabic script's potential for abstraction and artificiality fully satisfied the legal and emotional needs of religion. There were two basic types of script: the angular kind known as Kufic (since it was believed to have been invented at Kufa, a city in Iraq that briefly served as the capital of the early Islamic caliphate); and a rounded, cursive form, the oldest variety of which was known as *nashki* (while a later, more elegant derivative of this was called *thuluth*). Arabic writing was the object of constant experimentation and of decisive importance in shaping the aesthetic taste of the nations of Islam.

But if it is not already clear, art did not have an autonomous function in Islam; it was subordinate to larger objectives, and the artist was deprived of freedom of expression. Even if we admit that our description is somewhat schematic and "orthodox," having emerged in a rather late period, yet it is indicative of the

THE DUTY OF HOLY WAR

You are enjoined to make war against the infidels even though this may displease you: for you may well be displeased by that which is to your good, as it may be that you like a thing which instead is harmful to you; but God knoweth and you know not.

You will be asked if it is just to make war in the Holy Month. Reply: "To make war in that month is grave sin. But it is yet graver sin in the eyes of God, in that month to turn away from the Way of God, to blaspheme against Him and against the Holy Temple and drive out His people, since idolatry is worse than killing, and they will not cease to fight against you until they succeed in making you an apostate to your Faith. As for those amongst you who, having abandoned the Faith, die denying God, vain will be their works in this and the other world, and they will be condemned to the fires, where they will remain throughout eternity.

"But those who believed and who went out of their native land and fought in the cause of God, can hope in the pity of God, for God is pitiful and forgiveth."

Koran (II:216–18)

fundamental tendency. The taboo on the representation of the human form in Islam was, particularly in the early centuries, more theological than practical. Indeed, the *Koran* expresses no explicit condemnation in this regard, except perhaps in connection with statues representing idols. The rigid prohibition was to be generated by tradition, with the aim of striking out all references to paganism. Even then the condemnation was not respected in the same way at all times and places; exceptions were to arise, for example, in the Syria of the Umayyads, the Mesopotamia of the Abbasids, and in the Iranian region. Nevertheless, it is clear that, with a few rare exceptions, neither the human nor animal figure was represented in places of worship, the mosques, where ornamentation was always to be abstract. Figurative elements — statues, reliefs, or paintings, either within architectural settings or on smaller objects — were for the most part reserved for private and secular works. They sprang from the desires of the aristocracy, and were based on the glorification of the sovereign; it was not by chance that such figurative elements, even in palaces, were largely confined to the private sectors, not to the public areas.

Miniature paintings, however outstanding they were to become within the artistic realm of Islam, are not, as Massignon has observed, a typically Moslem art, and the fact that they flourished may be explained by the circulation of these works among an elite. As a result, the social position of those who worked in the field of the visual arts was not a high one; this was in part a reflection of ancient attitudes, a suspicion throughout the sparsely settled Arab lands of all those connected with manual activities, who were often in a servile condition. As in our own Middle Ages, the artist was for the most part cloaked in anonymity. It was only in the fifteenth and sixteenth centuries, and outside the Arab world — particularly in the Iranian and Turkish worlds — that the artist and artisan began to come into focus, and that they were accepted into the class of leaders, even honored. But even though some of them equaled in fame those supreme artists of Islam, the calligraphers, they never had the political or social weight enjoyed by the poets and literati in Islam's early centuries.

Under Islam, then, art plays a basically ancillary role to religion, but in the face of all its local conditionings it is anything but uniform, giving rise to a surprising variety of styles reflecting the ethnic, cultural, technological and other traditions of the countries in which it developed. One of the most eloquent testimonials of this is the architecture, which among other things is one of Islam's most vital manifestations as well as practical servants. Islam was essentially a city religion, and as a result it found in the city its basic elements, which were to take shape ever more clearly in the first decades of the conquest, when, emerging from Arabia, the new religion found it necessary to render its triumph in tangible forms. Georges Marçais defined these elements as the mosque, the public baths, and the bazaar.

The Islamic monument par excellence, of course, is the congregational mosque, where particularly in the early stage the community met to fulfill the legal precept of prayer in common but also to participate in all the important decisions regarding society. The baths, previously unknown in Arabia, were a loan from the Roman-Byzantine world that Islam adapted to the needs of ritual ablutions. Concentrated in the bazaar were all activities of an economic, handicraft-industrial, and commercial nature; it was divided into sectors according to the various occupations. The bazaar was a legacy of the classical and oriental worlds, but under Islam the people of the bazaar were mere instruments of the government, a fact that was to deprive Islamic craftsmen of all powers of contract, although the bazaar in other ways did serve as a force for more progressive tendencies. Closely bound up with the economic activities of the bazaar were two other types of structures. One was set aside for the storing of goods to be sold later, and in the Near East this was usually called a *qaisariyya,* a term derived from Greek and referring originally to a state warehouse; the other, known by the Persian name *khan,* was for merchandise in transit; functionally and structurally the *khan* was like the stage posts of the caravans along trade routes, and is usually translated as caravansary.

The care dedicated to such commercial structures was entirely covered by the wing of the Islamic religion, and we might refer to a passage from Maxine Rodinson that throws light on this attitude: "Tradition and the *Koran* contemplate with equal favor economic activity, the seeking of profit, commerce, and hence production for the market. It is even possible to find dithyrambic formulas addressed to the merchant. It is narrated that the Prophet himself said: 'The sincere, honest merchant will be found [on Judgment Day] among the prophets, the just, and the martyrs'; 'on Judgment Day the honest merchant will sit in the shadow of the throne of God'; and 'merchants are the couriers of this world, the faithful custodians of God on earth.' According to Holy Tradition, commerce is a privileged way of earning one's livelihood. 'If you draw profit

1. *Allahu akbar!* God is Supreme! (repeated four times)
2. *Ashhadu an la ilaha illa 'llah!* I bear witness that there is no other god but God. (repeated twice)
3. *ashhadu anna Muhammadan rasulu 'llah!* I bear witness that Mahomet is the Messenger of God! (twice)
4. *hayya 'ala 's-salat!* Come to Prayer! (twice with face turned right)
5. *hayya 'ala 'l-falah!* Come to Prosperity! (twice, face turned left)
6. *Allahu akbar!* God is supreme! (twice)
7. *La ilaha illa 'llah!* There is no other god than God!

In the *adhan* calling the faithful to dawn prayer, after phrase 5 comes the cry: *as-salatu khairun min an-naum!* Prayer is better than sleep! (repeated twice)

from what is permissible, your action is a *jihad* [that is, equal to the holy war or any other effort on behalf of the divine cause]. If you use these earnings for your family and your relatives, it will be a *sadaqa* (a work of charity). And in truth, an honest *dirham* (a silver coin) from commerce is worth more than a *dirham* earned in some other fashion.' "

Meantime, there were still other basic structures of the Islamic world. The holy war and the need to consolidate frontiers gave rise to the *ribat,* a fortified monastery fitted out with small cells (where the warrior-monks [*ghazi*] lived) and equipped with a prayer hall and a watchtower that served as both a minaret and a symbol of Islam. As the ambitions of Islam expanded, the *madrassa* was developed: this was a theological college where the custodians of orthodoxy specialized in the teachings of religious disciplines, particularly Islamic law. Along with these, hospitals, homes for the aged, and refectories, were often built for the community. As for the many types of private homes built throughout the immense territory of Islam, even they mirror Moslem social demands in their basic designs, such as in the large vestibules or the areas reserved for women. With some few exceptions — in Mecca, Cairo, and Baghdad — dwellings were built horizontally, a feature intended to mortify the pride of builders, doubtless under the impact of the lesson in humility in a saying attributed to Muhammad: "Building is the most pointless of the undertakings that can devour the riches of a believer." (Even for buildings for the community, fragile materials were often used.) Note, though, that unlike Christianity, Islam had no objection to wealth as such, nor to the enjoyment of terrestrial blessings; if God placed man in this world, he should be able, within the conditions of the Law, to enjoy it.

The residence of the sovereign, the palace, which also became identified with the seat of the government, the *dar al-imara,* likewise mirrored the social demands of Islam. And even though it did not tend to have those characteristics of solidity that as a rule were sought for in structures of a religious nature, the palace bore a distinct imprint "so that it might symbolize the temporal authority to which Islam attributes an incontestable, permanent value. Islam recognized this authority whether it was accompanied by a spiritual magisterium, as was the case with the authority of the Caliph under the Prophet's aegis and delegated later by the Caliph to his representatives, or whether it was a simple military power, established by force but obeyed by the subjects in that it defended the prestige of Islam and assured its triumph. Every structure erected for the direct use of the reigning dynasty therefore reflected the majesty of sovereign power expressed in the vastness of the courtyard onto which it faced and in the nobility of the ceremonies exalting its splendor." (Sourdel-Thomine). For the most part, therefore, art in the Moslem realm was to be of palatine inspiration, closely bound up with the tastes and tendencies of the ruling prince.

In keeping with its ideals, Islam promoted an active urban life and founded many cities (while destroying quite a few others, it must be said). All in all, the phenomenon was a spectacular one, particularly if compared to the urban panorama of medieval Europe, where only a few cities — Constantinople is an example — attained a population of ten thousand; the Islamic world included numerous large cities, with populations that frequently exceeded one hundred thousand, such as Baghdad or Cairo. Yet it is not easy, although often attempted, to speak of the "Islamic city," for this is a notion that escapes a precise definition. According to the most recent research, the cities of Islam, taken as physical entities and human communities, were in no way different from the usual medieval city. Beyond this, however, it must once again be stressed that Islamic institutions were all concentrated in the cities and that these latter shaped all of Islam's activities.

But the most tangible embodiment of all of Islam's realities and ideals remains its architecture. Although unified in its motivations, it cannot be claimed that its manifestations were unified, for they were spread out over more than a thousand years and involved three continents rich in totally different artistic traditions. We are to be viewing here only a highly summary and schematic picture of all this, and even at that the subject's complexity has posed many problems. Since the architecture documented in these pages is for the most part that of the "official" kind, an expression of the power and the sovereigns of the time, we have preferred to adopt a division into sections usually based on the major dynasties that kept united, if only for a short time, or that divided up, the *dar al-Islam.* This criterion has not always proven entirely satisfactory, but within limits it enables us to perceive some chronological and geographical order behind the monuments of Islam.

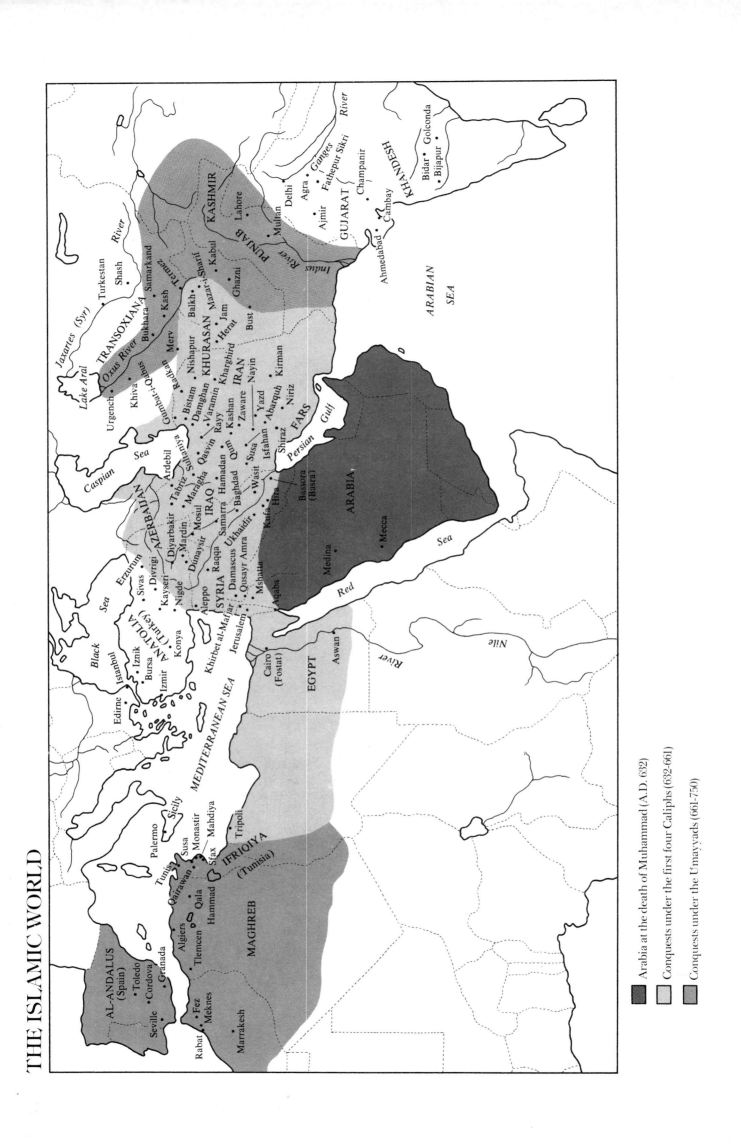

THE ISLAMIC WORLD

Turkestan • Shash
Jaxartes (Syr) River

Lake Aral

Urgench •
Khiva •
Gumbat-i-Qabus •

Caspian
Sea

Ardebil •
AZERBAIJAN
Tabriz •
Maragha •
Diyarbakir • Mardin •
Dünaysir •

Erzurum •
Sivas •
Divrigi •

ANATOLIA
(Turkey)

Kayseri •
Nigde •
Konya •

Istanbul • Iznik
Bursa •
Izmir •

Edirne •

Black
Sea

Palermo •
Sicily

Tunis •
Qairawan •
Algiers • Tlemcen • Qala
Hammad

AL-ANDALUS
(Spain)
Toledo •
Cordova •
Seville • Granada

Rabat •
Fez • Meknes

Marrakesh •

MAGHREB

MEDITERRANEAN SEA

Susa
Monastir
Sfax • Mahdiya
IFRIQIYA
(Tunisia)

Tripoli •

EGYPT

Cairo
(Fostat) •

Aswan •

Nile River

TRANSOXIANA
Oxus River
Samarkand •
Bukhara •
Kash •

Merv • Rabkan

Nishapur •
Bistam •
Damghan •
Varamin •
Rayy •
Qasvin •
Qum •
Hamadan •
Suhaniya
Susa •
Isfahan •
Shiraz •

KHURASAN
Mazar-i-Sharif
Balkh •
Herat •
Jam •
Kharghird •
Nayin •
IRAN
Zaware • Abarquh
Yazd •
Kirman •
Niriz •
FARS

Termez •

KASHMIR
Lahore •
Multan •
Kabul •
Ghazni •

Bust •

PUNJAB
Indus River

Delhi •
Ajmir • Agra • Fathepur Sikri
Ganges River

GUJARAT
Ahmedabad •
Cambay •

Champanir •

KHANDESH
Bidar • Golconda
Bijapur •

ARABIAN
SEA

Baghdad •
Samarra
IRAQ
Mosul •
Raqqa •
Ukhaidir •
Kufa •
Hira
Wasit •
SYRIA
Damascus
Aleppo •
Khirbet al-Maffar •
Jerusalem •
Qusayr Amra •
Mshatta •
Aqaba •

Persian
Gulf

Bassora
(Basra) •

ARABIA

Medina •
Mecca •

Red
Sea

Arabia at the death of Muhammad (A.D. 632)

Conquests under the first four Caliphs (632-661)

Conquests under the Umayyads (661-750)

ISLAM

ORIGINS OF ISLAMIC ARCHITECTURE

A miniature by Ab al-Razzaq, belonging to a manuscript executed at Herat in 1494–95, a copy of the *Khamsa*, "The Five Poems" (also called "The Five Treasures"), the work of the celebrated Persian poet, Nizami of Ganja (1141–1204). In the first of these poems, the poet sings of the Prophet Muhammad's ascension to heaven, which according to legend began at the Kaaba in Mecca, represented conventionally at the bottom of this miniature. The trip took place during the night, and Muhammad's swift mount, Buraq, appeared to have the head of a lovely angel.

It is one of several ironies in this survey of the inextricable relationships between a religion and its architecture that we must start with this generalization: the Arabs who launched the Islamic religion as an international imperial and cultural force knew no genuine architecture of their own. The modest dwellings in the scattered sedentary centers of the Hijaz region of Arabia such as Mecca and Medina hardly deserve the term "architecture." Indeed, the building abilities of the mass of Bedouins who made up the early Islamic contingents did not go beyond tent construction. Of the mosque, or *masjid* — that is, the place of prostration, but in reality not only the place of worship but also the political and social center of Islamic life — these early Arabs had no idea, architecturally speaking, and its eventual form was the result of an evolutionary process that involved an entire generation.

That the Arabs had no familiarity with architecture is shown by the tradition that when the Quraysh tribesmen wanted to rebuild the semi-demolished Kaaba of Mecca in 608, they had to rely on a certain Baqum, a shipwrecked sailor who was apparently an Ethiopian. Referred to by the sources as "carpenter and master builder," Baqum used the lumber of his wrecked ship for the Kaaba's walls, employing a typically Ethiopian technique based on a mixture of wood and stone. For the reconstruction of the great mosque of Kufa in 670, ordered by the Umayyad governor Ziyad ibn Abihi, the historian Tabari (who died in 923) tells us that indigenous builders "of the temples of ignorance" were called in — that is, non-Moslems, since the governor "declared himself incapable of expressing what he wanted."

The first mosques we know of are those founded in the cities of Iraq, and these are without architectural pretensions. That of Bassora (Basra), the simple Arab military camp that later gave rise to the important city, was simply traced out on the ground, perhaps protected by bundles of sticks around the perimeter. In 638 a roof was added on the *qibla* side — that facing Mecca. The Kufa mosque of 638 was a square plot of land, its dimensions of some 330 feet on each side having been determined, it was claimed, by the range of four arrows shot by an archer toward the four cardinal points. It was not enclosed by a wall but by a ditch. The *qibla* side was covered by a roof supported by columns.

The mosque founded at Fostat (the first Moslem settlement near what was to become Cairo) in 641–42 by Amr ibn al-As, the conqueror of Egypt, was a small edifice measuring 95 by 55 feet, with two doors on each side except that of the *qibla*. Still missing was the court (*sahn*), which was not added until later. The roof was flat, most likely supported by palm trunks. Yet crude as this structure was, it was based on the model of the ancient Egyptian hypostyle halls — just as the mosque at Kufa was probably based on the ancient Persian pillared halls of the *apadana* type. In the Syrian region, the Arabs preferred to use the actual churches they expropriated from, or in some cases shared with, the Christians.

Even from what has been sketched here, it is evident that the early Moslems had no clear or consistent concept of an architectural design for a mosque. But we must bear in mind that the primitive mosque was not merely a place of worship but also the place where the community gathered on all important occasions. It was in the mosque that they were called upon to take decisions, discuss them, or submit to them; it was a place open to all Moslems, who conducted their business there; it served as a tribunal and as a place for teaching the *Koran*. In other words, the mosque began as the city forum, and even when a slow evolution accentuated its sacred function (as Leone Caetani has demonstrated), it remained a multi-functional place. This is more easily understood if one remembers that the mosque participates in the functions of the "parliament" of the Arab tribes, the *majlis* (synonymous, prior to Islam, with *masjid*); according to Lammens, in fact, the mosque derived directly from it, since the *majlis* had the privilege of inviolability (*hima*) and sacredness (*haram*). The mosque was therefore fundamentally a meeting place in which it become essential to indicate the direction of the *qibla,* to orient the faithful in their prayers, a direction that Muhammad had marked out by driving a lance into the ground. It was only later that the *qibla* was to be dignified by the *mihrab,* a niche where prayers could be focused; the earliest known evidence of such an element dates to the outset of the eighth century.

Opinions on the significance of the *mihrab* are highly controversial. Indications are that, typologically it may be an imitation of the Torah niche of the eastern synagogue; but as we shall see, other possibilities cannot be ruled out. In the *masjid al-jamaa* ("community mosque"), and only in it, one finds the *mimbar,* which was originally a kind of throne, the symbol of sovereignty and the seat of the head of the community (whether the caliph or one of his representatives). From this seat, the *khutba* was delivered, "the discourse" that in the early days of Islam was a sort of political speech, and which only later became a homily, just as the *mimbar* was to become specifically religious in nature. The *khutba* was not necessarily limited to the religious service on Fridays (the day that, after a long period of evolution, came to be set as Islam's holy day), but was delivered each time the head of the community found it necessary to call the community together for the *salat al-jamaa*; this had nothing to do with the ritual prayers, but was a political duty from which no male Moslem could be excused and which took place only in the *masjid al-jamaa.*

The demands of the Moslem religion are minimal, especially as regards the religious edifices. The primary conditions are that the direction of prayer toward Mecca be indicated, and that the space be sufficiently large to accommodate the community. Praying can be done in the open air, as in the primitive mosque of Bassora or in the *musallahs* (places where the *salat* is performed on certain occasions). Nevertheless, for the sake of convenience — and also, it might be admitted, to make the place of worship and gathering more worthy — a portion of the space intended as the *masjid* was soon covered with a roof. This covered space was the prayer hall, and was to take on the aspect of a "long hall," that is, with the entrances on the main side and at right angles to the axis of the *qibla.* The adoption of this type of hall, which came to the fore in the Mesopotamian communities according to the scholar Ugo Monneret de Villard, is to be sought in ancient Babylonian architecture. But the nearest prototype may be seen, in Lambert's view, in the Eastern synagogues, such as those known to us at Dura Europos.

The call (*adhan*) to the canonical prayers, a crucial part of the modest Moslem rite, was made at Medina from the roof of the Prophet's house. At Damascus, where in the early period the Moslems had appropriated the ancient temple of Jupiter, the *adhan* was chanted from one of the four towers of the original *temenos,* the perimeter of the sacred enclosure. It was only much later that plans were drawn up for special structures in the form of towers, which served not only the practical purpose of the call to prayers but also offered a tangible testimony to the victory of Islam. It was not by chance that these towers, commonly known as minarets, came into being precisely in the Syrian-Egyptian area, where the populations of the cities were primarily Christians or Jews. The first examples were those erected at the four corners of the Amr ibn al-As mosque at Fostat, which was rebuilt and enlarged by Caliph Muawiya in 673.

The mosque composed of a court faced on one side by a broad hall and surrounded on the other three sides by porticoes, which was to become the accepted type for centuries, was realized for the first time by "pagan" architects with the aforementioned reconstruction of the Kufa mosque in 670. This design had also been adopted earlier in the Eastern synagogues, and it is accepted that these were themselves based on Hellenistic plans. A role in the formative process of the mosque may also have been played by the model of the forum-basilica complex of the Roman cities of the Near East, in which the basilica was of the broad-shallow type — as at Kremna and Smyrna, and perhaps at Antioch. Nor should it be forgotten, as Monneret noted, that this type is found in the temples in southern Arabia, although it is still difficult to ascertain

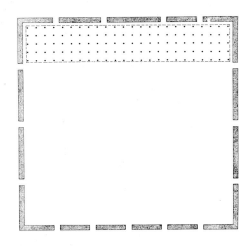

Kufa (Iraq): Plan of the primitive mosque; a simple roof covered the qibla *side. Legend claims that its dimensions were determined by shooting an arrow in four directions.*

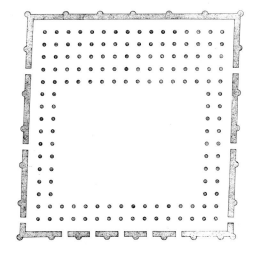

Kufa (Iraq): Plan of the Great Mosque rebuilt by the Umayyad governor, Ziyad ibn Abihi. It has five naves parallel to the qibla wall, but it did not have a mihrab, *or prayer niche, a later innovation.*

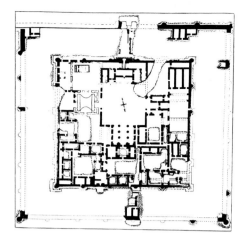

Kufa (Iraq): Plan of the dar al-imara, *or government house, dating to perhaps 670. It has the appearance of a Sassanian regal palace, with the typical four-*iwan *design, the main* iwan *preceding a domed throne room.*

THE EUPHRATES IN FLOOD

The Euphrates under the breath of the winds, when its waves foaming strike the banks,
    fed from every *wadi* full and noisy, with heaped remains of poppies and trunks of trees,
    where the sailor surprised clings to the helm, exhausted, anxious,
    is not more generous than Him in bearing gifts, nor does today's gift preclude tomorrow's.
    Such is the praise I bear you, and if it is welcome to you I did not mean, God forbid, to ask you for a gift.
    It is rather an act of asking for pardon; and if it were of no use, he who speaks it would be destined to disgrace.
    NABIGHA ADH-DHUBIYANI (poet at the courts of the Ghassanids and Lakhmids)

Medina (Saudi Arabia): Schematic reconstruction of the Prophet's house, over which a famous mosque was later built (see plan, page 21).
1 *Chambers of the women of the household*
2 *The roofed area, oriented toward Mecca, under which Muhammad prayed and conversed with his companions*
3 *Roofed area under which guests slept*

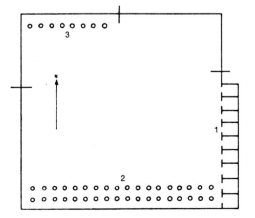

whether there was a genuine Yemenite contribution to the mosque's architectural evolution.

Although often exaggerated — and, conversely, at times flatly denied — we must also take into account the influence, if only indirectly, of the house of the Prophet at Medina. It was a modest structure: a square plot of land some 165 feet on each side, surrounded by an outer wall of unbaked bricks and only about 10 feet high. Outside the east side, and facing the court, were the miserable mud huts of the Prophet's wives. Part of the north side was covered by a roof of mud and branches supported by palm trunks; these huts housed the poorer of the Prophet's followers who had emigrated with him from Mecca. Another portico, facing Mecca, had been built on the south side, and it was here that Muhammad spoke with his disciples, performed the *salat,* and received visitors. Inside the house, in one of the rooms on the west side, the Prophet was buried.

As Caetani has clearly demonstrated, the house of Muhammad was of a completely private nature, and it substantially remained so up to the death of the third caliph, Othman, assassinated in 656; however, it was enlarged while the Prophet was still living, in 628, and then in 644 by Caliph Omar, and once again in 649–50 by Othman. Caetani has also noted that it was only gradually that Muhammad's house became public in nature, and eventually sacred: "The great change took place after Ali had moved the seat of government outside Arabia and Medina had fallen to the rank of a provincial town and a place of memories. When the bustle and worldliness of the capital of a great empire gave way to the monotonous calm of provincial life, people no longer came to Medina in quest of positions, wealth, or honors, but only out of obsequiousness to the memories of the great past. . . . And it was in this period, in part through the grafting of religious ideas of non-Arab peoples, that there developed the concept of the holiness of the house of Muhammad and that there took place the transformation from a private abode to a sacred and public temple." It was precisely because of this value as a relic that the house of the Prophet was to exert, as we shall see, some influence on the architectural definition of the mosque.

The religious and political characteristics of mosques — inseparable under Islam, manifested by the diverse functions of the *masjid al-jamaa* in the early stage, and never to be completely lost — are also underscored by the fact that the great majority have alongside the *dar al-imara,* the seat of the government, the residence of the caliph or whoever represented him in the community. The *dar al-imara,* even though it eventually concentrated the functions of what we today call government departments or ministries, maintained its fundamentally private nature as the dwelling of the chief. Meanwhile, the *masjid al-jamaa* continued to play essentially a public-community role, although it would perhaps be going too far to say with the French scholar Jean Sauvaget that the mosque is "a kind of public annex to the palace."

Despite the general lack of archaeological documentation of the earliest period of Islam, we have the good fortune of knowing what is considered the oldest Moslem *dar al-imara,* the one brought to light by Iraqi archaeologists at Kufa. Although this should probably not be attributed to 637–38, as some have claimed, it may be the one that, according to Tabari, was planned by a noble Persian of Hamadan, a former Sassanid functionary, Ruzbih ibn Buzurgmihr ibn Sasan, in the opening years of the rule of the Umayyads (about 670). The palace presents a typical design of the Sassanian type, containing a court faced by four *iwans* on the axes of a cross, with the focal point being the main *iwan* that led into a square hall, probably covered with a dome, an architectural feature typical of ceremonial Sassanid architecture. The *iwan,* by the way, which will play such an important role in Islamic architecture, was a large, usually monumental, niche or portal facing a court.

We may sum up this brief overview of the origins of Islamic architecture by saying that, from the great patrimony of traditions with which it was making contact, Islam gradually chose what was most suitable, preparing itself, as soon as the needs became clear and the times permitted, for a new and vigorous synthesis.

THE FORMATIVE PERIOD: THE UMAYYADS

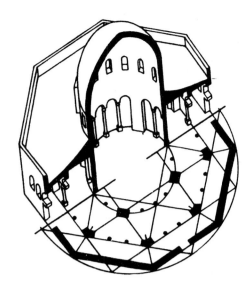

The struggles for the succession to the caliphate culminated in 661, as we have noted, with the death of Ali and the defeat of his Shiite partisans by Muawiya of the Umayyads, an offshoot of the Quraysh tribe to which the Prophet had belonged. One of the innovations of Muawiya was to adopt the hereditary criterion for the designation of the caliph, which at least greatly diminished the possibility of bloody conflicts in the future. The Umayyads thus became the first dynasty of caliphs, and were to hold sway for about a century in the new empire founded by the Arabs. The first Arab historical sources are of a much later period and, virtually without exception, they are unfavorable to the Umayyads, who are portrayed as ungodly and worldly. But modern historiography has granted them more credit, pointing up the fact that, in effect, it was under them that "arabism" reaped its first successes.

The Umayyads found themselves committed to a tremendous effort to lay the basis of the Islamic state, organizing the undisciplined Arab tribes and suppressing revolts and sedition. In the world outside, meanwhile, in Asia and Africa, there was an urgent drive toward those wars of conquest that, by the first half of the eighth century, had laid down the confines of the "classical" Islamic world, from the Atlantic Ocean to the Indian Ocean. The Umayyads pursued a tolerant policy in integrating the defeated, protecting these latter on the payment of taxes and drawing from their ranks most of the functionaries indispensable to the structure of a centralized state. The Umayyads also promoted various arts and crafts, and after their model — the Byzantine-Eastern sovereigns — everything assumed the characteristics of a dynastic art aimed at the materialization of the authority of the state and hence at the exaltation of the prince and the satisfaction of his needs and tastes.

In establishing the importance of the Umayyad period in the field of arts, we may draw on fairly extensive monumental and archaeological data. These permit us to consider Umayyad art as the formative period of Islamic art, during which the fundamental new trends or new transitions were undertaken or developed in a complex process of integration and interaction. The shift of the capital from Medina to Damascus under Muawiya was a development of the greatest importance, for it not only answered the political needs of the moment and struck a first blow against Arab hegemony but also was one of the first steps toward the universalization of Islam. The art of the Umayyads is known to us primarily through Syria, their chosen region, where there had already been fruitful contacts between the Semitic and Hellenistic-Roman worlds. The contact was established on a terrain that the Arab tribes of the Ghassanids, tributaries of the Byzantine authorities, and those of the Lakhmids, tributaries of the Sassanids, had to a large extent prepared for the synthesis Islam was to bring about — namely, between late-ancient and Eastern art.

The documentation on Umayyad art is confined basically to architecture, and to all intents and purposes it begins with a monument unique in Islam: the Dome of the Rock (*Qubbat al-Sakhra*) erected by Abd al-Malik (685–705) in Jerusalem. Placed almost in the center of the leveled-off area of Haram al-Sharif, where the Temple of Solomon had stood, it was built atop a rock that, according to tradition, was that of the sacrifice of Abraham — of whom the Arabs considered themselves descendants. It is an edifice of the pre-Islamic type — more properly, the Syrian type. Its harmonious proportions in design and elevation resulted from the application of a proportional system based on the principle of the star-shaped polygon, which was developed by Greek culture, and served as a basic element of Islamic decoration. Some of the details — the

Jerusalem: Cut-away plan of the Dome of the Rock, an octagonal structure with its interior divided into a double ambulatory marked off by an octagonal peribolos, of columns alternating with pillars, and a second, circular peribolos. The latter supports a cylindrical drum with blind windows that forms the base for the high wooden dome lined with metal.

Jerusalem: Reconstruction of the al-Aqsa Mosque, a basilica-type structure — that is, the naves run perpendicular to the qibla wall. This reconstruction was done by Creswell and is based on the Abbasid restoration of Caliph al-Mahdi of 780.

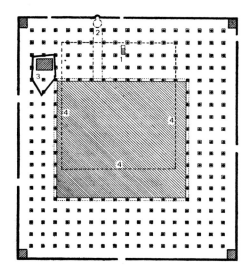

Medina (Saudi Arabia): Schematic reconstruction of the mosque of the Umayyad period that incorporated the ancient house of the Prophet.
1 The mimbar, or pulpit, which occupied the place of the seat from which Muhammad had spoken; it was left in its original position even after the mosque was enlarged
2 The mihrab, which is not on a principal axis of the structure but is aligned with the original qibla
3 Muhammad's tomb, with its irregular enclosure — so designed to prevent its being used to orient prayer
4 Limits of Muhammad's original mosque

wooden stays connecting the capitals, the small dome, the windows adorned with pierced frames — tie the monument to Byzantine traditions. On the exterior, however — now covered by ornamentation of a later period — we find a cornice with small arches and twin colonnettes in the Iranian tradition, one that had probably penetrated into Syria as early as the Ghassanid period, as is borne out by the decoration of the gate of Amman and the bas-reliefs of Qasr al-Abyad. The interior of the Dome of the Rock was lined with a profuse decoration, marble at the base and mosaics in the upper section. Mosaics also covered the outside until they were replaced in the middle of the sixteenth century by glazed tiles. The widespread use of mosaic ornamentation in sumptuous and sophisticated forms is a Byzantine tradition, as embodied in the imperial foundations on the sites of the great sanctuaries of Christianity, rather than a local Syrian or Palestinian tradition. This is to be explained by the motives behind the construction of the Dome of the Rock, which was an expression of the political will of the great king, Abd al-Malik.

We must start by accepting that this Abd al-Malik carried out such far-reaching reforms in the framework of the Arab state that he conditioned the entire subsequent history of Islam, turning it away from dangerous influences. He developed an Islamic type of coinage, abandoning Byzantine and Sassanid models, and he promoted Arabic not only as the official language of religion but of the state as well, thus laying the groundwork for the linguistic unity that was to constitute one of the strongpoints of Islam. Late traditions were to make the Dome of the Rock an object of pilgrimage — replacing the Kaaba at the time of the sedition of the anti-caliph, Ibn al-Zubayr, who had taken over Mecca — and the site where Muhammad was believed to have taken flight for his extraterrestrial trip on the back of the mystic Mount Buraq. Of special significance is the Dome of the Rock's ensemble of mosaics, which consist of ornate plants of a naturalistic type, derived from the classical tradition or conventionalized in keeping with Iranian taste, and of royal symbols such as crowns and jewels of the Byzantine and Sassanid type, in union with the inscriptions, a characteristic element of the aesthetic-ethical aims of Islam. As Oleg Grabar has demonstrated, these mosaics proclaim the military victory over Islam's two early enemies, Byzantium and the Sassanids, and project the spread of the new universal religion. The Dome of the Rock was therefore conceived as a full-fledged triumphal monument, one more facet in Abd al-Malik's campaign of propaganda on behalf of the Islamic faith and state.

It was also intended to vie with the Christian monuments in Palestine, a claim explicitly supported by the tenth-century geographer Muqaddasi, a native of Jerusalem. In fact, the Dome of the Rock was but part of a complex that included the al-Aqsa mosque, which although also probably founded by Abd al-Malik, has been extensively rebuilt (and was devastated by a fire in the late 1960s). A study of the various reconstructions reveals that the primitive al-Aqsa mosque was composed of naves perpendicular to the qibla wall. But such a structure, evidently based on the great Constantinian Christian basilicas, is an exception among the Umayyad mosques of Syria. The basic form of these latter mosques can be summed up as follows: a colonnaded court (sahn) facing a prayer hall that extended to a considerable width and that was usually divided into three naves parallel to the qibla wall and often cut by a transept on an axis with the mihrab. The most famous example of this Umayyad-Syrian type is the Great Mosque of Damascus. The type we may call Iraqi is characterized by a considerably deeper hypostyle prayer hall. But in fact both types can be considered variants on one basic goal — namely, how to organize a space capable of accommodating a Moslem community while affording protection from the sun and rain and while indicating the direction of the prayers and the location of the imam (prayer leader).

The Iraqi type of mosque was long known only through a number of descriptions — for example, that of the Bassora mosque (665) or of the Kufa mosque (670). But now we have a clearer idea, thanks to the excavations of 1936–46, of what we may consider the oldest known congregational mosque: that of the Umayyad city of Wasit, Iraq, built in 703–4 by the celebrated governor al-Hajjaj. Reduced to its mere foun-

dations, it has a square design of about 325 feet on a side, with the court surrounded on three sides by a colonnade and on the other side giving onto a prayer hall with eighteen columns in rows five deep. The columns were hewn from blocks of sandstone, and some were sculptured with ornamentation in the Sassanid style. Missing from the *qibla* wall is the *mihrab* niche. This element, which was to become so important in later mosques, was introduced a short time afterward, during the enlarging and rebuilding of the mosque of the Prophet at Medina in 707–9 under al-Walid I, who decorated the niche with a profusion of marble and mosaics, the work of Greek and Coptic craftsmen. The Medina mosque, frequently restored and rebuilt, has lost its original form (although this has been reconstructed by Sauvaget); it involved a number of special arrangements due to the fact it was built over the old house of the Prophet and that it was conditioned by memories of him. The *qibla*, for instance, did not govern the principal axes of the structure, these being dictated by Muhammad's tomb. One of the most significant innovations was the introduction of the *mihrab* to indicate the *qibla*, under the aspect of a concave niche framed by an arch; from that time on, this was to become one of the permanent elements of the religious architecture of Islam. Various theories have been proposed with regard to its origins. Particularly convincing is that of Stern, according to whom the *mihrab* commemorates the place occupied in the original prayer hall by Muhammad as *imam*, while its form stems from Roman memorial architecture. However, we cannot rule out the theory of Sauvaget, who

Jerusalem: The Dome of the Rock (Qubbat al-Sakhra). Built by Caliph Abd al-Malik (685–705) on the rock that tradition had identified as that used in the sacrifice of Abraham, the forefather of the Arabs. According to later traditions, it was from this rock that Muhammad departed for his celestial trip on the mystic Mount Buraq. Beyond such symbolism, the Dome of the Rock is a monument celebrating the victory of Islam over two great enemies — Byzantium and the Sassanids.

Damascus (Syria): The Great Mosque of the Umayyads, built under al-Walid I between 705 and 715. This is a view of the facade of the prayer hall facing the court, dominated by the transept with its pediment.

A NIGHT'S REVELRY

What a marvelous night I spent in Dair Bawanna, where wine was poured and people sang!

Just as the cup went round so spun we dancing, and those who did not know thought we had become mad.

We passed close to scented women, and song, and wine, and there we stopped.

We partook of their communion, and we bowed down to the crosses of their convent, like unbelievers.

AL-WALID IBN YAZID
(Omayyad Caliph, d. 744)

IF THE HOUR HAS COME

Lord, if the hour of my death has come, let it not be on a stretcher covered with green drapery.

But let my tomb be the belly of a vulture that lives in the air of heaven amid waiting birds of prey.

May I fall a martyr, prostrate amongst many fallen, stricken in a terrible step!

Knights of the Banu Shaiban, linked to one another by the fear of God, entering the field when armies clash.

Leaving the world, they have left all struggle, and have passed to the place promised in the Holy Book.

AL-TIRIMMAH (Omayyad poet)

LOVE POEMS

My spirit clung to hers before we were created, and after we were drops ripening to life, and in the cradle.

It grew as we grew, with lusty vigor, nor, when we die, will it break faith with the sworn pact,

but it will live on in every later state and visit us in the shadow of tomb and sepulcher.

Wind of the north, do you not see me delirious with love and visibly exhausted?

Give me a breath of the breeze of Bathna, and condescend to blow on Jamil;

and say to her: "Little Bathna, enough for my soul is a little of you, or even more than a little."

I swear I'll not forget you so long as a sun's ray shines in the east, so long as a mirage deceives in the unending desert.

So long as a star hanging in the sky will shine, and leaves grow on the branches of lotus bushes.

JAMIL (Omayyad poet, d. 701)

considered the *mihrab* a reduction of the terminal apse of the basilica audience halls, a reflection of the time in primitive Islam when religion and the state were linked. This view finds support in the image on a coin, perhaps of Abd al-Malik, and possibly dating back to about 695.

The Great Mosque of Damascus, which Islam rightly considers one of its marvels — all the more so as it has survived with its original structure fundamentally intact — is the most grandiose example of the congregational mosques of Umayyad Syria and one of the most complete architectural realizations of this period. Built under al-Walid between 706 and 715, it was erected on the site of the sacred enclosure of the Temple of Damascene Jupiter, which governed its dimensions (520 by 330 feet). The porticoes that surrounded the perimeter of the ancient *temenos* on three sides, and the prayer hall on the south side, marked out a great court of some 400 by 160 feet. The prayer hall was divided into three naves parallel to the *qibla* wall by arcades resting on the inside on two series of columns and on pillars along the court. This court facade is dominated by the pedimented facade of the transept, which cuts through the three naves along the axis of the *mihrab*. Rising above the transept is a dome that replaced the older one of 1082–83, destroyed in a fire. The original dome, also of wood, must have been closer to the *mihrab,* in line with the *maqsura,* an enclosure, usually a wooden grill or grating, reserved for the sovereign and his family, which had been introduced by Caliph Muawiya or by Marwan (683–85) to protect themselves from possible attacks. A series of windows illuminated the prayer hall and transept; the roof was a truss construction with double slopes. In the west part of the court is a small octagonal room covered by a dome, raised from the ground by means of eight columns and originally decorated with mosaics; in this structure, one recognizes the *bayt al-mal*, the small edifice where the treasure of the Moslem community was kept, in accordance with a practice of primitive Islam — although we do not know whether this was continued through the Umayyad epoch.

The mosque at Damascus was adorned with a high molding with Byzantine-type marble paneling and with a mass of mosaics, most of

which have been lost in the fires that have devastated this monument. But what remains is sufficient to enable us to appreciate the high quality of the workmanship — and to make us regret its irreparable loss. The mosaic decoration, with its absence of all human and animal imagery, consists of urban landscapes and a profuse vegetation, realized in accordance with the illusionistic style of the classical tradition but done in the refined Byzantine technique. In all likelihood, the execution of the mosaics was entrusted to Byzantine craftsmen, as had been done with those of the Medina mosque, for which Abd al-Malik had requested assistance from the emperor of Byzantium, who sent both materials and mosaicists.

The Great Mosque erected by al-Walid had the aim not only of satisfying the need of the increased Moslem population of Damascus but also that of offering his subjects a monument capable of vying with the great basilicas of Christianity, then so numerous in Syria. The themes of the mosaics have had various interpretations, but they too are seen to conform with this larger aim. The geographer Muqaddasi, at the end of the

Damascus (Syria): A section of the interior of the Great Mosque of the Umayyads. The precious marbles and splendid mosaics that cover the interior were almost completely destroyed by a fire in 1893, but the remaining portions still enable us to appreciate their excellence. The mosaics, executed with Byzantine techniques, are composed of a texture of colored and gilded glass. There are no human or animal figures, but an abundance of leafy trees and cityscapes, the latter often with fantastic or stylized architecture (such as that just visible above the central door in the photograph). The subjects of the mosaics probably symbolize the world pacified under the sway of Islam.

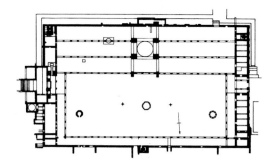

Damascus (Syria): Plan of the Great Mosque of the Umayyads. This mosque is one of the most complete and grandiose architectural manifestations of the masjid al-jamaa *of this period. Typical is its structure, with the prayer hall divided into three naves parallel to the* qibla *wall, cut by a broad transept facing onto the great porticoed court.*

Anjar (Lebanon): Plan of the city. The urban design here bears witness to the permanence of the pre-Islamic traditions — specifically Roman, as in the great porticoed roads and the division into insulae.
1 Government palace, with two apsidal halls opposite one another
2 Mosque
3 Baths

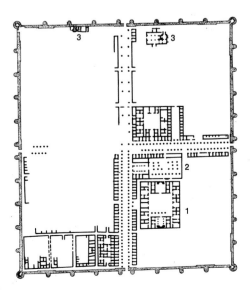

tenth century, asserted that "there is neither a tree nor a well-known city that is not represented on the walls of this mosque," and it seems highly probable that the imagery symbolized the world pacified under the sway of Islam in an idyllic version of a "Golden Age." It was a triumphal theme, therefore, in keeping with that expressed in the architecture and mosaics of the Dome of the Rock, but in the Damascus mosque the accent was on power, the concrete domination of the world as signified by its cities and vegetation. This is the key to a better understanding of the structure of the Umayyad mosques of Syria, too. This type of edifice, seen as the absolute center of the faith and the focal point of political power, finds in the Great Mosque of Damascus its most complete formulation, under the thrust of Islam's emerging needs and in line with the Umayyads' policies of empire building. These needs were fully satisfied by the Syrian architectural school, which employed elements typical of its own architectural lexicon, but refreshed the meanings and created a coherent ideological, ceremonial, and aesthetic language.

The mosque's two-sided nature — religious and political — is also illustrated by its close location beside and links with the palace of the government; this relationship was a feature throughout the Umayyad period and to some extent during the subsequent Abbasid era. A situation of this same kind could also be found at Anjar, a small town founded in the early years of the eighth century on the Beirut-Baalbek road and which affords an extremely rare example of an urban complex of this period. The town has survived with its basic plan intact, because it was abandoned with the fall of the Umayyad dynasty. In its plan, the town testifies to the survival of pre-Islamic traditions — specifically, Roman — with its square surrounding wall equipped with four gateways serving two main colonnaded streets crossing each other at the center at right angles. The mosque at Anjar, having only two naves and a rather small court, indicates that the architectural formulation was still in a tentative phase. The palace is the type with a central court, faced on the short sides by two apsidal halls — evidently audience halls — one of which has a three-nave basilica arrangement. On the long sides, the court is lined by a series of apartments. Standing near the city's north gate is the building that housed the public thermal baths, with a great hall flanking the thermal area itself. Such baths stem from similar Roman structures, which the Arabs adapted to their own needs, ablutions being essential to Islamic ritual.

Desert Palaces of the Umayyads

Beyond such pre-Islamic influences on the religious structures in Syria and Palestine, the Umayyads undoubtedly continued the territorial organization of the preceding eras. For example, we also know of milestones erected by Abd al-Malik that bear witness to the system of roads. The Umayyads also took up the project of reclaiming the land of the sub-desert area that had constituted the support of the Roman frontiers, guaranteeing trade and presenting a bulwark against the infiltration of nomads from the south. Survivals of this intensive activity include numerous Umayyad structures based on the most ancient Roman-Byzantine and Ghassanid models, which push into the desert following the line of approximately six inches average rainfall, a line that cuts a sort of great arc from the Euphrates near Raqqa as far as Aqaba, a fertile protective fringe of the east horn of the Fertile Crescent. These structures, known under the name of "desert palaces," or "castles," are not the result, as was once thought, of a romantic nostalgia for the desert by the new conquerors. The leaders, for one thing, belonged to the urban aristocracy, although it is true that the Umayyad caliphs, particularly for political reasons, had little liking for the life of the crowded, restless cities of Syria, whose inhabitants for the most part were not then Muhammadans. As Menneret and Sauvaget have suggested and the latest research has confirmed, virtually none of the Umayyad castles was intended

merely as a residence for the prince; these castles also functioned as farming centers, the direct descendants of the rustic villas of the late Roman empire. The castles, in fact, were equipped with well-developed systems for the collection of rain or spring water, guaranteeing the water supply not only of the palace itself but also of the surrounding fields. In addition to these more luxurious foundations, directly attributable to the caliph or members of his family, a number of minor structures are known; more modest in their architecture, they undoubtedly belonged to private individuals.

The Umayyad desert palace may be described more or less as a square enclosure with round corner towers and one entrance, with a court in the center of the interior, colonnaded or otherwise, and faced with rooms for the inhabitants. It appears that in the development of this type of edifice, stemming from the *castras* of the Roman-Byzantine frontiers in their external aspects, an important contribution was made by the semi-nomadic Ghassanids. Indications are, in fact, that these latter are responsible for the transmission of a number of typically Iranian elements — for example, the round towers. The residential chambers of the castle (*bayt*, originally meaning "tent"), usually composed of four rooms facing in pairs onto a small court, is of the Syrian type. And virtually a constant in such Islamic palaces was a prayer hall.

One of the oldest of such castles is that of al-Minya, near the Sea of Galilee, attributed to al-Walid I; there we find a somewhat irregular layout of rooms. Particularly worthy of note is a mosque with three transverse naves and a basilica-type hall, decorated with exceptional profusion, and with the *bayt* alongside. Among the most complex and most highly developed examples of this type of caliph's residence — although not in the desert — is that of Khirbet al-Mafjar, near Jericho, Jordan. It was never completed, except for its bath area, but appears to

Khirbet al-Mafjar (Jordan): This palace, near Jericho, is attributed to the time of the Umayyad Caliph, Hisham (724–43). This view is of the great pillared hall of the thermal complex; its mosaic floor employs geometric designs in the classical manner.

Khirbet al-Mafjar (Jordan): Plan of the palace complex.
1 Porticoed court
2 Basin with pavilion
3 Palace
4 Mosque
5 Thermal area, including the great hall with its polystyle pillars
6 Audience hall

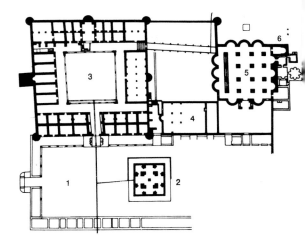

Mshatta (Jordan): A section of the opulently sculptured facade of the Umayyad palace of Mshatta, near Amman. (This section is now in the Staatliche Museum of East Berlin.)

Khirbet al-Mafjar (Jordan): Reconstruction of the audience hall.

date back to Caliph Hisham (724–43) or to one of his two successors, Yazid III or al-Walid II. Pressed into service here was the pre-existent Roman aqueduct, both for the use of the palace, to which a great thermal-bath was annexed, and for the irrigation of both the fields in the Jordan River valley and the crops in a vast enclosure around the palace itself. The water was also used to power a number of mills for grinding cane to extract sugar, a valuable product, the use of which did not begin to spread until the sixth century, when the Sassanids introduced it from India to Persia.

From a deep vestibule preceded by a door between two towers, one entered Khirbet al-Mafjar's porticoed court, in the middle of which was a square basin surmounted by an octagonal pavilion; this court preceded the approach to the palace itself and served as an outside link to the mosque and to the thermal baths that extended along the north. The baths were dominated by a great salon, with walls broken up by semicircular niches, and was divided by four rows of polystyle pillars and surmounted in the center by a dome. Unlike the other Umayyad baths, and those of a later period, the great hall maintained its function as *frigidarium;* the hall also served as a resting place, and could be entered from a small apsidal hall intended for the sovereign's audiences. The *calidarium,* mounted on hypocausts, is made up of a round hall with deep radial niches. The palace was richly decorated with stucco and mosaics. The decoration in stucco — a technique borrowed from the Sassanids — includes both geometric and floral motifs, but a large part was also comprised of animal and human imagery, amid which there even appeared a statue of the caliph, represented frontally, in keeping with the Iranian custom. Particularly significant were the mosaics, including the magnificent one that has survived in the audience hall, which imitates a carpet with its representation of two animal groups beside a tree, and the

floor mosaics of the great hall, or *frigidarium,* with geometric motifs in the classical tradition.

Floor mosaics of the geometric type also decorated the palace of al-Minyah and the baths of Qusayr Amra. This latter, quite bare and unadorned on its exterior, presents a number of variants compared to that of Khirbet al-Mafjar. The chief interest lies in the pictorial decoration, now almost completely destroyed, which covered the walls — paintings in the late-Roman and Byzantine style and including scenes of bathing, gymnastics, naked women occupied at various chores, construction scenes, personifications of History and Poetry, and, on the ceiling of the *calidarium,* the Zodiac. In the exedra of the great room with parallel vaults, which was intended as an audience hall, is the figure of a prince on the throne, represented in accordance with the iconography of the Byzantine Pantokrator ("All-Powerful God") — although some claim to see in these paintings more of the Sassanian and Eastern influence. Contiguous to this figure are six personages in rich apparel, four of whom are identified by Greek and Arabic inscriptions, including the Emperor of Byzantium, the Emperor of Persia, the Negus of Abyssinia, and the last Visigoth king of Spain, Roderick, who fell in battle against the Arabs in 711. The other two are perhaps to be identified as the emperors of China and India. But in any case, all six figures seem to represent and symbolize the defeated enemies of Islam. The dating of this important pictorial ensemble is controversial, but definitely later than

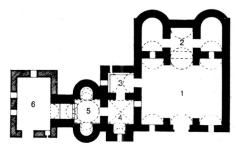

Qusayr Amra (Jordan): Plan of the palace-complex.
1 *Audience hall, with three barrel vaults supported by transverse arches*
2 *Exedra of the throne, where the figure of the prince was painted*
3 *Apodyterium (dressing room)*
4 *Tepidarium*
5 *Calidarium (On the dome of which the zodiac was painted)*
6 *Room with the heating system*

711; it was traditionally assigned to al-Walid I (705–15); more recently it has been assigned to the reign of Hisham I, between 724 and 743.

While Western motifs and styles are prevalent in the pictorial decorations of Qusayr Amra, in the later ones of Qasr al-Hair al-Gharbi, of the time of Hisham I, along the Damascus-Palmyra highway, some of the floor paintings show a clear Iranian influence, not only in the themes chosen — courts and hunting — but also in the styles employed, a phenomenon already observed in the decoration of Khirbet al-Mafjar. Also attributed to Hisham is Qasr al-Hair al-Sharki (reported for the first time by the seventeenth-century Roman traveler, Pietro della Valle) in the desert between Palmyra and the Euphrates; it was composed of a citadel and a palace, annexed to which was a caravansary of a very simple type, one of the oldest of Islam. And also attributed to Hisham is a series of structures near Rusafa-Sergiopolis, the ancient holy place of the Christian Arabs, a caravan post on the road to Raqqa, which appears to have been Hisham's new capital. It is of interest, too, that it was precisely with Caliph Hisham I, although Syria and Palestine remained the chosen region of the Umayyads, that there began a shift of focus toward the eastern territories, Mesopotamia in particular, from the economic as well as political point of view, anticipating the goals of the future Abbasid caliphs. In the eastern part of the Fertile Crescent as well, the Umayyads undertook great projects of improvements and agrarian reclamation, with imposing works of construction or restoration of the canals for the waters of the Euphrates and with the introduction of new crops. Perhaps dating back to this epoch, in fact, was the cultivation of cotton in Jazira (Upper Mesopotamia), a practice imported from Central Asia and a crop that was to become ever more widely cultivated, replacing the traditional flax.

Belonging to the final phase of the intensive building activity of the Umayyad dynasty is the grandiose, unfinished palace of Mshatta, not far from Amman, Jordan; its dating has given rise to many controversies, but it is now generally accepted as belonging to the Umayyad period. From the outside the construction looks like the usual Umayyad desert castle, save for the dimensions (some 480 feet square), and its walls are flanked by towers. Inside, the distribution of space is different, more complex, foreshadowing the great Abbasid palaces. The interior area is divided into three equal parts; work on the side sections was never begun, but in the middle section, also tripartite, we recognize an entrance area comprised of a mosque and a forecourt, its walls broken up by niches. At the end of this latter is a residential area for the caliph, composed of four *bayts,* in the midst of which is the audience hall that faces the court through a triple barrel-vault, like a triumphal arch. The middle nave of the basilica-hall ends with a tri-apsidal room, an indication of the merging of the Syrian and Persian-Mesopotamian traditions. The outer facade, except in the part corresponding to the prayer hall, was enriched by a riotous ornamentation of sculptured bas-relief (now to be seen in Berlin), with floral-type ornaments enlivened by various animals both real and imaginary. The decoration reveals the hand of various artisans, due no doubt to the system of conscription — that is, of recruiting manpower from various parts of the empire, a system widely used by the Umayyads. This explains, in the decoration of Mshatta, the presence side by side of Syrian-Coptic and Persian-Mesopotamian elements.

With the fall of the Umayyad dynasty, the artificial oases of the sub-desert areas of Syria and Palestine were largely abandoned, as were their various Umayyad palaces. The areas of Islamic sedentary settlement began to shift toward the periphery of the Fertile Crescent, with an implacable movement that only in recent times has once again changed direction. Indeed, this phenomenon seems to have emerged as far back as the last of the Umayyads, both because an "eastern policy" had become increasingly clear and because the maintenance of the artificial oases was no longer profitable, involving a heavy financial commitment that the coffers of the dynasty could no longer sustain. With the advent of the Abbasid dynasty, Syria and Palestine lost their status as privileged regions, passing into the background in relation to the eastern part of the empire — Mesopotamia in particular — and the traditional rivalry between Syrians and Iraqis can be dated back to this epoch. But these regions still deserve credit for having initiated the process of synthesis of various artistic elements of the ancient world, even though this synthesis was to assume more autonomous characteristics in the new crucible of Mesopotamia, where Moslem art was to take on its definitive Eastern characteristics.

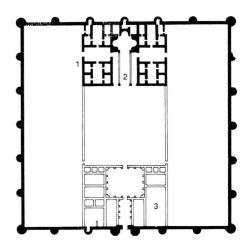

Mshatta (Jordan): Plan of the Umayyad palace.
1 *Residential area, formed of four apartments*
2 *Basilica-type audience hall, ending in a square room faced with three apses and preceded by a triumphal arch with three barrel vaults*
3 *Prayer hall*

Mshatta (Jordan): Reconstruction of the triumphal arch that formed the front of the audience hall.

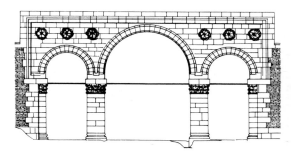

Of four things comes the life of the heart, the
spirit and the body: flowing waters and
gardens, wine and the beautiful face of the
beloved.

Wine is passed round amongst us in a cup of
gold which Persia has enriched with the most
various figures:
  On the bottom is Cosroe, on the sides are
wild cows which are being hunted by horsemen
armed with bows.

Does it not overjoy you that the earth is in
flower and that you can drink good wine of
honest blend?
  How will you forgive yourself if you ab-
stain from drinking a nectar sired by the black
grape, born of the green mother vine?
  Hasten: the gardens of al-Karkh are in-
viting and the exterminating hand of war has
not yet siezed upon them:
  there will you find birds of several kinds
that do not, it seems, disdain to speak;
  when they sing there fails not to lodge in
every soul that joy which heals all ills.
  How many taverns have I visited in a night
whose mantle was as black as pitch!
  And the tavern-keeper with ruffled hair,
rising from the bottom of his couch staggering
from drunkenness with sleepy eyes,
  says to me: "Who are you?" and I reply to
him: "I'm a respectable person whose qualities
are known by more than one name;
  I've come here to find ambrosia and to
marry her." "Out with your money, then," said
he. "Her marriage portion must be paid on the
nail!"
  And when it was clear I was no beggar, nor
would I pour my own wine, nor yet wait,
  he brought me wine as pure as musk, clear
as a tear flowing down a cheek from an eye not
blackened with bistre.
  The taverner failed not to pour wine nor I
to drink; at my side was a girl, a charming
creature with a white complexion.
  And how many songs she sang to us, and
yet no blame attached to us. Blame me no
more, then, for any censure leads again to
drink.
      ABU NUWAS (d. 813 or 815 in Baghdad,
          the most exquisite Arab poet)

Heed not ruins, the kite flies over them, on
their antiquity disasters weep.
  Leave the rider of a she-camel a space of
land on which such steeds are made to trot.
  Take not from the desert Arabs nor en-
tertainments nor customs; meager and miserable is their life!
  Let milk be drunk by people ignorant of
all the refinements of life,
  in a land where spiny bushes and acacias
grow and the animals there are hyenas and
wolves.
  On curdled milk, yes, spit freely, for it is
no sin.
  Far better than that is pure wine, poured
in a circle by a skilled cup-bearer,
  that has lain long in a barrel, burning
though no flame is seen.
                          ABU NUWAS

ARCHITECTURE OF THE ABBASID EMPIRE

The first era of great Islamic conquests having come to an end in the
first half of the eighth century, the state founded by the Arabs enjoyed
relative calm along its borders, a situation that permitted it to face up to
the grave crisis of adjustment triggered by the social, financial, political,
and religious difficulties that had swamped the Umayyad regime. Particularly serious was the social problem generated by a disparity of rights
between the Arab aristocracy and the new converts, these latter being
kept in a position of inferiority in spite of the ideal of equality of all
Moslems. No less grave were the economic and financial difficulties of the
Umayyad state, in part because of the drop in revenues — the result of
the decline in conquests — but primarily because of the inadequacy of
the state organization. The breakdown was triggered off with a revolt in a
peripheral region, Khurasan, the northeastern and most Islamic region
of Iran, under the ideological cover of a vendetta against the Umayyads,
always considered by some as usurpers of the claims of the family of the
Prophet to the caliphate. The beneficiaries of the revolt were the Abbasids, descendants of one of Muhammad's uncles, and the first Abbasid
assumed power in 750.

The Abbasid caliphate was to stand firm during some five centuries,
although after its initial moment of splendor its effective power became
progressively weaker, until in the end it was little more than an honorary
title. In 1258 even this nominal power ended with the murder of the last
Abbasid caliph by the Mongols during the sack of Baghdad. But with the
Abbasids, Islam did become a universal culture. The Islamic state ceased
to be exclusively Arab. Adherence to Islam — not the fact that one
belonged to a privileged race, the Arabs — was now the basic require-
ment for participation in public affairs. Within this new framework, the
Iranian element, to be sure, would enjoy particular prominence. One of
the first acts of the new Abbasid caliphs was the abandonment of
Damascus as the official capital of the empire; the capital was moved to
Mesopotamia (modern Iraq), where in 762 the second Abbasid caliph,
al-Mansur, founded Baghdad. This shift of the center of power to the
east was a reasonable and politically necessary development, and the
attention already given to Mesopotamia by the last Umayyad caliphs was
indicative of the political and economic weight that the eastern provinces
were assuming in the new framework of the Islamic state. From the
standpoint of the history of artistic culture, moreover, this development
defined the process of the "orientalization" of Islam, with Iranian
influences in particular ascendancy and with a receptivity toward ever
wider graftings from central and eastern Asia.

Islam, which had come into being amid an urban, commercial society,
however small and remote, would best fulfill its function as a dynamic
civilization by choosing a seat of power in Mesopotamia, that veritable
crossroads of empires, traversed by the ancient trade routes of the three
great continents, Asia, Africa, and Europe. Mesopotamia, heavily
populated for its time and with a network of both old and new urban
settlements, with the new capital and its concentration of wealth, provided Islam with a formidable center of propulsion. The concept of
power typical of the Umayyads assumed a still greater importance among
the Abbasids, manifesting itself in accordance with the models of the
ancient Eastern monarchies. The caliph resided in a sumptuous court,
isolated from the people, and his entire activity was concentrated on the
materialization of his power with the aim of glorifying his own name.
Developing in the shadow of the caliph was a bourgeoisie of merchants,
bureaucrats, landowners, scholars, and artists. Although this bourgeoisie
was never to succeed, despite its constant alliances with the prince, in
wielding true political power — in fact, this group ended by being

completely removed from the sphere of power by the military in the tenth century — it was nonetheless to serve as the preponderant contributor to forming the refined, active, and often brilliant society that was to set the tone for the living styles and aesthetic canons of Islam.

Unfortunately, nothing remains of the Baghdad of al-Mansur, but from the descriptions that have come down we know that the city was circular in shape, in keeping with a Near Eastern tradition that reached from the Assyrians to the Sassanids. The city was conceived primarily as a means of assuring the security of the sovereign, whose residence, which is identified with the government palace, was isolated in the center of the city. The Baghdad of al-Mansur had a diameter of some 9,000 feet, and was defended by moats and by two pairs of concentric rings of walls, in which four gateways opened out from roads that bisected the town. The dwellings of the people, served by radial streets, were placed in subdivided rings distributed in four sectors, so that in case of disorders they could be cut off from one another. The gateways were rather complex, employing an elbow, or right-angled, type of access, probably stemming from Central Asian models; each was topped by an audience hall designed to accommodate a large garrison. In the city's center stood the government palace, Bab al-Dhahab ("golden gate"), connected to a large congregational mosque. Little is known for certain about the appearance of this palace; we do know, however, that it had two stories, that it was square, and that it contained a ceremonial complex conceived in accordance with the Sassanian pattern — an *iwan* followed by a hall with a dome. According to some sources, the palace had a central hall with a dome to which four *iwans* were joined; this variety was also of Sassanian origin, but realized in accordance with a Central Asian elaboration. Apparently of this latter type was the government palace of Merv, erected in 748 by Abu Muslim, the leader of the revolt against the Umayyads; and in the century that followed, we shall find this type of palace also being built at Samarra.

The oldest monument that has survived from the Mesopotamia of the Abbasids is the palace-fortress of Ukhaidir, mentioned for the first time by Pietro della Valle in a report on his return trip to Italy in 1625. According to the reliable theory of Creswell, it was built after 778 by a powerful Abbasid prince who aspired to the caliphate, Isa ibn Musa. It was built entirely of chips of calcareous stone held together by means of a strong mortar, unlike most of the other Iraqi edifices, which are of baked or unbaked brick or simple compressed mud. The Ukhaidir palace conforms with the eastern tradition in its basic design, the development of its elevations, and in the vault system of the roofs. It consists of a great turreted wall interrupted by flat niches, in the Sassanid tradition. On the north side of the interior is the palace proper; along its main sides are the *bayts,* or residential chambers, of the typical Iranian variety — that is, with an *iwan* flanked by two side rooms preceded by a portico facing an open court. To the right of the entrance, as at Mshatta, is a prayer hall. The central nucleus, marked off by an aisle, included a huge court of honor with the ceremonial complex dominated by a towering *iwan,* followed by a domed hall.

Attributable to the reign of Harun al-Rashid (786–809) (according to Herzfeld) or to that of al-Mansur (754–75) (in Creswell's view), is the fine Baghdad Gateway at Raqqa, Syria — the city that for a time, beginning in 796, was the capital of that famous caliph, Harun al-Rashid. Built entirely of baked brick, the entrance has an acute arched vault framed by two large niches. Running along the top is a strip of niches with a polylobed internal profile, a design that was widely used at Samarra, the caliph's residence in the ninth century and that was to become one of the characteristics of Abbasid architecture. Particularly noteworthy on this Baghdad Gate is the geometric decoration of the niches, achieved by a combination of bricks, a type of ornamentation destined to undergo a complex evolution in Iranian territory.

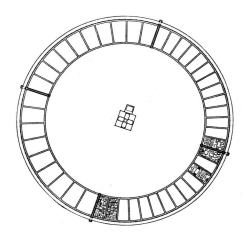

Baghdad (Iraq): Plan of the city designed by Caliph al-Mansur and founded in 762; nothing of this old city remains except for a few descriptions on which the above schematic plan is based. At the center were the masjid al-jamaa *(chief mosque) and the* dar al-imara *(palace). The circular design has an ancient tradition in the Middle East, and incorporates a cosmological, magical significance. According to the historian Tabari, the city was first laid out on the ground with ashes so that Caliph al-Mansur could have an idea of what it would be like. The moment to begin the work was chosen by an astrologer.*

SOFT NIGHT OF SEPTEMBER

Were it not for the fruits of September, of all kinds harvested, and for the clearness of the water and of the air,
    my soul would be untroubled when the earth will enclose it within the two dismal walls of the grave.
    Soft night of September, we lay on cool couches brushed by a light wind,
    when that nocturnal traveler, the moon, revealed in full her face, bright through the clear air.
    Soft a breath of its breeze in the morning bearing tidings of basil plants.
    O speak out all the praise you will, of this familiar month, in which each day dawns a miracle of God.

            IBN AR-RUMI (836–96?)

Ukhaidir (Iraq): Plan of the fortified palace in the Wadi Ubayd desert (about 120 miles south of Baghdad).
1 Court of honor
2 Audience hall, made up of large iwan *followed by a domed hall*
3 Mosque

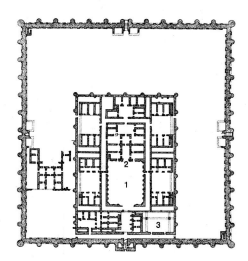

Samarra (Iraq): The Great Mosque of al-Mutawakkil as viewed from its adjacent minaret. All that really remains are the surrounding walls with parts of the semi-circular buttresses, which originally had an upper band with niche panels. The walls had sixteen doorways. All the supports of the roof — octagonal pillars on square bases, connected by teak beams — have been lost. It is the world's largest mosque.

Samarra of the Abbasids

The most extensive testimony to Abbasid art and architecture, however, comes from Samarra, situated some fifty miles north of Baghdad, along the Tigris River. The massive forces of slave troops, mainly Turks, whom the caliphs began recruiting — starting principally with al-Mamun (813–33) — to meet the needs of the army and to form a personal guard corps had produced tensions in cosmopolitan Baghdad, where clashes between the troops and the civilians became ever more violent. In 836, in an act typical of an absolute monarch of the era, Caliph al-Mutasim decided to shift the court and all the administrative offices to Samarra. The site was not particularly suitable for a large settlement, primarily because of the difficulty in supplying water; but this challenge then dictated the city's unusual form — some 22 miles long on the banks of the Tigris, and only about 3 miles wide. It is interesting to note, too, that Samarra represented a grandiose example of land speculation, the plots in question being those the caliph gave as concessions to the crowd of functionaries and notables who were obliged to populate the new city.

The caliph, wishing to preserve some tranquillity, had sought to put as much space as possible between himself and the people of Baghdad to avert the danger of civil uprisings, and the principle of security was to inspire the criteria of the design of the new city. There were no walls, it is true, but the streets were immense and communication within the city was difficult. The troops were isolated in their self-sufficient quarters, and obstacles were placed between various sections. Yet the city enjoyed only a brief existence. After some fifty years, Caliph al-Mutamid (870–92) moved the capital back to Baghdad, and Samarra rapidly fell into decay. The causes of its swift end are to be found in the lack of an authentic social cohesion, which alone could have guaranteed its survival and which itself resulted from the network of security measures that consumed virtually all the caliph's energies.

If moving the capital from Baghdad to Samarra were surely an eloquent sign of disarray in the power of the Abbasid caliphate — a disarray that was to receive its "finishing touches" in the following century — it nevertheless represented a moment of some splendor in the realm of art. The building mania of the Abbasids here ran wild, both in the number and grandeur of the structures. All the buildings erected by the caliphs aimed at underlining the power of a secular prince, and on a colossal scale. It was not by chance that Samarra includes among its buildings some of the world's largest, for the construction of which it was necessary to resort to the conscription system, with workers and materials brought in from all over the empire. The various edifices rose quickly, most being of unbaked brick or compressed mud — although baked bricks were used at crucial points — and embellished with a profusion of surfaces decorated with stucco, paintings, mosaics, and even imported marble.

The enormous field of ruins at Samarra is still known only in part; what familiarity we have is owed primarily to the excavations of the Germans Sarre and Herzfeld in 1912–13, which were followed later by those of the Department of Antiquities of Iraq. Various centers are to be distinguished both on the north and south ends of the city. Qadisiya, octagonal in shape, appears to have been the first residence of al-Mutasim, who then abandoned it, finding it inadequate; he moved farther north, practically to the center, to a place known as Jausaq al-Khaqani. Here are found, among other structures, two great hippodromes and the Great Mosque built by his successor, al-Mutawakkil (847–61), who also erected the palace of Balkuwara for his own son, al-Mutazz. In 859, al-Mutawakkil, possessed by a veritable building mania, decided to build a city all for himself, choosing an area a bit to the north, which he called Mutawakkiliya, or Jajariya. Here are found the ruins of his grandiose palace, still unexplored, and of another mosque, known as Abu Dulaf.

These two mosques at Samarra — the Abu Dulaf and the previously mentioned Great Mosque at Jausaq — are of the Iraqi type: that is, they have fairly deep prayer halls, without any particular emphasis, either in

Samarra (Iraq): The minaret of the Great Mosque of al-Mutawakkil, also known as al-Malwiya, "the spiral." This minaret, more than 165 feet high, is situated some 90 feet from the mosque's north side. It was originally connected to the mosque by a viaduct that went from the base of the minaret.

THE BAKER

Never will I forget a baker I passed by, rolling out his pastry in the twinkling of an eye.
    From when I saw it a ball in his hand to when it was spread out round as the moon,
    passed no more time than a circle takes to spread on the surface of a pool, when you throw a stone.

             IBN AR-RUMI (836–96?)

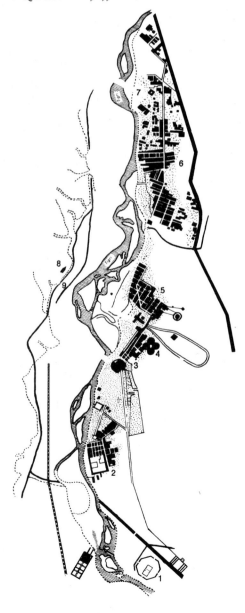

Samarra (Iraq): Plan of the city.
1 *Qadisiya*
2 *Balkuwara*
3 *Great Mosque*
4 *Hippodromes*
5 *Jausaq al-Khaqani*
6 *Jafariya (or Mutawakkiliya)*
7 *Mosque of Abu Dulaf*
8 *Qasr al-Ashiq*
9 *Qubbat al-Sulaybiyya*

layout or elevation, on the ceremonial parts. In fact, the nave corresponding with the *mihrab* is only a bit wider than the others. It is also interesting to note that a close connection is no longer maintained between these mosques and the government palaces. The Jausaq mosque, with its 400,000 square feet of surface (some 800 by 500 feet), is the world's largest. It is found inside a large enclosure, the *ziyada,* where annexes such as baths and latrines were also located, the purpose being to isolate the mosque from direct contact with the life of the city. All that remains of the edifice is the perimeter wall of baked brick, set off by semicircular towers and decorated along the top by square panels with round medallions in the center, the whole lined with stucco. On the inside, a deep portico surrounded the court on three sides, while the hypostyle prayer hall was situated on the fourth side, with twenty-five naves set off by octagonal pillars, and marble columns at the four corners. The pillars were not connected by arches; the flat roof was of teakwood beams. Still standing outside the facade — at the end opposite that of the *qibla* and its *mihrab* — is a conical minaret, on a square base, known as al-Malwiya ("spiral"), since it is served by an external spiral ramp. Modeled on a Babylonian ziggurat, it is topped by a cylindrical body with niches, probably used to support a wooden pavilion.

A similar minaret is found at the other great mosque of al-Mutawakkil, erected at Jafariya and known as the Abu Dulaf; its dimensions of 700 by 450 feet make it somewhat smaller than the Great Mosque. Virtually nothing is left of the walls, which were of unbaked brick, but the interior is fairly well preserved. The prayer hall is of an unusual type, being divided into seventeen naves at right angles with the *qibla* wall. The naves do not actually reach the wall, however, for it is preceded by two naves running parallel to it; in conjunction with the nave on the axis of the *mihrab,* these latter form the so-called T design. Exceptional in Mesopotamia, this design was widely used in North Africa, where we find the oldest example in the Great Mosque of Qairawan, dated to 836.

None of the palaces at Samarra, except the Qasr of al-Ashiq ("the lover") on the west bank of the Tigris, appears to be fortified, security being entrusted, as we have indicated, to a whole series of administrative and organizational measures. In general, the palaces, veritable citadels, are not unified structures but are made up of many different parts distributed inside a great quadrangular enclosure dominated by the ceremonial axis of the nucleus intended for the caliph. The palace of al-Mutasim, for instance, the Jausaq al-Khaqani, built between 836–38, is an immense, intricate conglomeration of edifices spreading over an area about one mile long. From an open space outside a great gateway, one had access to an oblong forecourt, and after traversing a number of other courts one arrived at the official area, situated along the Tigris. The nucleus of the caliph's area was represented by a great domed hall faced by four *iwans,* the ceremonial design already referred to. Through a series of rooms placed on the complex's main axis, one arrived at the Bab al-Amma, the gateway formed by three grandiose *iwans* (still standing). According to Sourdel-Thomine, this was not the entrance to the palace, as is generally thought, but a sort of belvedere on the Tigris, to which one descended by a monumental stairway, at the foot of which was a great pool.

In a better state of preservation is the palace of Balkuwara, built between 854 and 859 for al-Mutazz, the son of al-Mutawakkil. Unlike the other palaces at Samarra, this has a more cohesive design. It is divided into two parts. In the access section are two courts, with monumental doors leading to a third court inside; this latter's main facade, with three *iwans,* regulates entry into the ceremonial area. In the second external court is a three-nave mosque. On the sides of the palace area is a complex of structures intended for the family of the prince and with open spaces for games. Such palaces were as a rule furnished with cool underground areas (*serdab*) suitable for coping with the sweltering heat of summer, basins with fountains, and gardens with rare plants. Large walled-in spaces, such as that east of the Jausaq palace, some three miles long, represent the remains of the hunting grounds where animals were collected for the sovereign's forays. Also worthy of note were the private

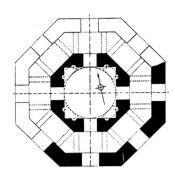

Samarra (Iraq): Plan of the Qubbat al-Sulaybiyya.

COURTLY LOVE

Oh that I might know who she was and how night is come! Was hers the face of the sun, or that of the moon?
   Was it a vision of the intellect, made manifest by its own working, or an image of the spirit made manifest to me by thought?
   Or an image, formed in my soul, of my own hope, which my eyes believed they did perceive?
   Or yet none of these, but was it instead an event, produced by destiny to cause my death?
      IBN HAZM (994–1064, Andalusian poet)

I have recalled you with longing in al-Zahra, between limpid horizon and sweet face of earth
   whilst the breeze languished at sunset, almost diseased with pity for me.
   The orchard smiled from its silver waters like necklaces taken from your breast.
   It was a day like the days of our past joys, those we gathered furtively whilst Fate was sleeping . . .
   Oh my splendid jewel precious and beloved, like the precious trinkets lovers buy!
   Exchange of mutual requited love was in the past the lists wherein we jousted;
   but now am I more than ever worthy of praise for faithfulness to your love: you are consoled, and I am alone in love for you!
      IBN ZAIDUN (1003–1070, Andalusian poet)

Samarra (Iraq): Plan of the Mosque of Abu Dulaf.

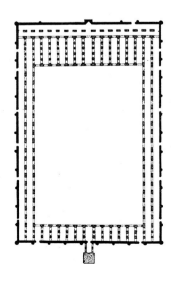

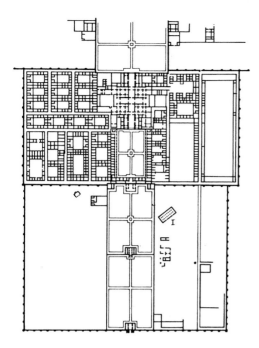

Samarra (Iraq): Plan of the Balkuwara palace. Note the axial construction and the succession of courts, in one of which is situated the mosque (1); it is easily recognizable in its asymmetrical position, obligatory because of the orientation of the qibla.

Samarra (Iraq): Plan of the central part of the palace of Jausaq al-Khaqani.
1 Main entrance
2 Courts
3 Audience hall with four iwans
4 The three iwans on the Tigris, known as Bab al-Amma

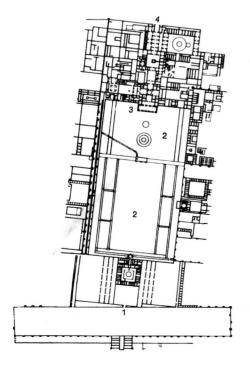

homes, all of which were of the same design: a court faced by the main hall in an inverted-T design. In the more affluent homes we find a second court, identified as the *harem*, the "forbidden area," the women's quarters. These homes were always fitted out with baths, and sometimes with *serdabs*. All appear to have had flat roofs.

At Samarra we also have the oldest known Moslem mausoleum, given the name Qubbat al-Sulaybiyya. Within it was the tomb of Caliph al-Muntasir, who died in 862, erected for him by his Christian mother; alongside him were buried the caliphs al-Mutazz (died 866) and al-Mutahdi (died 869). The mausoleum is made up of a square, domed chamber, set within an octagonal ambulatory covered with a barrel vault; Creswell has rightly compared the plan to that of the Dome of the Rock in Jerusalem. Although the mausoleum is made up of a square, domed chamber, set within an octagonal ambulatory covered with a barrel vault; Creswell has rightly compared the plan to that of the Dome of the Rock in Jerusalem. Although the mausoleum was to become one of the typical elements of Islamic architecture, use of such edifices did not spread, as we shall see, until the tenth century. In fact, the oldest Moslem doctrine advocated "equalization of tombs" — that is, leveling them to the ground to call attention to the equality of all men in death — and as such was absolutely against all funerary structures. What remains to be discovered is from where the Abbasids adopted this usage, for not even the Byzantine emperors were buried in mausoleums.

From even such a quick review of these various Abbasid monuments, it should be clear that, in relation to those of Umayyad Syria and Palestine, we find ourselves facing a completely different spatial concept. The organic, unified use of space, which was still operative in the Great Mosque of Damascus, or in the *frigidarium* hall at Khirbet al-Mafjar, tends in Abbasid architecture to break up into various independent, cellular units in keeping with the Iranian sensibility, which aimed at a concrete and not an illusive definition of space.

Before leaving the Abbasids, we must take a brief look at the rich, often lavish, decorations of their architecture. The most favored portions of structures were lined with marble and mosaics, and a large part of the palaces was set aside for ornamentation with carpets and fabrics and rendered still more precious by the addition of gold and gems, descriptions of which, full of wonder, have come down to us. The bulk of the decoration was entrusted, however, to multicolored stucco, which as a rule formed the molding of the walls in all the rooms of any importance as well as serving as cornices and ceiling work for doorways and arches. This form of decoration, indeed, affords some of the most important evidence for defining the aesthetic characteristics of Islamic art.

Three different types of stucco decoration have been recognized in the classification scheme of Creswell, although they do not belong to any chronological order. The first two, A and B, were executed by molding the ornamentation on the stucco while it was still fresh, cutting deep grooves in the surface so that the motifs would stand out clearly on a dark background. Style A is obviously derived from the late-classical Umayyad tradition, with which we are familiar from the work at Mshatta. The motifs are based on a variation of the vine stems and acanthus leaves, and these are rendered in a naturalistic style, although there are also many abstract forms employed. In Style B, the forms are flatter and the vegetal elements are rendered in a decidedly less naturalistic manner. The various elements are split into sections and isolated and then rearranged in an abstract geometry, distributed inside panels and medallions. The origins of Style B are in the Sassanian artistic tradition, and, so Dimand believes, there may also be Indian influences. Style C, known as the "Samarra style," is the one that more properly deserves to be called Islamic. The ornamentation was executed with a technique different from that of the other two: whereas they were done with molds, Style C was often carved as well as molded, and the carving was done so as to produce sloping margins, or what is known as beveled carving. Furthermore, the vegetal motifs — acanthus leaves, blossoms, twining tendrils — had gone through a process of conventionalization and abstraction. They were endlessly repeated, tapestry-style, on the surfaces, and with many combinations; the background had virtually been eliminated, being confined to filigree around the various motifs. The relief, always rather low, produced under the light not deep shadows but more nuanced effects. This resulted from the particular stylistic treatment of the surfaces, which came out slightly swollen because of the oblique angle of beveled carving.

The Samarra style was to find certain echoes even outside Mesopotamia, but its importance is fundamentally due to its becoming a determinant factor in forming that most characteristic element of Moslem decoration, the arabesque. As for the origin of beveled carving, this is to be sought in the Central Asian environment. There is little question that the style spread through Mesopotamia as a result of the massive presence of Turks in the army of the Abbasid caliphs. The Central Asian influence manifests itself, moreover, in various other aspects of Abbasid culture, including the stylistic cadences of the murals that adorned the edifices of Samarra. Unfortunately, only a few fragments of these murals have survived, for the most part in the harem of the Jausaq palace, including among other subjects numerous figures of semi-nude dancing girls. In addition, mention should also be made of the wood sculptures, particularly those in teak, imported from India, and also of the faience ornamentation. This latter is known to us through a number of interesting fragments of tiles made by the highly sophisticated technique known as metal luster painting, with which the Mesopotamian artists, especially those active in the ateliers of Baghdad, achieved results of great value — on pottery as well as on tiles.

Cairo: The al-Qatai Mosque, built by Ibn Tulun (876–79), here showing the north side of the court. Its minaret, frequently rebuilt, calls to mind that of the Great Mosque of Samarra in its spiral form.

BROTHER OF GLORY AND HONOR

Sweeter than old wine, sweeter than offering drinking-cups, is the clash of swords and javelins, the launching of one army against another . . .

I will bring confusion amongst the muzzles of the battle-horses, whilst war rises erect, more so than a leg above a foot,

together with a champion who awaited me until I handed over to him the power I wrested from the underlings,

a sheikh who holds optional the five canonic prayers and permissible to spill pilgrims' blood in holy land.

The lions of the squadrons, by him stricken in the thick of the fray, lay off the attack, whilst he never desists.

My flashing blade makes the earth forget the lightning in the air, and flowing blood takes the place of rain.

Dive into the mortal fray, O my soul! Leave fear of death to sheep and flocks!

If I leave you not bleeding on the tips of lances, may I not be called brother of glory and of honor.

AL-MUTANABBI (905–65)

The Tulunids of Egypt

A particularly interesting aspect of the imperial Abbasid style is to be found in Egypt, whose governor, Ahmad ibn Tulun, son of a Turkish slave, declared himself independent from the caliphate and gave rise to a brief dynasty in Egypt (868–905). This dynasty has left one quite exceptional monument: the al-Qatai mosque (876–79), built in the garrison town that ibn Tulun founded and which was to grow into Cairo. In the use of brickwork in the walls and stucco in the decoration, in the *ziyada* that isolates it from contact with the life of the bazaar, and in its spiral minaret, this mosque faithfully followed its Mesopotamian models, an imitation we see again in the Tulunid-epoch houses excavated at Fostat. The mosque, although maintaining the Iraqi principle of a fairly deep hall, also has naves — five, arranged parallel to the *qibla* wall. They are set off by a number of rectangular pillars, with corner colonnettes connected by slightly pointed arches, which support the trusses of the flat roof. Since the pillars are particularly large, with their major axis running parallel to the *qibla,* the view of the *mihrab* is impeded from virtually every point in the mosque.

Of a quite different nature is another of the significant monuments of Abassid Egypt, the Nilometer (literally, for measuring the rise and fall of the Nile) on the island of Rhoda, near Cairo, designed in 861 by the celebrated mathematician al-Farghani (known to the West in the Middle Ages as Alfraganus). Built entirely of stone, its exquisite taste in handling volumes speaks to us of a special feature of the Egyptian architectural school, one that we shall be discussing later. The Nilometer also preserves one of the oldest and most elegant Arab monumental inscriptions in Kufic characters.

Cairo: Plan of the al-Qatai Mosque.

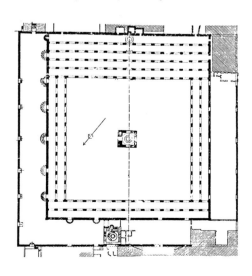

DISINTEGRATION OF THE ABBASID EMPIRE AND BIRTH OF THE REGIONAL SCHOOLS

The reign of Harun al-Rashid at Baghdad (786–809) marked the apogee of the political power of the Abbasid caliphate, but also the beginning of its rapid decline. As a result of a mass of political, religious, and socioeconomic factors, the caliphate was soon to be fragmented into a complex, unstable number of state entities. Andalusia (Spain) and the Maghreb (Morocco and Algeria) had already broken away in the eighth century, followed by Ifriqiya (Tunisia) at the outset of the ninth. During the course of the ninth century, Egypt was lost, having broken away under the Tulunids; in the following century, the country was taken over by the dynasty of Shiite caliphs, the Fatimids, rivals of the Abbasids. In the ninth and tenth centuries, a number of principalities, independent de facto and de jure, came into being in Central Asia and Iran. One of them, that of the Buids, natives of the Caspian area and of the Shiite faith, was to become masters of Iraq in the tenth century, taking the Sunnite Abbasid caliph under its protection; this arrangement was to last until the coming of the Seljuk Turks in 1056.

Despite such stormy vicissitudes, these centuries experienced the

Cordova (Spain): The Great Mosque of the Umayyads: a view of the prayer hall of Abd al-Rahman I. The naves are marked off by columns supporting horseshoe arches. Between them are light pillars linked by rounded connecting arches, seen here. A distinctive feature is the construction of the arches in stone alternating with baked brick, a technique in the Syrian and Byzantine traditions, and one that produces a fantastic striped effect.

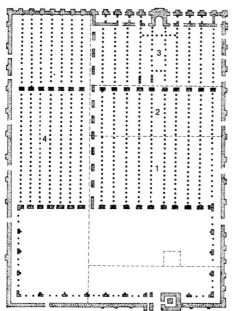

Cordova (Spain): Plan of the Great Mosque, showing its various phases of construction.
1 Work of Abd al-Rahman I (785)
2 Work of Abd al-Rahman II (848)
3 Work of al-Hakim II (961)
4 Work of al-Mansur (987)

flourishing of Islam's great intercontinental and overseas trade, with the basic routes passing through the Fertile Crescent. Islam's basic economy was still healthy and active, as indicated by the prospering of numerous transformation handicraft enterprises on a scale that was often para-industrial. First and foremost was the production of textiles, which in the Middle Ages (as has been pointed out) was comparable to the steel industry in our own times. The caliphs' state, on the other hand, was plagued by a grave financial crisis. Based on a regime that favored large land holdings, it failed to benefit from the new sources of wealth produced by commerce, which in effect was a privileged element because of the previously described Moslem doctrines. At the same time, various provinces emancipated themselves from the central caliphate, revenues fell off, and the costs of maintaining an army, by now totally mercenary, became increasingly steep. Agriculture, earlier the chief source of wealth of the Abbasid state, fell into disarray, even in the productive territories of the Fertile Crescent that were still under its authority. The causes of this disarray are to be found in the improper cultivation of the lands, the lack of a resident feudal society, and the established custom of paying mercenary troops by granting them the revenues from the land, which the mercenaries exploited intensively. This custom caused the peasants to leave the farms, giving rise to the growth of crowded cities, and so triggering off the process of "desertization" of former farming areas that is one of the most awesome phenomena of Islam. This last-named process slowly but implacably developed up to about the middle of the nineteenth century, particularly at the hands of the Bedouin Arab tribes

and Turkish nomads who swarmed out of Central Asia beginning with the eleventh century.

But the ninth and tenth centuries that marked the beginning stages of the disintegration of the caliphate simultaneously represent the period of the maximum cultural enrichment of Islam in its spiritual and religious life as well as in the arts and sciences. The leading authors of this vigorous period of intellectual activity were the Islamized non-Arabs, and during this period a number of regional artistic schools took shape. Although they shared a fundamental unity of Islamic inspiration, they tended to express themselves in their indigenous languages, exploiting whatever vital dynamic Islam had to offer while accepting ancient local traditions. At the same time, these converts submitted to influences that their wide contacts made possible, hoping to sustain their prestige by emulating the splendors of the Abbasid empire, which remained as an ideal stimulus and point of reference.

The Umayyads of Spain and the Cordova Caliphate

Toledo (Spain): Sketch of one of the ribbed domes of the Mosque of Bib Mardun (now the church of Cristo de la Luz). Of eastern origin in its technique, this dome dates to the end of the tenth century.

It is probably no coincidence that those provinces most removed from the center of the caliphate, the westernmost ones of Andalusia, the Maghreb, and Ifriqiya, were the first to render themselves independent of the central authority of Islam. The Visigoth kingdom in Spain had been liquidated by the Arabs as early as 711, after a struggle that lasted only two years. The turbulent new province of al-Andalus became the refuge of one of the handful of Umayyads who had escaped from the slaughter carried out against them by the Abbasids; this refugee was Abd al-Rahman, who in 756 chose al-Andalus to set up an independent emirate with its capital at Cordova. In 929 one of his successors, Abd al-Rahman III, proclaimed himself caliph, a title kept by this dynasty until it disappeared some ninety years later. Of the architecture of these Umayyads of Spain, great patrons of art and prodigious builders, there remain only a few monuments, but these provide a fairly clear idea of the period and style. The art of the Cordova caliphate was then to spread through the Maghreb from the middle of the eleventh century on, giving rise to the style now known as Hispano-Mauresque.

One of the edifices that provides major reference points for Islamic architecture in the West is the Great Mosque of the Umayyads at Cordova. After the two great mosques at Samarra, this is the world's third largest mosque — although its dimensions are the result of various phases of construction. Begun by Abd al-Rahman I in 785, it was enlarged by Abd al-Rahman II in 848 and by al-Hakim II (961–99), and finally by the powerful minister al-Mansur in 987. Its prayer hall has eleven naves at right angles to the *qibla* wall; that is, it is of the basilica type, like the al-Aqsa at Jerusalem. In the beginning, the court probably did not have a colonnade. The subsequent transformations of the mosque were to maintain the basic design even while broadening it by adding new elements alongside. But the final enlargement, by al-Mansur, ended by destroying the symmetry in relation to the *mihrab* simply because of the limits of the terrain. The interior, simple in design as it is, a feature characteristic of the West, employs a particular spatial dynamic in the original system adopted to increase the height of the naves — probably based on solutions used in the construction of the Roman aqueducts (such as that at Merida, Spain). The naves are set off by columns supporting horseshoe arches, perhaps in keeping with a Visigoth tradition; between the arches' upper curves, light pillars are linked by semicircular arches. These latter produce distinctive effects of perspective and spatial dilation; these effects were further enhanced by the polychrome masonry — light stone alternating with red brick, as in the Syrian and Byzantine tradition. Then the enlargement ordered by Hakim II introduced into the area of the *maqsura* the polylobed, or hexafoil, arch of eastern influence and the crossed arches connecting the area of the lower arches with those of the upper tiers. This architectural feature of the crossed arch, of great decorative value, appears to have been an original development, and it later became part of the vocabulary of the Arab-Norman architecture of Sicily and the southern part of the Italian mainland. Based on the example of the Aghlabid mosques of Qairawan and Tunis, both in Tunisia, a suggestion of the T-design was added by Hakim, and the central nave was covered by domes at about the point where the ancient *mihrab* of Abd al-Rahman had been, in front of the new *mihrab*. The domes were supported by ribbing of the Persian or Armenian style.

Domes of the same type formed the covering of another Umayyad mosque, the Bib Mardun (now the Church of Cristo de la Luz) in Toledo, Spain, dated to 980 (or 999); it has an unusual design, being divided into three triple-winged naves and having nine domes (although examples of this design are to be found from Ifriqiya to eastern Khurasan). Also engaging is the facade of this Toledo mosque, decorated with brickwork

Following page:
Qairawan (Tunisia): The interior of the great Aghlabid mosque, viewed from its minaret. Note the T design, typical of mosques in the western part of the Islamic world; it is formed by the greater height of the median nave and the one along the rear, running parallel to the *qibla* wall. The older of the two domes, that in front of the *mihrab* (in the background) has a lobed outer surface and an octagonal drum with slightly concave sides.

with arches and interlaced elements surmounted by a high decorative strip that reveals (according to the French scholar Henri Terrasse) an Abbasid-Mesopotamian influence.

The excavations initiated in 1910 (and still in progress) at Madinat al-Zahra, some five miles from Cordova, acquaint us with various aspects of the civil architecture of the Umayyads of Spain. Founded in 936 by Abd al-Rahman III, who gave it the name of his favorite, Madinat al-Zahra was the residential and administrative city of the caliph. But its foundation was not dictated by security reasons — as had been the case with Samarra for the Abbasids, or Abbasiya and Raqqada for the Aghlabids of Tunisia — but for reasons of prestige and luxury. For years, enormous sums of money were squandered on this city — about one-third of all the revenues of Andalusia. The city, which was destroyed in 1010, was divided into three quarters situated on terraces descending to the Guadalquivir River. So far, the northern quarter has been partially explored, including a series of caliphs' palaces. Various structures clearly show an eastern influence, although their symmetry is less rigid. Particularly striking are the two audience halls, basilica-type rooms divided by arcades. The more recent one, the work of Abd al-Rahman III, has three naves preceded by a colonnade forming a sort of inverted T-design; it calls to mind the Mesopotamian *bayts* and may well be the result of eastern influences. The decoration of these structures was chiefly of marble and stucco, sculptured in the Umayyad tradition of Syria, with both floral and figure motifs. The geometric ornamentation of the floors, however, suggests the influence of Byzantine art. All in all, the Umayyads of Spain developed within the framework of Islam a hybrid architecture, drawing from the classical Iberian and Visigoth tradition and from the Syrian tradition with its Eastern-Abbasid graftings, this last-named element entering both directly and though Egypt and Tunisia.

Tunisia in the Ninth and Tenth Centuries: Aghlabid Architecture

The first stable base of the Arabs in North Africa was in Ifriqiya (modern Tunisia), with the center at Qairawan ("encampment"), founded in 670 by the great military leader of the Umayyads of Syria, Okba ben Nafi. Here, at Qairawan, he erected a mosque that became one of the most venerated places of Islam: the *qibla* walls of all the other mosques of North Africa are said to have been oriented to its sanctuary wall. Nothing, however, remains of the original mosque, for after a series of vicissitudes, it was completely reconstructed by the Aghlabid emirs in the ninth century. These latter, having received the hereditary governorship of Ifriqiya from Harun al-Rashid, ruled over it as virtually independent sovereigns from 800 to 909. It is to the Aghlabids that we owe several of the most seductive Islamic works in North Africa, and the Great Mosque of Qairawan was perhaps their most illustrious achievement. In its present form it is basically the work of Emir Ziyadat Allah who planned it in 836. It was enhanced by Abu Ibrahim Ahmed in 862–63, who decorated the *mihrab* in marble and luster tile, and by Ibrahim II (875–902), who added a truss roof to the prayer hall. The mosque covers a vast area in the form of an irregular rectangle. The portico (which is a late Hafsid and Ottoman reconstruction) is interrupted on the north side by an imposing minaret on a square base and with two receding sections; the architectural model for such a minaret is probably a watchtower. The deep prayer hall is covered by a flat roof supported by arches resting on columns, which set off seventeen naves at right angles to a transept, which is parallel to the *qibla* wall. With the middle nave, larger and higher than the others and surmounted by two domes, the transept forms the T design; indeed, it constitutes the earliest example of this, earlier than that already described in the mosque of Abu Dulaf at Samarra.

The origin of this T design was tied in with an influence from the ancient Christian basilica-type architecture, but indications are that it was independent of it. The scholars Pauty and Lezine contend that there was an influence from the Umayyad reconstruction of the mosque of the Prophet at Medina: the transept, parallel to the *qibla* wall, is believed to reflect the primitive gallery Muhammad had erected in his home as an oratory. In the reconstruction of the Medina mosque by al-Walid, this gallery was given a ceiling with especially rich ornamentation, just as lavish decoration was added to the ceiling of the gallery on an axis with the *mihrab;* the junction of the two galleries was marked by a sort of shell-shaped shield. In Tunisia, this formula was given an original interpretation, being increased in height with a double purpose: aesthetically, to break the modular uniformity of the prayer hall; liturgically, to express the accentuated value being assumed by the ensemble of the *mihrab,* the *mimbar,* and the *maqsura.* In these and other elements, the great mosque of Qairawan was to constitute the fundamental model of the North African mosque, which with minimal variations was to last up to our own time.

Particularly striking at the Qairawan mosque is the dome atop the *mihrab,* with its lobed-rib structure resting on a drum with lobed niches. As was pointed out by George Marçais, an influence from Mesopotamia is to be seen in this dome, its type of decoration, and the use of brickwork in various elements. Also worthy of note are the decorations of the *mihrab* framed by luster tiles, of Mesopotamian origin, and internal marble paneling after the Syrian tradition. The original facade of the court was also decorated with sculptured reliefs. We have a more exact idea of what they were like by viewing the facade of the Mosque of Three Doors, also at Qairawan. Although reconstructed, this facade retains its profuse decoration with Kufic inscriptions and bas-relief with floral motifs. The carvings are of a special kind, evidently based on a local tradition, but without the relaxed style of the Syrian or Mesopotamian arabesque — although they are to be traced back to this source as a type. Similar to the Great Mosque of Qairawan is the Zaytuna Mosque of Tunis, dated to 864, although its drum ornamentation was based on classical Roman formulas.

Within the architecture of Ifriqiya, a place apart is held by what may be referred to as the "Susa school." It is a sober, austere architecture of a military type in which one can discern the influence of Syrian models. Distinctive characteristics include the use of stone in the walls, pillars as supports instead of columns, and vaults in the roofs. Examples of these characteristics are to be found in a number of mosques and *ribats* (forts for monastic knights). In the prayer halls of the *ribats,* in the diminutive oratory of Bu Fatata (838–41), and in the Great Mosque of Susa (850–51), the naves perpendicular to the *qibla* wall are covered with barrel vaults, resting by means of overpassing arches on cruciform pillars, which also support the reinforcing transverse arches. Another example of this roofing system is the only known Abbasid structure in Palestine, the Ramlah cistern of 789. In the Great Mosque of Susa — built in 850, as we are informed by the simple but elegant Kufic inscription running along the facade of the court — we find two domes on the central nave, one at the position of the primitive *mihrab* and one on the *mihrab* of the extension. This extension doubled the area of the prayer hall in the second half of the tenth century, in the Fatimid era. On one side of the mosque are two large round towers, probably all that remain of the four original ones, since the mosque played a role with the nearby *ribat* in the defense of the port and city.

Such *ribats* were typical edifices of the frontier territories — essentially full-fledged, fortified monasteries that housed the combatants of the faith — and their heavy distribution on the coast of Tunisia, exposed to the Christians, is understandable. The *ribats* appear to be square blockhouses with towers, and have only one entrance. In that at Susa, the entrance was through a small porch-like structure surmounted by a small dome. The lodgings were small cells along the sides of the edifice, occupying two floors, the upper one of which was the prayer hall. Although influenced by Mesopotamian models, the Susa *ribat* was itself to influence

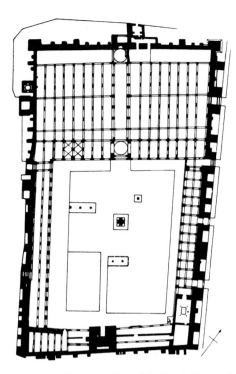

Qairawan (Tunisia): Plan of the Great Mosque. In its Aghlabid version, this mosque was to constitute the model for almost all mosques throughout the Maghreb, or North Africa.

Qairawan (Tunisia): Drawing of the interior of the dome in front of the mihrab *of the Great Mosque. It is ribbed inside and lobed outside; the connective niches are of eastern design.*

Qairawan (Tunisia): Facade of the Mosque of the Three Doors. The decorative carvings, although retouched, date back to 866.

Tunis (Tunisia): The Great Mosque, or Jami al-Zaytuna, "the olive mosque." View of the prayer hall. Built under the Aghlabid emir Abu Ibrahim Ahmed in 864, it has some similarities to that of the Qairawan mosque.

others erected in Tunisia. Research indicates that it was built between 770 and 796; during the reign of Ziyadat Allah in 821–22, it is thought to have received the characteristic round lookout tower, which also doubled as a minaret for the nearby Great Mosque — in imitation of the tower of the *ribat* in the neighboring city of Monastir, which had been built by the Abbasid governor in 796.

The Aghlabids, like their patrons the Abbasids, built their two residential and administrative capitals — Abbasiya and Raqqada — at some distance from Qairawan primarily for reasons of security. Abbasiya was founded in 801, and was named after the caliph's house; later they built the capital at Raqqada, this city also being designed as a place of amusement. Excavations (by the Tunisian government) at Raqqada have brought to light a great palace, made entirely of unbaked clay, a short distance from an enormous reservoir (uncovered earlier). At this reservoir, as at those of the caliphs' residences in Mesopotamia, the caliphs sailed their model flotillas and gave receptions. The Aghlabids were highly active in the field of hydraulic projects in an effort to restore the lands of Ifriqiya to their onetime prosperity; these began as merely utilitarian projects but in their structural integrity, a distinctive trait of most Aghlabid monuments, they achieved an expressive intensity that earns them a place among first-rate architectural works. Aghlabid architecture, in general, demonstrates a dependence on Eastern models — Syrian and Iranian-Mesopotamian — although they were adapted in an original way; also, it is not always possible to rule out some classical-Roman influence in the elaborations.

Susa (Tunisia): The Great Mosque, viewed from the tower of the *ribat*, the adjacent fort. The two building phases are clearly evident. The first, Aghlabid and dating back to 850, stops at the first dome, marking the position of the original *mihrab*. The prayer hall was duplicated in the second half of the tenth century, the Fatimid era; the *mihrab* of this added part is marked by the second dome.

Susa (Tunisia): Reconstruction of the prayer hall of the Great Mosque. The decorated lunette, on the left, coincides with the dome placed in front of the mihrab *of the original Aghlabid mosque.*

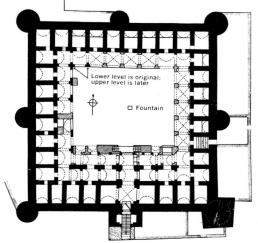

Susa (Tunisia): Plan of the ribat. *Note along the sides the cells that housed the warrior-monks.*

Mahdiya (Tunisia): Reconstruction of the original Great Mosque, of the Fatimid era.

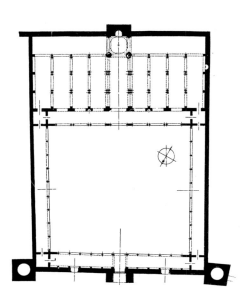

The Fatimids and Other North African States

Shiite propaganda, which proclaimed that the only people having a right to the caliphate were those descending from Fatima, daughter of Muhammad, and her husband, Ali, the fourth caliph, found a favorable public among certain Berber tribes centered around what is now the area of Constantine, Algeria. These tribesmen supported a Fatimid, or supposed Fatimid, *mahdi* ("one guided by God"), Ubayd Allah. This latter, proclaiming himself caliph, defeated the Aghlabids in 909, making himself master of an area corresponding to present-day Tunisia and Algeria. This gave rise to a dynasty, the Fatimid, that reigned directly over the territories that had originally supported the first Fatimid caliph, until in 973 this Fatimid dynasty moved to Egypt, tearing that rich province away from the Abbasid caliphate of Baghdad. The Fatimid caliphate remained in power in Egypt till 1171, but the original territories of the Fatimid "empire" came to be administered from 972 on by the Berber governors, the Zirids, who effectively replaced the Fatimids in this western region. In the middle of the eleventh century, as a result of clashes with these turbulent Zirids, the Fatimid caliph of Cairo unleashed in North Africa the invasion of the Banu Hilal, a nomadic tribe who, in the words of the great Tunisian historian and sociologist, Ibn Khaldun (1332–1406), "like an army of locusts destroyed everything before them," irremediably upsetting Ifriqiya's economy.

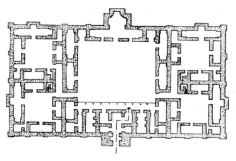

Ashir (Algeria): Plan of the palace of the Zirid emirs.

Qala of Beni Hammad (Algeria): Reconstruction of the Dar al-Manar, "the lighthouse palace." This is one of the most famous structures of the capital of this Berber state, which flourished thanks to the disarray of its Zirid rivals. Characteristics of this architecture are the broad vertical niches and small projections that shape the facade, elements also found in the Arab-Norman architecture of Sicily.

Relatively little has survived of the activities of the Fatimids in North Africa. Still insufficiently known are the palaces of Sabra-Mansuriya, near Qairawan, where there are groups of *iwan*-style halls of the Mesopotamian type. Only a few fragments remain of one of the two palaces known to have been erected by the two Fatimids in Mahdiya, the fortified city they founded in 915, situated in a strategic position along a small peninsula on the Tunisian coast. We have some idea of what the palace was like, however, from the palace of their Zirid vassals at Ashir, Algeria, built about 947 by an architect sent to them by the caliph. The design of the Ashir palace is clearly of eastern derivation and shows elements of both Syrian and Mesopotamian influences. It is characterized by lateral development, with the entrance in the porch on one of the long sides. Notable is the ceremonial complex at the back of the square court, on an axis with the entrance, made up of a domed, three-alcove audience hall preceded by an oblong antechamber with two apses, calling to mind the Mesopotamian inverted-T design.

Particularly beguiling from several points of view is the Great Mosque of Mahdiya, which unfortunately has been greatly damaged. Evidently it was of the usual Aghlabid type, although for the first time it includes an organically conceived gallery-narthex in front of the prayer hall, with a dome on the *mihrab* that was supported by polystylar pillars (similar to those of the baths of Khirbet al-Mafjar). But the main interest of the mosque lies in the fact that, for the first time in a religious edifice, we find an architectural arrangement of the facade that includes three doors and two quadrangular towers framing it. The middle door is distinguished by a monumental gatehouse of squared limestone, fashioned in harmonious proportions inspired by the Roman triumphal arch, from whose architecture the proportional relationships and the crowning of the cornice and the roof were clearly derived. The particular emphasis given to this entrance is most likely connected with ceremonial traditions of the Fatimid caliph, and this architectural feature in mosques was taken up again by the Fatimids in Egypt.

The portal of the Mahdiya mosque has a barrel vault with a horseshoe arch framed by niches on two levels, flat below and semi-cylindrical above. This use of niches as ornamentation, of Iranian-Mesopotamian derivation, was widely employed in the architecture of the Ifriqiya of the Fatimids and their Zirid vassals. Examples are the *mihrabs* of the Mahdiya and Susa mosques; the facade of the Zirid dome of the Zaytuna mosque in Tunis (991); in the east facade of the Sfax mosque, rebuilt in 998; and in the architecture of Qala, the capital of Beni Hammad, the tribal chief who established himself here as the rival of Qairawan. Located in the mountains of eastern Algeria, Qala became, after the ruin of Qairawan by the Banu Hilal nomads, an affluent center for a brief period, until it too was thrown into upheaval by the great Bedouin invasion. There still remains an important complex of ruins at Qala, in which three palace groups are found. The Dar al-Bahar, or "sea palace," is named after a grandiose water basin inside a colonnaded court, preceded by an imposing entranceway; arranged along the court were numerous rooms, now reduced to often unidentifiable foundations. The second structure is the Dar al-Manar ("the lighthouse palace") which still dominates the area; it is a rectangular mass enlivened by deep vertical niches; on the second floor is a cruciform hall, originally covered by a dome on a high drum, which was entered by an inner ramp. The third of the ruins at Qala is the "Palace of Greetings," where the excavations have been too recent to report definite conclusions.

Sfax (Tunisia): The east facade of the Great Mosque, dating back to 998. This mosque shows the successful application of the niche element, an ornamental feature of Iranian-Mesopotamian derivation.

Mahdiya (Tunisia). The portal of the Great Mosque, erected by the *mahdi* Ubayd Allah about 916. Made of squared limestone, and of harmonious proportions, this mosque is the most representative monument of Fatimid art in Ifriqiya, as Tunisia was then known.

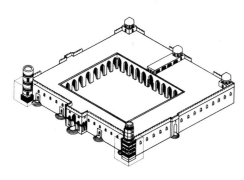

Cairo: Plan of the original al-Azhar Mosque.

Cairo: Reconstructed view of the original Mosque of Caliph al-Hakim (according to Creswell).

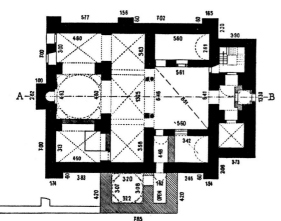

Cairo: Cross-section and plan of the tomb-mosque of Badr al-Jamali Amir al-Juyushi. The entrance through the little porch is surmounted by a minaret of three sections; the first of these has a muqarnas, *or stalactite, frieze of Iranian derivation.*

Architecture in Egypt Under the Fatimids

We have already noted how the Shiite caliphate of the Fatimids came to establish itself in Egypt in 969 as a rival of the Sunnite caliphate of Baghdad; under the Fatimids, until 1171, Egypt experienced a flowering of artistic activity and economic prosperity. The Fatimids supported the traffic from the Indian Ocean, endeavoring to draw it away from the Persian Gulf and through the Red Sea. They took advantage of the disarray in Mesopotamia, which coincided with favorable developments in the Mediterranean due to the intensive mercantile activity of the Italian maritime cities, in turn the result of the recovery of the European economy at the close of the tenth century. It was this economic activity that was to support the artistic endeavors of the Fatimids.

The building activity of the Fatimids was especially intense. In 969 they founded near ancient Fostat a military colony destined to become their capital, Cairo. In Arabic the name was *al-Qahira al-Muizziya,* "the victorious [city] of al-Muizz," the Fatimid caliph who conquered Egypt, thus touching off the great epoch of the former rulers of Ifriqiya. The first palaces the Fatimids built have disappeared, including al-Muizz and al-Aziz; both faced a square, like that at Mahdiya, the design of which they probably were imitating. In the structures that have survived, almost exclusively religious, it is possible to make out elements of the art of Ifriqiya as well as Iranian-Mesopotamian elements. But particularly beginning with the second half of the eleventh century, the widespread use of cut or freestone and a marked formal rigor bear witness to the consummate mastery of the architects of northern Syria and Upper Mesopotamia.

The first mosque founded in Cairo, in 972, was the al-Azhar, the seat of one of the most famous Islamic universities. Despite its various reconstructions, it is possible to trace its original plan, in which we may see a Tunisian legacy in the use of columns joined by arches, in the elevation of the transept furnished with two domes — one at the entrance and the other before the *mihrab;* the prayer hall with its five side naves is probably based on an Umayyad model. The stucco and wooden decorations of the transept, however, must be traced back to Abbasid art. In the slightly more recent mosque of al-Hakim (990–1013), the design, with its massive pillars of brickwork and corner colonnettes, goes back to Mesopotamian models via a Tulunid-Egyptian interpretation. But with the inclusion of a transept and its dome before the *mihrab,* the mosque utilizes the solution of al-Azhar, while introducing perhaps for the first time the feature of two domes at the far ends of the *qibla* nave. A Tunisian influence is undoubtedly to be found in the particular emphasis given to the facade, with the projecting entrance framed by two corner minarets. The entrance and minarets as well as the facade are decorated with stone bas-reliefs with Kufic inscriptions, geometric ornaments, and arabesques. The latter still call to mind, to a certain extent, the old Abbasid stucco models.

Meanwhile, a taste was developing in Egypt for stone architecture and for various refined elements of stone masonry, a taste already prefigured in the early Nilometer of Rhoda. This renewal of a technique and an architectural language is to be attributed, as we have said, to the influence of the schools of northern Syria and Upper Mesopotamia, which have left us some of the finest monuments of Cairo: the three great gates, Bab an-Nasr and Bab al-Futuh of 1087, and Bab Zuwayla of 1091. All of these were built under Badr al-Jamali Amir al-Juyushi, of Armenian descent, who, according to the historian Maqrizi, used architects from Edessa. The gates have a distinctly classical flavor in their handling of volumes and in the organic use of decorations, where the ornaments end up objectifying and exploiting the functional lines. Nevertheless, this object lesson from Syria and Upper Mesopotamia — as, shortly afterward, that from the great architecture of the Crusaders — was not to have an authentic,

independent development in Egypt but was to make itself felt in the decorations, in the use of freestone, and in the excellence of the techniques employed. A typical product of mature Fatimid architecture is the al-Aqmar mosque (1125), which makes use of the principle of the facade with entranceway; its decoration, although still organically connected with the structure and sufficiently sober, tends to enrich itself by such typically Seljuk decorative elements as the *muqarnas,* the stalactite-like components destined to be used so widely.

Parallel with the tradition then active in Iran, and with similar motivations, a great number of funerary monuments were being built in Fatimid Egypt. Their basic shape consisted of a cube surmounted by a dome, with connecting elements of niches with Seljuk-influenced *muqarnas;* the domes had various shapes, were often lobed, and in provincial versions — as at Aswan — assumed highly imaginative, picturesque forms. In the vicinity of Cairo we find a new type of tomb-mosque, that founded for himself by Emir al-Juyushi in 1085, where Mesopotamian and Seljuk cadences are particularly noteworthy — the profiles of the arches, capitals, cornices, and *muqarnas*. This tomb was built in accordance with a complex design: a vestibule area surmounted by a minaret; a court flanked by two rooms for visitors; then a triple arcade; after that, the prayer area, a square, domed hall; flanking this, two smaller rooms, one of which holds the tomb of the founder.

Sicily Under Islam

Although many people have a vague recollection of why Islamic art and architecture are to be met in Spain, it comes as something of a surprise to almost everyone when the Islamic presence in Sicily is confronted. The Aghlabids, the dynasty based in Tunisia, had actually captured Sicily in 902 — and a look at a map will reveal how inevitable this was — but within a few years the Fatimids were assuming power in Tunisia; when the Fatimids moved their capital to Cairo in 969, Sicily remained under the authority of these Egyptian-based Fatimids. The Fatimids essentially controlled Sicily until 1061, when the Normans took over, but even after this, and for some time, there were strong Islamic influences, both direct and indirect, on the arts and crafts of Sicily — particularly in textiles, ivory carvings, and mosaics. Unfortunately, though, virtually nothing remains of the building activity of the emirs of Sicily; we are dependent mainly on the later Arab-Norman architecture derived, although with accents of its own, from the Fatimid architecture of Ifriqiya and Egypt. There were also some contributions from Andalusia, although these emerged more clearly in the post-Norman Swabian era of Sicily. Worthy of attention from the Norman period are the pavilions and small palaces of Palermo — such as the Cuba, the Little Cuba, and the Zisa (from *al-aziza,* "the glorious"), works from the time of William II; the churches of La Martorana, of St. John of the Hermits, and of St. Cataldo; the cathedral of Palermo; that of Cefalu; and the Royal Palace of Palermo with its Palatine Chapel. Particularly famous is the stalactite ceiling of this Chapel, for its paintings represent perhaps the greatest cycle of Moslem painting to have come down to us. The paintings are difficult to classify, but they were evidently done about 1150 by artists drawing upon the Iranian-Mesopotamian tradition of princely motifs while working in the Fatimid style.

Damghan (Iran): The Tari Khane, a mosque of the Abbasid era, dated to about the mid-eighth century. Note the exceptional diameter of the stone pillars, a feature in the Sassanian tradition.

The Iranian Provinces

In the aftermath of the disastrous crisis that followed the Arab invasion of Iran in the seventh century, the ancient landed nobility, the Iranianized Arab aristocracy, and the Persian bureaucratic class that grew within the Abbasid administration were all cutting themselves off fat slices of power. The crisis of the Baghdad caliphate in the ninth century, which allowed the formation of numerous independent principalities, paved the way for the political rebirth of Iran, although by the eleventh century the latter was to fall, along with other territories, under the sway of new foreigners, the Turks. But Iran from 819 to 1055 experienced a period of outstanding economic and social progress. The resources of the various regions were no longer channeled toward Baghdad, but were for the most part placed back in use locally. Agriculture became particularly prosperous and handicrafts and commercial activities expanded greatly.

In the eastern Iranian provinces this work of emancipation was undertaken by the Tahrids (820–72) of Khurasan, who pushed on as far as Rayy and Kirman. They were followed by the Saffarids of Sistan (867–903), who radiated out in Khurasan, Afghanistan, Central Asia, and the Sind area of India; and finally by the Samanids (842–999), who starting from Transoxiana eventually extended their dominion over central Iran and Afghanistan. In central-western Iran, it was to be dynasties from the regions south of the Caspian who took command: first the Ziyarids, and then the Buids, who, belonging to the Shiite faith, ended by conquering Iraq and in 935, having become *amir al-umara* — that is, "servants of the caliph" — were to strip the Abbasid caliphate of all effective power.

From a cultural point of view, the most active centers in Iran were Samarkand and Bukhara in Transoxiana (now part of the U.S.S.R.). Under the Samanid emirs, great art patrons and refined connoisseurs, the neo-Persian language gained more ground as the medium of culture and administration, flowering with poets such as Rudaqi, Daqiqi, and above all, the famous Firdausi, who at the court of the Samanids began to

MOUNTAIN GAZELLE

How swiftly runs the mountain gazelle in the countryside!
    She has no friend; how can she live without a friend?
        ABU HAFS HAKIM (Tradition claims
                this is the first poem
                in the Persian language.)

THE SPRING

Paradisiac cloud, or idol, has dressed the land in the gala clothes of April.
    And the world so far is changed that, you might say, the tiger only in the struggle pounces on the roe buck.
    And the rose garden seems the paradise of Eden, its trees adorned with flowers like the houris of heaven.
    The earth seems brocade tinted with blood, and the wind seems a hand annointed with fragrant musk.
    Graceful hand which, in lines of wine and moss, portrays a friend on the grass of the lawn:
    An idol with ruby-colored cheek, red wine like a shining vestment in the temple!
    And you'd say the world is become like a peacock; there it is rough and rugged, here it is soft and smooth.
    And from the dust exhales a rosewater scent so that, you would say, roses are blended with the mud.
    But good Daqiqi of the world's uncounted things four has chosen, four gracious virtues of all good and ill,
    A lip that seems ruby and the soft lament of the lute, wine the color of blood, of Zarathustra the faith.
        DAQIQI (d.952, poet of the Samanid court)

AUTUMN IS COME

The mount is become another mount, of silver, and of gold is the pasture made.
    Yet the water is become shining, and shadowy the air.
    The dove coos no longer since the orchard is laid empty.
    Silent is the nightingale since the garden is laid bare.
    The pomegranate is like cornelian seals in a golden box, the apple is like signs of weeping on a silver face.
    The cold wind is come like the sigh of lovers at dawn, the song of the crow is come like an angry message from the beloved.
        RUDAQI

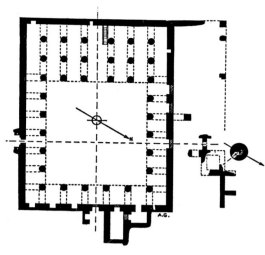

Damghan (Iran): Plan of the Tari Khane. The design is of the Iraqi type, but in its structure and spatial conception it fits completely into the Sassanian architectural tradition.

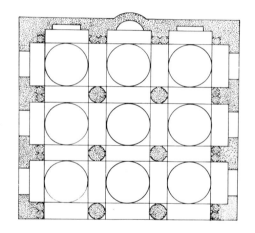

Balkh (Afghanistan): Plan of one of the oldest mosques known in the eastern territories of ancient Iran.

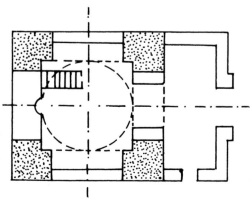

Yazd-i Kasht (Iran): Plan of an ancient chahartaq, converted into a mosque.

write the *Shah-Nama,* The Book of Kings, the summit of the ancient Persian epic. The Samanids, indeed, promoted the collection of ancient Persian poetry, albeit placing it within the framework of the historical development of Islamism, and it is of interest to note that it was primarily the eastern orthodox dynasties that became champions of Persian culture, while Arabic letters flourished under those of the Iranian Shiite influences. But we should not therefore think, as a result of some romantic view of history, that these feudal dynasties were the initiators of national states or cultures. Thus it is only with caution that we employ the expression "Iranian renaissance," which this period is usually called. The birth of Persian poetry was an aristocratic phenomenon, which ripened in the eastern Sunnite courts, especially in that of the Samanids, during the period of the maximum cultural enrichment of the entire Islamic world, the ninth and tenth centuries. Persian poetry, thus, grew out of an international Islamic culture that customarily used Arabic but, as if in a refined exercise, now began to employ a new language. It was a sort of "variation on a theme," to use the description of Alessandro Bausani, in which "the theme is the common, unified Islamic culture (which should not be identified with 'Arab culture' in view of its strong Persian element) and the variations are the individual national languages."

As for the visual arts, particularly with the shift of the center of power from Syria to Mesopotamia, the Iranian legacy was at once integrated into Islam, as a result of Islam's need to provide a ceremonial apparatus for the state that had been imposed by political exigencies. The Iranian artistic tradition had remained virtually intact, in part because most of the artists and artisans had suffered little or nothing from the Moslem conquest. The relative scarcity of archaeological evidence in the genuine Iranian territories — although it has become richer in recent decades — should not deceive us. The revelations of the Abbasid art of Samarra are proof of the vitality of an Iranian art that, in response to the needs of the new lords, renewed itself with a minimal ideological adaptation of its own expressive means.

In the eastern provinces of Islam, Iran, and the territories of outer Iran, we do not have adequate monumental remains — or at least they are not yet well enough known. But what we do possess is sufficient to give a general idea of the characteristics of this area, even if it is not always easy to define the individual regional characteristics. We are familiar with a certain number of mosques that demonstrate the spread of the Iraqi model, from the oldest surviving one, at Damghan, to those of Susa, Shushstar, Siraf, Nayin, Demavend, Lashkari Bazaar, and Chehelburj in the Merv oasis, all built in accordance with typically Iranian patterns. According to the sources, the oldest mosque of Nishapur, in Khurasan (like that of al-Mansur at Baghdad), had a prayer hall with a flat roof supported by exceptionally high wooden columns. This type of structure dates back at least to the Achaemenid period of the ancient world, and it was to hold its own in Iran for a long time to come. The mosque of Tari Khane at Damghan, begun in the eighth century, with its great round pillars and slightly elliptical vaults, stems completely in its brick structure and spatial conception from the Sassanian architectural tradition. In the later mosque of Nayin, the Masjid-i Juma, dated to about 960, the round pillars became slimmer and more daring, but its architectural decoration framed by stucco, although in a style derived from Samarra, was used in the Sassanid palace of Damghan.

Discovered in the Balkh area of Afghanistan (between 1966 and 1967) was a mosque of obscure origin but of the special type already met in Spain and Ifriqiya and examples of which are also to be found in Egypt and Iraq. It is of square design, open on three sides, and covered with nine domes resting on enormous round piers like those at Damghan; the piers are lined entirely with stucco in a style closely connected with the A and B styles of Samarra. This decoration makes it one of the most complete examples of these styles discovered east of Mesopotamia and dates the structure to about the middle of the ninth century.

The vitality of the Sassanian tradition manifested itself not only in building techniques and decorative practices but also in the very fundamentals of architectural planning. For the mosque, in fact, not only the Iraqi type was used but also types that were characteristic of and congenial to local architectural and ideological traditions. Although the examples that have come down to us are still few in number, we may say that for the mosque the *chahar taq* type was commonly used — that is, a tetrapylon formed by four supporting elements, connected by arches and covered by a dome. This was the simplest and most widespread type of sacred building in Iran, the one in which the sacred fire of the ancient Zoroastrian religion was exposed. With a minimum of adaptations, this building lent itself exceptionally well to the function of housing the *mihrab*. It is often known as a kiosk-mosque.

One Sassanian *chahar taq* pressed into use as a mosque, for example, was that of Yazd-i Kasht, in Fars; a tetrapylon was probably incorporated into the later structures of the Masjid-i Juma of Yazd; and isolated *chahar taqs* functioning as mosques continued to be built at least up to the sixteenth century. Stemming directly from a tetrapylon, of the variety where the central hall was included in an ambulatory, is the mosque of Hazara, near Bukhara, which dates to the tenth-eleventh centuries.

Another typically Persian architectural form, particularly in civil architecture and of wide ceremonial use — and no less typical than the domed hall that, as we have mentioned, constituted the throne room in Sassanian palaces — is the *iwan*, the monumental niche. It, too, was used as a mosque, and we have a fine example of this, although altered to some extent, at Niriz in Fars, dated to around 970, which in its original version had an interior with deep niches. Indications are that the Masjid-i Juma of Shiraz — built by the Saffarid Amr ibn Layth around 890 — was also made up of an *iwan*. Its roof, constructed as a series of transverse arches connected on top by small vaults that permitted the removal of the windows from the walls, employed a construction technique known in the Sassanian palace of Iwan-i Kharkha (Khuzistan) and which was to be continued in the subsequent Seljuk and Ilkhanid periods. The original designs of the Masjid-i Jami of Tabriz, built in the eighth century, and of the Masjid-i Arg of Bam, built in the ninth century, also probably employed the *iwan*. These two architectural forms — domed hall and *iwan* — which were to become the characteristic forms of all subsequent Islamic-Iranian architecture, introduced into Moslem architecture, which tends to be horizontal, a vertical aspect that, although moderate in relation to certain other cultures' architectures, was to remain a constant element in the eastern Islamic world.

The tenth century saw the emergence in Iran, particularly in the northern territories, of an edifice that was to be spread far and wide over the great bulk of the Moslem territories: the mausoleum. We have already noted a first, sporadic example at Samarra, the Qubbat al-Sulaybiyya. This diffusion of the mausoleum evidently must be seen in connection with the development of the worship of the tombs of Shiite "saints," such as at the mausoleum of Fatima at Qumm, dated to the second half of the ninth century, and that of Ali at Najaf, dated to the early tenth century. But a no less strong incentive was to come from the princes of the new dynasties born out of the dissolution of the Abbasid empire, for these princes were ever on the lookout for means of increasing their prestige and glory. In the Caspian area a type of tomb came into use that had a round or polygonal tower, covered by a dome with a sloping, tent-like roof, either conical or pyramidal. Worthy of note is that known as the Gumbat-i Qabus, built in 1006–1007 for Qabus ibn Vashmgir, one of the last Ziyarid princes of Gurgan, in northern Iran. It is a slightly tapered structure, some 160 feet high, its shaft enlivened by large triangular spurs. On the surface of bare brickwork, in the panels between the spurs, are simple but vigorous Kufic inscriptions. It is without doubt the most beautiful mausoleum of this type, a superb monument erected to the glory of a prince. Built not long afterwards were the round tombs of Lajim (1016–17) in Mazanderan, with a double inscription — in Kufic and Pahlawi characters; that of West Radkan, Khurasan, of 1020–27; and the Pir-i Alamdar at Damghan, of 1021.

Another type of mausoleum destined to become widespread was the

Nayin (Iran): The Masjid-i Juma, dated to 960, with a view of its Iraqi-type prayer hall. Its Sassanian pillars, although somewhat lighter and more slender, are entirely decorated with stuccowork, in a style derived from Samarra. On the right is the great wooden *mimbar*.

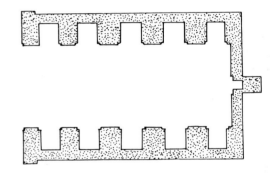

Niriz (Iran): Plan of the original Masjid-i Juma ("the Friday mosque").

Gurgan (Iran): Reconstruction of the Gumbat-i Qabus.

qubba type, made up of a square base covered by a dome. The oldest example of this type that has survived also constitutes the last outstanding work of Samanid architecture: the tomb of Ismail at Bukhara, begun about 907 and completed by 943. It is easy to trace the origins of this mausoleum back to the *chahar taq* type, just as previous Sassanian structures can be seen as the source of the gallery with small arches hiding the transition area of the dome and the four characteristic small corner domes. These latter — a motif that was to spread to the architecture of Moslem India — have no corresponding element in the interior, which enjoys a more extensive spatial dimension. The facade has four doors, each inside an architectural cornice, and the corners are resolved by columns, which, rather than being an echo of Abbasid architecture, hark back to a central Asian architectural tradition. The edifice is entirely of baked material, and both the internal and external decoration is obtained by playing on the possibilities of geometric combinations of baked clay left exposed and integrated with sculptured brickwork. This baked clay decoration, several examples of which we have already come across in Abbasid architecture, was to become characteristic of the later Ghaznavid and Seljuk art. Although stucco ornamentation is confined to a few details in the mausoleum of Ismail, elsewhere it was still widely used for interiors, as is shown by the numerous panels at Nishapur and at Samarkand, chiefly in the A and B styles of Samarra. Outstanding among the *qubba* mausoleums — the most extensively documented style in Central Asia — is that of Arab Ata at Tim in the Zarafshan Valley (U.S.S.R.), dated to 977–78; according to local tradition, it is the tomb of an Arab from the time of the original conquest. It presents one special feature, a facade somewhat higher and more accentuated than usual. The transition area of the dome, moreover, provides the oldest known example of niches with *muqarnas*, or stalactites.

The architecture of the Samanid palaces is still not that well known, but we can get some idea of the civil architecture of this period by studying the private dwellings of Central Asia of the sixth and seventh centuries. Basically the type called for a great quadrangular tower on a high sloping foundation bearing an elevated structure with walls enlivened by semicircular bastions, one adjoining the other and connected on top by niches that support a parapet. Indications are that there was only one door, which led to the two-story interior. The various rooms were distributed on the two floors in accord with one of the most common designs: a domed central hall, which formed the core for four other halls. This design was of the type that we know was typical of the *dar al-imara* of Merv and of the ceremonial part of the Samarra palaces. The bastioned type of castle was to remain in use at least up to the twelfth or thirteenth century. A stupendous example of the bastioned wall is to be found in the caravansary built by the Qarakhanids in 1078–89 and known as Rabat-i Malik, at Bukhara. The great development of commerce led to an intense campaign of caravansary building, numerous examples of which are to be found in Central Asia, some of them fairly ancient, such as that of Beleuli of the end of the tenth century, on the "road of the Khwarezmshah": running toward the Volga, this road served commerce with eastern Europe as far as the Scandinavian peninsula. Another ancient example was that of Basham, in southern Turkmenistan (U.S.S.R.) of the tenth-eleventh centuries. This had the peculiarity of being divided into two separate parts — one with an open court followed by one that was completely roofed over; this design might be the prototype of the Anatolian caravansaries of the thirteenth century, the Seljuk era.

It appears probable that in Khurasan the dwelling house also adopted, in its most advanced forms, the central court design with four axial *iwans*; this and the aforementioned form with the cruciform hall, may be considered a variant of one type. The four-*iwan* court was an Iranian form, its oldest example represented by the Parthian palace of Assur in Upper Mesopotamia of the first century A.D. In the Sassanid palace of Shapur I (A.D. 241–72) at Bishapur, in Fars, we also have an arrangement of this type, if we follow Godard in excluding the dome covering the great central hall. This pattern was to become the classic type in Iranian

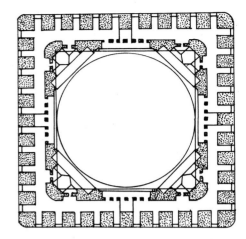

Bukhara (U.S.S.R.): The mausoleum of Ismail the Samanid, dated to the first half of the tenth century. This is a classical example of decorative effects obtained by playing on the geometric combinations of bricks.

Bukhara (U.S.S.R.): Plan of the upper gallery of the mausoleum of Ismail the Samanid.

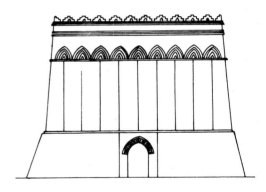

Merv (U.S.S.R.): Reconstruction of a house-tower with bastioned walls.

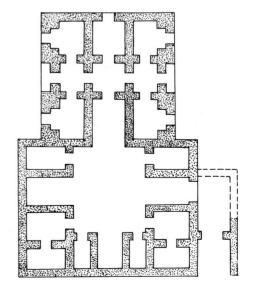

Basham (U.S.S.R.): Plan of the caravansary.

Ghazni (Afghanistan): The minaret of the Ghaznavid sultan Masud III; this drawing is based on a British photograph of the nineteenth century.

architecture. It is to be found, in fact, in the regal palaces of the Ghaznavid sultans, the Turkish dynasty that replaced its patrons, the Samanids, in the east of the Iranian highlands and established its capital at Ghazni, in Afghanistan.

We introduce the Ghaznavids here since they may be considered the political and even cultural heirs of the Samanids. For although the language of the government remained Arabic, it was at the court of Ghazni that Firdausi completed the *Shah-Nama,* the same court that saw the flourishing of a cluster of celebrated personalities such as the great scientist al-Biruni. Ghaznavid art, as yet not well known, may be considered the sister of the great Persian art that was to take hold in the Seljuk period. Our knowledge of the architecture of this Ghaznavid dynasty, which extended its dominion to India — where, in the end, it was to have its main interests, after it was driven out of Iran by the Seljuks — is centered chiefly around two great palaces. One of these dates back to the time of the dynasty's most illustrious representative, Mahmud (999–1030) and is located at Lashkari Bazaar, a royal city near Bust. The other was built by one of Mahmud's successors, Masud III (1099–1115) at Ghazni itself; it was completed in 1111.

These two Ghaznavid palaces were built primarily of compressed mud and unbaked brick, with selective use of baked brick in the lining and at points bearing the most stress. But while that of Lashkari Bazaar is fairly well preserved, thanks to the arid climate of the region, the altogether different climatic conditions of Ghazni and the destructive work of treasure hunters have wrought havoc with the fragile structure of the palace of Masud III, so that it is now virtually demolished. Both palaces are of quadrangular design, with a central court faced axially by the four *iwans,* their sizes varying in direct relation to their functions. The largest *iwans* are that of the entrance and that leading to the throne room, which faced each other in accordance with the principle of axial symmetry; this was an old Iranian principle that had come to the fore in Abbasid architecture, from which Ghaznavid architecture drew a number of

Bust (Afghanistan): Main arch of the *iwan* **of a great mosque, possibly to be attributed to the Ghaznavid era of the twelfth century.**

MY POETRY

With a caravan load of fabrics have I set out from Sistan, with cloth spun from the heart, woven by the soul.

Fabrics made of a silk called Words, with patterns painted by a painter whose name is Tongue.

Each thread with effort was torn from the breast; each weft or woof, tormentedly left the heart.

These, these are not cloths woven like other cloths; judge you them not similar to others!

This is not cloth that may be harmed by flood; this is not cloth that may be hurt by fire.

Its color is not ruined by the dust of Earth, nor can the passing of Time efface its pattern!

> FARRUKHI (d.1038, one of the most famous poets of the Ghaznavid Court)

ELEGY UPON THE DEATH OF THE SULTAN MAHMUD

The city of Ghazna is not the same city that last year I saw: what can have become of it, that all is now so changed?

The streets see I in tumult and the open places full of weapons and armor, of knights and horses.

Princes do I see beating their faces like weeping women, eyes do I see made rose-colored through weeping blood.

The king, this year, is come not back from his wars: an Enemy is descended upon this city, upon this land.

Or perhaps yesterday he drank too much wine, sleeps still and wakes not, stricken still by drunkenness?

Arise, O King! For from afar are come the messengers of princes and many gifts have brought and regal offerings.

But now, who can awake you from this sleep?

Aye, heavy sleep has taken you now, such that you raise not your head from this repose.

Yet was it not, O King, your custom to sleep so long; no man ever saw you sleep so soundly.

Still yet a little while should you have held court upon your throne that your trusted friends and family might yet have beheld your face.

Trembling for fear of you kings would hide in their castles.

Out of fear for whom, O Sovereign, are you now locked in the castle?

Poets in song and crowds in acclaim enflamed for you; you went away and suddenly that song departed into nothing!

> FARRUKHI

elements. The four-*iwan* design is repeated in the apartments of the private section, which, as was customary, was placed alongside the throne room. The facades facing the courts are interrupted by niches, particularly deep in the palace of Masud III, while the exterior facade had a similar design. As was the palace of Lashkari Bazaar, this latter was probably spread over two stories. The only entrance was aligned with the facade, meaning that it had no monumental gatehouse (or *pishtaq*).

The palace of Masud III contained a large prayer hall, directly adjacent to the court, but also communicating with a spacious waiting hall in the vestibular area; this hall, evidently matched by another on the other side of the vestibule, was square in shape and divided by four polystylar pillars. This prayer hall, in effect a mosque, was of the hypostyle type, with wooden columns resting on bases of sculptured marble. The space between the columns is wider on the axis leading to the *mihrab*, which is of the "Eastern type" — that is, with a square rather than rounded niche. The outer facade of the palace is broken by a large square tower, probably the base of a minaret. At Lashkari Bazaar, in consideration of the fact that the court was moved there temporarily, the exceptionally large mosque is situated outside the palace itself, along the west wall of the great forecourt, an arrangement calling to mind the Abbasid palace of Balkuwara. After the mosque at Balkh, this one at Lashkari Bazaar is the oldest known mosque of Afghanistan. It consists of the one prayer hall, open on three sides, and with little depth (it is some 280 by 35 feet), with two side naves set off by baked clay columns supporting a roof of small domes. The naves are intersected on the axis with the *mihrab* by a sort of transept, above which one sees a dome resting on four columns. A dome in front of the *mihrab* in a mosque with a broad hall is an innovation in the Iranian context, so far as is known; it provides a useful element to the

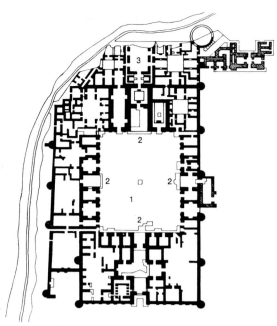

Lashkari Bazaar (Afghanistan): Plan of the palace founded in the time of Mahmud of Ghazni (999–1030).
1 Central court
2 Iwan
3 Throne room (where a number of striking paintings were recovered)

Ghazni (Afghanistan). Palace of Masud III.
1 Central court
2 Iwan
3 Throne room
4 Apartment
5 Prayer hall
6 Waiting hall
7 Great square
8 Shops

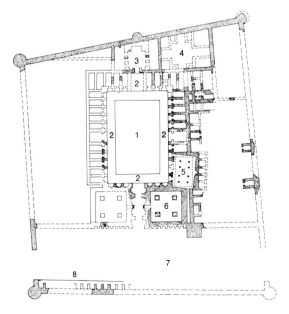

study of the early Iranian mosque, about which little is known. In nearby Bust, for instance, there seems to have been a four-*iwan* mosque, its only remains being the grandiose entrance arch of baked clay, enhanced with decorations. The dating of the arch to sometime in the Ghaznavid period has not, however, been proved.

In discussing these two palaces, we have mentioned their ceremonial areas, which unfortunately have not come down to us intact. Particularly outstanding is that of the palace of Masud III, although it is reduced to little more than its foundations. In it we find a great *iwan* standing in front of the throne room, which was square in shape, with a rectangular niche in the rear covered by a stone hood over the throne itself. A number of fragments in the baked material of this hood suggest that the throne room, flanked by massive pillars, was covered by a dome. If this surmise is correct, this is the first time within the Iranian-Islamic framework that we run across the use in a regal palace of this device of ceremonial Sassanian architecture, which is documented by a whole series of palaces, from those of Firuzabad, Qala-i Dukhtar, Qasr-i Shirin, and Damghan, to the first known *dar al-imara*, that of Kufa in 670, and which we shall find again in Seljuk mosques.

The decoration was chiefly brickwork, at times functioning structurally but more often executed independently in panels and then applied to the walls. It consisted of interweaving geometric motifs and arabesques and large Kufic and Nashki inscriptions, with the whole painted in a lively polychromy of blue, red, and yellow. In the Lashkari Bazaar palace, a large role was also played by stucco, which decorated the facade as well, while in the more recent Ghazni palace, stucco was generally reserved for the panels inserted into the brickwork decoration. At Ghazni, marble was also used lavishly, an unusual material for this period, perhaps to be attributed to an Indian influence, although nothing Indian is seen in the technique or in the style. The marble work at the palace of Masud III included molding of the outer facade and the court, and it was decorated with arabesques derived from the tree of life within a stylized architectural cornice bordered by a Kufic inscription containing a poem glorifying the Ghaznavid sultans. Of particular significance was the fact that the language of the poem was Persian — not Arabic, the epigraphic language par excellence throughout the Islamic world. The inscription is one of the oldest examples, and among the most revealing, of the epigraphic use of Persian, and is a document of great cultural value. The poetic vision set down in the epic meter of *The Book of Kings* by Firdausi reflects the two great ideals on which Ghaznavid society was based: on the one hand, the defense and expansion of orthodox Sunnite Islam; on the other, an appeal to legendary Persian traditions through the forms of poetry.

Also found at the palace at Ghazni was a profusion of architectural bas-reliefs — hunting scenes of the Sassanian type, animals, dancing girls, and bodyguards in Central Asian costumes — contributing a completely new chapter to the history of Moslem art. In the central province of Lashkari Bazaar, the materials were less luxurious; nevertheless, the throne room has provided us with a series of pictures depicting bodyguards in rich apparel, treated in a style derived from the late-classical experience of Central Asia, a unique survivor of the murals that, so we learn from early sources, frequently were a part of the interior decorations of Ghaznavid palaces.

Still standing at Ghazni are parts of two towers, that named after Masud III and that of Bahram Shah, as we are informed by the Kufic inscriptions on the ornamental borders, a particularly elegant variety of Kufic elaborated in Khurasan. All that remains of the towers, which stood near two still unexplored mosques — and are therefore probably minarets — are the base sections in the form of star-shaped polygons; nothing is left of the cylindrical shafts that attained heights of up to 200 feet. (In the case of the tower of Masud III, its height is known because of a nineteenth-century photograph, taken before the top was destroyed.) This type of minaret, tall and slender, with its cylindrical shaft on a usually polygon base, appears to have emerged in northwest Iran at the close of the tenth century and the beginning of the eleventh.

THE SELJUK PERIOD

The eleventh century brought a fundamental development that was to initiate a new period in the history of Islam: the wide-scale penetration of the Islamic world by Turkish peoples, and the creation of a Turkish empire, that of the Seljuks, which was to condition the entire subsequent unfolding of affairs in the eastern half of the Moslem territory, from the Mediterranean to Central Asia. The Seljuk Turks — so called after their eponymous founder, who had become converted to Islam — were of the Ghuz group of Turks, known later as Turkemans, and hailed from the Central Asian steppes. Having spread out through Transoxiana and Khurasan, they defeated the Ghazanavids near Merv in 1040 and seized northern Persia and Azerbaijan. They then passed into Mesopotamia where, as Sunnite Moslems defending orthodoxy, they entered Baghdad in 1055 and drove out the last Shiite Buids. The Seljuk chieftain, Tugrul Beg, was recognized by the caliph as "king of the east and west" as well as sultan, and was accorded great powers. Under his successors, Alp Arslan and Malik Shah — both renowned military leaders with a strong sense of state organization — the Seljuks attained the summit of their power. In 1071, the defeat of the Byzantines at Manzikert opened the doors of Anatolia, which became the goal of the restless tribes from Central Asia; having "Turkocized" Asia Minor, they soon made themselves independent of the Seljuks to the east and established the Sultanate of Rum ("the west," specifically the territories that belonged to Byzantium), which was to last until the outset of the fourteenth century.

Their conquest of Syria and Palestine led the Seljuks to a clash with the heretic Fatimids and then with the Crusaders, who occupied Jerusalem in 1099. To the east, the Ghaznavids had to all intents and purposes become their vassals. Despite the efforts of Alp Arslan and Malik Shah, and their Persian Grand Vizier, or prime minister, the famous Nizam al-Mulk, to set up a strongly centralized state, the Seljuk empire was based essentially on a kind of feudalism (a term used for convenience, but which should not be thought of here as literally the same as the Western socioeconomic institution), with its cohesion guaranteed by the army. At the death of Malik Shah (1092), the empire broke up into a large number of rival autonomous principalities ruled by *atabegs* — generals, but originally men who served as sort of regent-tutors of the young Seljuk princes destined to govern the various provinces. The last of the great Seljuks, Sanjar, son of Malik Shah, whose reign was long and full of strife (1118–57), was left with nothing but part of Iran. Sanjar, waging a campaign against the new waves of Turks pressing into his realm from the northwest, was to die in battle against his fellow Oghuz tribesmen, who were still nomads wandering through northeast Iran. Meanwhile, the Ghorids of central Afghanistan were in a phase of expansion, the Khwarezmshah tribesmen were girding themselves for an invasion of Iran, and the time of the great Mongolian invasion of Genghis Khan (1220) was drawing near.

When the Seljuk Turks first invaded these various territories, they wrought no substantial harm; indeed, in the wake of the tangled situation of the ninth and tenth centuries, these territories enjoyed a relative peace and, for a moment, there was even a tendency toward their political reunification. But, through the confusion of local events that soon followed, one can descry a number of characteristics of a positive nature that make it possible to describe this as "the second epoch of Islamic classicism" (O. Grabar), after the initial one of the Umayyads and Abbasids. It was, in fact, a time of great new integrations and syntheses that emerged out of the new contacts among the Turks, the Christians of Asia Minor, and the Indians. The Sunnite orthodoxy gained new vigor, and a powerful mystical element in Islamism emerged — Sufism. While the figure of the sovereign became identified with the sultan, who wielded part of the universal power originally reserved for the caliph alone, the

QUATRAINS FROM THE RUBAIYAT OF OMAR KHAYYAM

I
Awake! for Morning in the Bowl of Night
Has flung the Stone that puts the Stars to Flight,
   And lo! the Hunter of the East has caught
The Sultan's Turret in the Noose of Light.

II
Dreaming, when Dawn's Left Hand was in the Sky,
I heard a Voice within the Tavern cry,
   "Awake, my Little Ones, and fill the Cup
Before Life's Liquor in its cup be dry."

XI
Here with a Loaf of Bread beneath the Bough,
A Flask of Wine, a Book of Verse — and Thou
   Beside me singing in the Wilderness —
And Wilderness is Paradise enow.

XIV
The Worldy Hope men set their Hearts upon
Turns Ashes — or it prospers; and anon,
   Like Snow upon the Desert's Dusty Face
Lighting a little Hour or two — is gone.

XXVI
Oh, come with old Khayyam and leave the Wise
To talk; one thing is certain, that Life flies;
   One thing is certain, and the Rest is Lies:
The Flower that once has blown for ever dies.

LI
The Moving Finger writes; and, having writ,
Moves on: nor all thy Piety nor Wit
   Shall lure it back to cancel half a Line,
Nor all thy Tears wash out a Word of it.

LVIII
Oh Thou, who Man of baser Earth didst make,
And who with Eden didst devise the Snake;
   For all the Sin wherewith the Face of Man
Is blackened, Man's Forgiveness give — and take.

   OMAR KHAYYAM (eleventh-century mathematician and poet; the translation here is the famed rendering of Edward Fitzgerald)

Isfahan (Iran): A view of the court of the Masjid-i Juma. This is the oldest known four-iwan mosque, datable to the late eleventh century (although most of what is now seen dates from later). On the left is the south *iwan*, the main one, which is followed by the domed hall that precedes the *mihrab*. The ar-rangement of the *muqarnas* of the south *iwan* dates to the time of Huzan Hassan (1475). The glazed faience decoration was frequently retouched in the Safavid era, under Shah Tahmasp and Shah Abbas III (1661). On the right is the west *iwan;* its ornamentation dates to the late Safavid era (eighteenth century).

caliph regained his dignity and spiritual authority. It was a time of extreme intellectual vivacity in which Iran was once more to play a decisive role, bringing forth an al-Ghazali, the theologian, a Nizami, the poet, and an Omar Khayyam, the poet. It was the era in which "shape was given to all the elements that were to characterize Moslem culture down through the centuries to our own day." The coming of the Seljuks generated a dynamic renewal that manifested itself in a mixing of the social classes, a far-reaching increase in urban development, and intensive commercial and cultural contacts that restored a sort of unity to the entire territory involved, from the Mediterranean to Afghanistan.

From the standpoint of artistic achievement, the Seljuk period was one of Islam's most brilliant, astonishing for the profusion and variety of its output. For Islamic Iran, it unquestionably represented a period of

Isfahan (Iran): The south *iwan* of the Masjid-i Juma as viewed from across the roof of the east *iwan*. The dome in front of the *mihrab* was erected some time before 1088–89 by Nizam al-Mulk, the great prime minister of the Seljuk sultan Malik Shah (1072–92).

Right:
Above:
Isfahan (Iran): A section of the interior of the pavilion of Taj al-Mulk, on the north side of the Masjid-i Juma, erected in 1088–89. Originally it was not part of the same complex as the mosque but was only connected later on. The dome rests on the square section of the drum by means of elegant niches with *muqarnas*. Around the impost of the dome is a simple but monumental inscription in Kufic characters. This is an unsurpassed masterpiece of brickwork architecture.

Below:
Isfahan (Iran): View of the interior of one of the wings of the Masjid-i Juma.

Pages 70–71
Above:
Bukhara (U.S.S.R.): The Masjid-i Magok Attar, a mosque of the twelfth century. To be noted in the rich decoration of the facade is the motif of round pillars, a reminder of the bastions of castles.

Below:
Jam (Afghanistan): A minaret erected near the ancient capital of the Ghorid dynasty, Firuzkuh, during the reign of the sultan Ghiyas al-Din Muhammad (1163–1203). It is more than 200 feet high. Standing out from the complex brickwork decoration is the fine Kufic inscription in glazed blue faience. Another inscription, now lost, adorned the polygonal base.

Right:
Bukhara (U.S.S.R.): The Kalan Minar (great minaret"), built in 1127.

maximum splendor: between the eleventh and thirteenth centuries, Iran experienced the definitive integration of its traditional, typological, and aesthetic legacy with the new elements. But in general, although there developed a substantial unity throughout the area of Seljuk predominance, we can define not only the numerous local variants but three great artistic provinces with distinctive characteristics: the eastern one, represented by Iran and its Central Asian extensions; that of Mesopotamia and Syria; and that of Asia Minor, the Sultanate of Rum. Building activity under the Seljuks was particularly lively, an emanation not only from the prince and the military class wielding power but also the urban, mercantile, and intellectual bourgeoisie, all of whom supported it for reasons of social, cultural, or economic advancement. And of course a significant contribution was made by religious institutions, in spite of the lack of an authentic religious hierarchy; they were active in the support of and in the framework of a political program of orthodox religious education promoted by the state, geared to the aim of curbing all heretical movements — particularly that of the Shiite-Ismailite sect — in that they saw the actions of all these as a threat to peace and security. But the religious institutions themselves were now influenced by Sufic-mystical currents incorporated into orthodoxy, and the end result was the multiplication of religious structures — mausoleums, convents, oratories.

The Great Seljuks

The Seljuk era was a period of both rich architectural inventiveness and the establishment of types, and although both trends were to remain active until the modern age, they were not always especially productive. Their matrixes are to be sought principally in the framework of Iranian culture, although much investigation remains to be done. (Still to be defined, for instance, is the authentic Turkish contribution to Seljuk architecture, it being more often assumed than demonstrated, or the relations with Armenian architecture.) But we may properly think of Iran during the eleventh and twelfth centuries as the time of "the great Seljuks," with the center at Isfahan.

The model of the kiosk-mosque that, as we have seen, may be considered native to Iran, continued to be viable in the Seljuk era, and we have numerous outstanding examples, such as the original phases of the main mosque of Ardistan (1072–92), that of Qazvin (1106–14), that of the Madrassa Haidariye of Qazvin, and that of the mosque of Gulpayagan (1105–18). The dome of this last-named, by the way, with its slightly squashed shape, its slender external ribs, and the lozenge decoration on the drum, has suggested to some a Turkish influence based on their tents. The most outstanding development in the architecture of the Seljuk era, however, is represented by the introduction of a new type of mosque, which may be considered the classical Iranian mosque, based as it is on the four *iwans* around a central court. The reasons why this type was adopted are not known for sure. The commonly accepted theory is that of Godard, according to whom the four-*iwan* mosque, which took its precise shape in the twelfth century, is derived from the house plans of Khurasan, transmitted through the *madrassa,* or theological colleges; in any case, this has given rise to one name for this type of mosque, the *madrassa*-mosque. According to van Berchem, the design first appeared in Khurasan at the outset of the tenth century as a private school, housed in the residence of the teacher himself. Toward the middle of the next century, the schools emerged from the private sector to become a political institution under control of the state, in accord with the political pro-

grams of the Seljuks, as dictated by their prime minister, Nizam al-Mulk. He, in turn, drew his inspiration from the Ghaznavids, for whom the religious school had become essentially an instrument for the reeducation of people in orthodoxy. The oldest *madrassa*, founded by Nizam al-Mulk, was that inaugurated in 1067 at Baghdad, but no trace remains — as is the case with many others resulting from his initiative. One exception is the remains of one, datable between 1080 and 1092, at Kharghird, Khurasan, which has four *iwans* but is otherwise much like a private dwelling.

The first mosque to adopt this four-*iwan* plan, as far as we know, is the renowned "Friday Mosque" of Isfahan, the Masjid-i Juma, which is believed to have taken on this aspect after 1120–21, when it was rebuilt on the site of the Iraqi-Abbasid one, destroyed by fire. But the Isfahan mosque, even prior to this reconstruction, had been the object of activity of the Seljuks in the person of Taj al-Mulk, a rival of Nizam al-Mulk; the former had built, in 1088–89, on the axis of the *qibla*, but on the opposite side, a highly elegant domed pavilion, one of the masterpieces of Iranian architecture, and which was to be a sort of ceremonial entrance to the mosque, although not directly connected to it. It is to Nizam al-Mulk, however, that we owe the present domed hall overlooking the *mihrab*. This hall can be traced back to the type of kiosk-mosque built during the reign of Malik Shah (1072–92), but dating back to some time before the Taj al-Mulk pavilion. The two edifices were undamaged in the fire of 1120–21, and the great domed hall of Nizam was organically included in the reconstruction of the mosque, which adopted — due to the influence of the *madrassa*, according to Godard — the four-*iwan* design, with one of the *iwans* placed before the domed hall. This breathed new life into an ancient Sassanian formula, which had been associated particularly with royalty — the *iwan* serving as a vestibule to a domed ceremonial hall. The association can obviously not have been merely mechanical or accidental.

Merv (U.S.S.R.): The mausoleum of Sultan Sanjar (1157), in the *qubba* style. The dome looms over the bare, powerful base, thanks to the high drum that included two series of arcades; the dome's connecting area is hidden by a gallery once richly adorned with glazed blue faience.

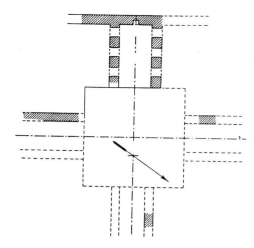

Khargird (Iran): Plan of the Nizamiye, a madrassa believed to have been built by Nizam al-Mulk between 1080 and 1092. The four-iwan design was that usually used in Khurasan homes and came to be used throughout much of the Islamic world in the design of madrassas. The madrassa, a school intended for religious teaching, became under the Seljuks a means of continuing the program initiated by the Ghaznavids, and as such the school was a political institution under the control of the state, an instrument for reeducation into orthodoxy. Each iwan is believed to have housed one of the four schools that taught the proper way under Islam.

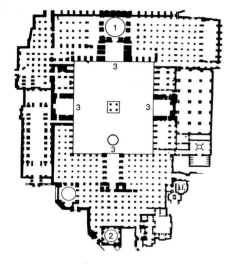

Isfahan (Iran): Plan of the Masjid-i Juma.
1 Great domed pavilion of Nizam al-Mulk, resting on heavy polystylar pillars
2 Domed pavilion of Taj al-Mulk
3 Iwans added after fire of 1120–21

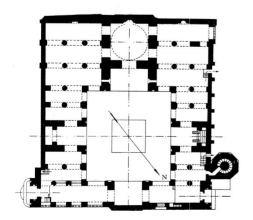

Zaware (Iran): Plan of the Masjid-i Juma. This is the first known mosque in Iran built from the very outset with four iwans; it is modeled on the great mosque of Isfahan.

Bearing in mind a number of stimulating observations about this matter, particularly those by Oleg Grabar and Richard Ettinghausen, we shall offer a few theories of our own. This type of mosque does not satisfactorily meet the needs of Islamic community prayer, for its design is similar to that of private dwellings and their derivatives: the palace of the sultan and the caravansary, both of which appear to have contained an iwan complex plus a domed hall. Such types of buildings had come to the fore prior to the madrassa and the Seljuk mosque. The variants in design of this last-named respond, therefore, to the special demands of the earlier edifices, with their fundamental function, to one degree or another, of accommodating a considerable number of individuals. As was first indicated by Monneret de Villard, and later illustrated by Etting-hausen, the four-iwan mosque was not only intended for prayer but also for teaching, for the lodging of teachers and students, for housing the library, and for all the charitable activities in a stopping place for pilgrims, the ill, and such. The mosque, in other words, also functioned as a hospital in its historically original sense, a hospice; this would explain the development of the two stories of roofed-over spaces, which can hardly have been designed merely as strolling areas.

In adopting the domed hall in the mihrab area, the designers certainly were not unaware that the tetrapylon form was taken over from Islamic Iran as an isolated prayer hall. But in the Iranian environment, such a form was also used as the focal element of a wide type of hall, at least up to the outset of the eleventh century, as in the mosque of Lashkari Bazaar. There, however, given its close dependence on the royal palace, the domed element may also have had a ceremonial function; in other words, the domed room may have indicated the place set aside for the prince during prayers. It seems highly probably that the concept of the domed hall linked to royalty was not lost in Islamic Iran, especially if we consider that, in line with Sassanian usage, the exceptionally heavy royal crown, weighted down with symbols, was not actually worn by the Ghaznavid sovereigns but suspended over their heads. The crown of Masud I (1030–41) was held up by four statues, and conceptually speaking it was in fact a dome. The throne room of Masud III in his Ghazni palace (completed in 1111) was made up of an iwan standing in front of a hall that was probably domed.

It is quite likely that during the Seljuk era, in keeping with the strong sense of the state obvious in the goals of this dynasty, a quest was undertaken in building the capital's main mosque to accommodate a wide range of needs — which had long ago outstripped those of community prayer alone — while at the same time to symbolize power. And the sultan's palace was found to be the most suitable model, from a functional point of view as well as from that of the complex of symbolical values its form represented. The formative process of the Juma mosque of Isfahan was not a result, hence, of the chance recovery of an older architectural device, but of an intentional integration. The fact that in the old Iraqi-type Iranian mosque there was no dome marking the mihrab is not so important, perhaps, as the fact that the new type was adopted without delay; the construction of the provincial city of Zaware (1135–36) is one example, and in 1158–60 the need was felt to remodel in line with this royal pattern the kiosk-mosque of Ardistan, which dated back to the time of Malik Shah.

In line with the importance it assumed in the architectural economy, the dome became the object of a series of technical and formal experiments of great interest to architects. Systems were worked out that made it possible to build vaults without wooden supports, achieving results of high artistic value, the ribbed dome being one of the most characteristic examples. An effort was made to diminish the weight of domes, too, rendering them more airy and elegant, and architects began to tackle the problem of double-shell domes, which were to prove so popular in the Timurid era. Particular attention was focused on the joining area between the square base and the circular dome, with the extensive use of the drum enhanced by muqarnas, or stalactite elements, a feature destined to become typical of so much Moslem architecture. The origin of this last-named element, which is more decorative than functional, must be sought apparently in the eastern parts of Iran. We have an early, if not first, example in the tri-lobed connecting sections of the previously described mausoleum of Arab Ata, at Tim (about 978), where we also find the first example of a monumental entranceway (*pishtaq*), also destined to become a typical element of Iranian architecture.

This period also gave rise to the feature of the double minaret flanking the entrance, one of the oldest examples of which is found at Tabas, Iran. As for the free-standing minaret, Iran saw the emergence of a type featuring an exceptionally tall, smooth cylinder broken only by small balconies; the oldest example of this type appears to be that at Damghan, built in 1058. A particularly well-preserved example of the superimposed-shaft minaret is the one at Jam, in central-western Afghanistan, a work of the Ghorid dynasty. Also more or less popular, especially to the east, were those minarets with their shafts enhanced by semicylindrical grooves, a type emulated both in India and in Anatolia. In Central Asia, architects experimented with another variety, characterized by more massive proportions and a markedly tapered shaft, such as that of Bukhara's Kalan mosque, put up in 1127 by a Qarakhanid sovereign, and that of the Vabkent mosque, built in 1198–99.

The funerary monuments were still of the type based on an edifice with towers, such as that of Rayy, built in 1139. The octagonal variety came into widespread use chiefly in central Iran. One of the oldest is that of Abarquh, dated to 1058; outstanding, too, are those discovered in Kharaqan, also of the eleventh century; while in northeast Iran a type with a square base appeared, an example of which is the Gumbat-i Surkh of Maragha (1147–48). The *qubba* mausoleum was spreading all over Khurasan, finding its happiest expression in the Sanjar mausoleum near Merv, built in 1157. Running along a high square base of bare brickwork is a gallery masking the area of the corner connecting elements. It is from this gallery, by means of a high drum enlivened by two series of arcades, that the dome begins its upward curve, its interior enhanced by an elegant ribbing that originally was covered by glazed blue tiles. This type links up with the tomb of Ismail the Samanid at Bukhara; but it has more direct antecedents in mausoleums such as that of Abu Said at Meana (Uzbekistan, U.S.S.R.), dated to around 1050. In Central Asia other types of sepulchral constructions were used, such as those of Dehistan, which are round or octagonal with an unusually deep *iwan;* examples include those of Misriyan and of Khwarezm, where rising up from a square base is a towering drum covered with a conical or pyramidal roof. This type of mausoleum is known as *gumbat* or *turbe.*

Little has remained of the secular or civil structures of this period in Iran. Nothing at all is left, for instance, of the sultans' great palaces that, as mentioned, must have been of the Ghaznavid variety. Worthy of note is a bath at Nigar, south of Kirman, which adopts the type of *suspensurae* of the classical baths; but the design is more a local variant of plans worked out in Syria in the Islamic period. Particular attention was focused on roads, and it was in this era that numerous bridges were built or reconstructed, such as that at Tus. But the most outstanding monument resulting from this activity was the Rabat Sharaf, a caravansary on the great road of Khurasan between Nishapur and Merv. According to Godard, it was built in 1114–15 and restored forty years later, evidently after it had been damaged during the Oghuz uprising. It was a sumptuous structure, entirely of baked brick, with two colonnaded, four-*iwan* courts, one following the other — a design also found in the caravansary of Akcha Kale in the Kara-Kum desert, dated to around the eleventh–twelfth century, and which with variants has come down to the modern age in, for example, Afghanistan. The double court provided the opportunity to select the clientele; the innermost court, the richest in its comforts, also included, at least in the Rabat Sharaf, two apartments with the four-*iwan* design, evidently intended for the most important persons.

Seljuk architecture made extensive use, particularly in its more ambitious structures, of baked brick, spreading even to regions where there had been different traditions, such as Fars — which had made abundant

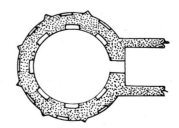

Dehistan (Iran): Plan of a mausoleum of the eleventh–twelfth centuries. Characteristic of this type of sepulcher is the extremely deep iwan *that serves as a vestibule.*

use of stone and mortar — or in Azerbijan. The decorative possibilities of baked brick were stressed by the prominence given the open-faced texture of the walls, developing the principle so perfectly enunciated in the tomb of Ismail at Bukhara. Often the mortar joints receive a molded decoration, which little by little was to be replaced by specially sculptured bricks. The ever wider use of terra-cotta elements, shaped beforehand, was to lead to the development of a sort of mosaic decoration, in which geometric motifs began to approach arabesques, and the decoration was unshackled from the actual construction of the walls to be executed separately and applied to the monument later. In some cases the decoration was directly sculptured into the wall. Some measure of organic correspondence between structure and decoration was always maintained, although in certain small monuments the decoration reached the point of excess, tending to destroy the integrity of the walls as walls. There is no question, however, that the Taj al-Mulk pavilion at Isfahan, of 1088, where the decorativeness of the open-face brickwork was aimed at bringing out the structure's functional and expressive lines in an elegant, concrete definition of the space, remains the unsurpassed example of this type of brickwork architecture. The decoration is further enhanced by large inscriptions, which in this period were to find their widest and most consistent use; Khurasan, in fact, developed its own variation of monumental Kufic, embellished by a high ornamental fringe.

The use of stucco, intended primarily for interiors, was never abandoned completely, but this, too, was to remain within the architectural demands rather than freely covering the available wall surface. About the middle of the twelfth century, as a result of the loss of relief in the brick decoration, the stucco was to spread out like a veil over the walls, reproducing more economically the effects of the brickwork weaving. Panels of stucco, these also colored, were included in the geometric pattern formed by open-face brickwork, and this device marked the beginning of the use of glazed ceramics to decorate the exteriors. The oldest example of this latter is the terra-cotta inscription enameled in turquoise blue on the Damghan minaret, dating to the middle of the eleventh century. This technique and its application were to triumph in the centuries to follow. This era also saw the spread of the use of glazed tiles as decoration of interior walls, a practice foreshadowed at Samarra. Initially, at the close of the eleventh century, use was made of molded tiles and monochrome glazing, with motifs derived from textiles — or so it appears from evidence at Ghazni; then, in the second half of the twelfth century, tiles began to be painted with metallic luster, coinciding with the flourishing in Iran of this advanced technique in pottery. Painting must have played a significant role, too, but little has survived, and the bulk of contemporaneous miniatures have been lost; nevertheless, thanks to the abundant ceramic output of this period, we can to some extent reconstruct the painting of Seljuk Iran as one of rather dull colors and with courtly themes.

Khurasan (Iran): Plan of the Rabat Sharaf caravansary.

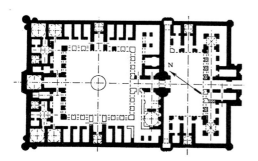

Iraq and Syria Under the Seljuks

Even in these regions of ancient, well-established traditions, the artistic mastery of the Seljuks gained great renown. The architecture of the region was primarily of stone, availing itself of various different materials in order to obtain sober polychrome effects, although the great domes with inner and outer stalactites, in accordance with the Iranian type,

unaysir (Iraq): Plan of the Great Mosque. This plan represents an original variant of the ancient Umayyad design with naves parallel to the qibla wall, both because of the use of a nave-narthex and the particular emphasis given to the dome that precedes the mihrab and that, seen from without, dominates the entire edifice. The dome design reveals an influence from Iranian-Seljuk art. The Dunaysir mosque is rightfully considered one of the masterpieces of Artuchid architecture.

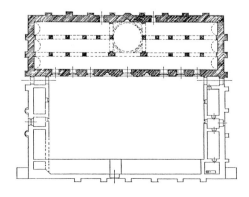

employed brickwork. A number of Iranian types of construction, in fact, were taken over, such as the minaret and the four-*iwan* design for the *madrassas*, while in Iraq the use of the open-face brickwork became widespread. From Iraq of the thirty-fourth caliph, al-Nasir (1180–1225) — a bizarre personality with good organizational qualities, who in the crumbling of the Seljuk empire managed to save a position of independent power for himself — we have the remains of a palace in which unquestionable Seljuk influences appear. Worthy of note are the vaults in which a special interpretation is given to the *muqarnas*, a feature that in Iraq was to assume forms that were distinctively typical; this can be noted first and foremost in a number of mausoleums, with square or polygonal bases that support extremely high pyramid roofs built up of *muqarnas*, not only inside but outside. Particularly famous is the mausoleum of Sitta Zubayda, the wife of Harun al-Rashid, apparently rebuilt around 1200, and that of Imam Dur, from the end of the eleventh century.

As for the activities of the dynasty of Zenghid tribesmen who dominated Syria and Upper Mesopotamia under the *atabeg* of Aleppo and Mosul, attention should be called to the Great Mosque of Mosul of Nur al-Din — the famous Norandin, opponent of the Crusaders — in which we have a "chessboard" structure covered by small domes and barrel vaults, alternately at right angles to one another, and probably the Iranian-type minaret of brickwork. Also to be considered in connection with Nur al-Din are a number of monuments in Damascus, which he conquered in 1154: the *maristan* (hospital) with a four-*iwan* design; and the *madrassa*, to which is attached his tomb, dating to 1172. The *madrassa* has two *iwans* that stand opposite each other and face the court, a design that is perhaps to be traced back to the private dwellings of Egypt. An engaging innovation was a basin in the middle of the court, connected to a fountain gushing water in the back of the *iwan*, opposite the entrance. This was an addition that perhaps stemmed from an Iranian influence and that, as an interior ornament, has also been recognized in a house at Fostat (Egypt), built in the Tulunid period. Both fountain and basin also appear in the main hall of the Zisa at Palermo, begun in 1161 under William I, the Norman, and finished under William II (1166–89).

Some recognition must also be given to another dynasty of Turkish princes, that of the Artuchids, who managed to hold on to Upper Mesopotamia to the last years of the fourteenth century, including the cities of Hisn Kayfa, Mardin, Kharput, Amida (Diyarbekir), and Dunaysir. Their architecture was chiefly in stone, and although receptive to a number of Iranian elements, it moved along a road of its own. Its masterpieces included the imposing towers of Ulu Badan and Yedi Qardesh in Diyarbekir, both enhanced with large inscriptions that accentuate their classic form. The great mosque of Diyarbekir, which we know from its version of 1114–15, harks back to the Damascus type — three naves parallel to the *qibla* wall, broken by a great transept with a truss roof facing a court, surrounded by two tiers of columns. This type was to remain an exception, however, and a different variety of mosque emerged in this region, one made up of a great domed hall on the *mihrab*, between two series of naves parallel to the *qibla* wall, the whole preceded by a sort of gallery-narthex, and the court tending to be relatively smaller. The masterpiece of this type is the Great Mosque of Dunaysir, of 1204; its solid rectangular mass, dominated by a high dome resting on a windowless drum, narrows down at the facade with its elegant and harmonious architectural details.

The Seljuks of Rum

The invasions of the Turkish tribes during the eleventh century brought into the confines of Islam a new territory, Anatolia, or Asia Minor (essentially modern Turkey). In this region a series of Turkish principalities were formed, such as that of the Danishmendids of Sivas, Kayseri and Malatya (1092–1178); the Saltukids of Erzurum (1092–

1202); and the Mengujekids of Erzinjan and Divrighi. But it was one tribe of Turks that ended by gaining the most power over this territory, the Seljuks. These Seljuks, relatives of those who controlled Iran and Mesopotamia, were known as the Seljuks of Rum, their name for "the west," or the territories of the Byzantine empire, whose forces they defeated at Manzikert in 1071. The Seljuks then proceeded to establish their capital at Iznik (ancient Nicaea) between 1082–97, and after that at Konya and Sivas, from 1097 to 1302.

The independent, well-organized Sultanate of Rum, relatively secure along its borders, succeeded in taking advantage of the considerable resources offered by its territory and by the prosperity of commerce in the Mediterranean and, with the reactivation of the ancient road network, to which they dedicated particular care, the Seljuks restored the area to a foremost rank in transit traffic. The exceptional wealth the country came to enjoy gave rise to an intensive building activity, supported not only by the sovereigns but by the entire aristocracy. Although it welcomed Iranian lessons on a wide scale — and in general, Anatolian-Seljuk culture was to be basically Iranian — Turkish architecture of Anatolia had characteristics of its own in which there were varying degrees of Byzantine, Syrian, and Armenian traditions, resulting in quite valid, original works. For all edifices of a religious or charitable nature, the building materials par excellence were to be primarily stone and marble, which were abundant and of high quality in Anatolia; brickwork was also to play a key, if less apparent, part.

Characteristic of Anatolian-Seljuk architecture is the type of mosque, which followed a development of its own. Taking shape at the time was a design that utilized a long rather than wide hall. The main domed area tended to broaden out, both on the axis of the *mihrab* and along the wall of the *qibla,* while the domed area in front of the *mihrab* opened out onto the prayer hall, and ended by prevailing, thus foreshadowing solutions that were to be perfected by Ottoman architects. As a result of climatic factors, the open court soon lost its importance, finally disappearing altogether. All that remained was a symbolic aperture in the central nave, as had been the case in the mosque of Ulu Jami in Kayseri, built in 1140,

Konya (Turkey): The Mosque of Ala al-Din (1156–1220), here seen from the north side. This is a complex structure consisting of an enclosure in the form of an irregular quadrangle. It was placed atop a hill and included a great prayer hall with seven naves parallel to the *qibla* wall, and a second smaller prayer hall with a domed area of Seljuk derivation, in front of which are two mausoleums, one unfinished and the other with a high pyramidal roof. The exterior, unusually sober in appearance, has the look of a medieval castle. Particularly outstanding is the superb two-colored portal, the work of some architect from Damascus.

Divrighi (Turkey): Plan and cross-section of the Ulu Cami.
1 Mosque
2 Hospital

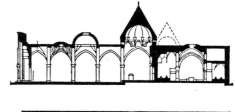

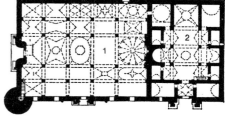

Konya (Turkey): *Madrassa* of Karatay (1251), a close-up of the portal with its *muqarnas* niche. The influence of Syrian architecture is to be seen in the form, the decoration, and the polychromy.

in that of Divrighi, 1229, and of Nighde, 1233. In the complex mosque of Ala al-Din at Konya, the court is a space without an organic connection with the prayer area. Based on Iranian models is the Great Mosque of Malatya of 1224, with the domed area of the *mihrab* preceded by a great *iwan* made of baked brick with decorations of enameled ceramic. This Iranian type is also to be found in the mosque of Khawand Khatun at Kayseri, built in 1238; with the mausoleum, the *madrassa*, and the baths, this mosque forms a complex of charitable institutions. Such multifunction foundations are typical of the period, and particularly of the Turks of Anatolia, when princes and other powerful individuals vied with one another in sponsoring charitable works, with the aim of extolling the efficiency of the state as well as its piety. Outstanding among these works is the Cifte *Madrassa* of Kayseri, with the mausoleum of its founder connected to a hospital, dating to 1205; the Sivas hospital of 1217–18, the largest structure of its kind from Seljuk Anatolia; and Divrighi's mosque with the adjoining hospital, of 1228–39.

This building activity did not even cease when the "golden age" of the Rum Sultanate came to an end in 1243, when the Mongols reduced the Seljuks to what was virtually a condition of vassalage. Dating to the second half of the thirteenth century are works such as the sumptuous *madrassa* of Karatay at Konya, built in 1251, and the *madrassa* of Inje Minareli of 1258, both of the type of Iranian *madrassa* in its Anatolian adaptation — that is, with the court covered by an enormous dome, which included an aperture for illumination. In these two monuments the brick dome is joined at its base by great fan-type triangular connecting elements of a type that, although already tested in the Great Mosque of Isfahan, was to become associated with Islamic architecture of Anatolia. The dome of the Karatay *madrassa* is completely lined inside by sumptuous blue-black and white glazed mosaics, which give the wall mass a particular lightness and foreshadow the Ottoman treatment of space. Of a more specifically Iranian design is the Cifte *Madrassa* of Erzurum, built in 1253, having an open court with two tiers of galleries, its arches supported by columns along the inside facades; compared to its model, the Turkish structure is quite original in the use of space and volumes. Turkish minarets of this period were also derived from Iranian prototypes, with particular favor accorded those with a shaft fashioned of semicylinders, such as that of Inje Minareli at Konya, or the pair at the portal of the Cifte *Madrassa*. This Iranian architectural formula, the portal framed by a pair of minarets, was widely used in Anatolia.

Also resulting from Iranian influence, through the mediation of

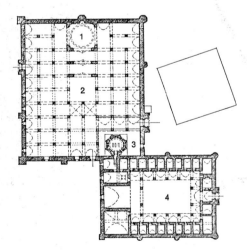

Kayseri (Turkey): Plan of the Khawana Khatun complex.
1 *Mosque*
2 *Court*
3 *Sepulcher of the founder, a woman*
4 *Madrassa with two iwans placed opposite one another*

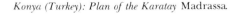

Konya (Turkey): Plan of the Karatay Madrassa.

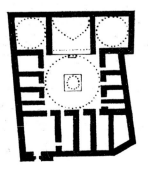

Konya (Turkey): The interior of the great dome covering the room aligned with the court of the Karatay *Madrassa*. **This is a splendid example of the faience ornamentation so widely used in Seljuk Anatolia.**

Armenia and Azerbaijan, was the type of mausoleum built of freestone and sculptured with rich decorations, either cylindrical, square, or polygonal resting on a base with the sepulchral crypt and with a conical or pyramidal roof — in effect, what we have already identified as the *gumbat,* or *turbe,* of the Seljuks to the east. We know a particularly large number of these at Akhlat, Divrighi, Tokat, Sivas, Nighde, Kayseri, and Konya, bearing witness to a great formal and decorative inventiveness. Particularly striking is the mausoleum of Tercan, surrounded by a great round wall; its origin, as far as the type of structure is concerned, is a matter of heated controversy among the specialists.

As has been indicated, the first half of the thirteenth century was a time of flourishing traffic for the Rum sultanate, which rebuilt the main roads — particularly the one leading north–south, joining the ports of the Black Sea, Sinope and Samsun, with Adalia on the Mediterranean — and equipped them with an efficient series of caravansaries, also known as *khans.* Built of freestone, these latter often look like fortresses. Various types are known, but the most typical one is that called the Sultan Khan, because it was built thanks to the munificence of the sovereign. The Sultan Khan type may be generally considered Anatolian, although it may have been based on some Central Asian prototype, such as that at Basham. It is a two-part edifice made up of a court, usually colonnaded, in the back of which, on an axis with the entrance, is the access to the second part, a hall with naves and a dome for illumination and ventilation, a feature that made it possible to cope with Anatolian winters. Particularly outstanding is the Sultan Khan along the Konya-Aksaray road, of 1229, and the Sultan Khan of the Kayseri–Sivas road; both include a small room intended as a prayer hall, or mosque, a feature always found in such buildings, although its location may vary.

The bulk of the secular structures of the Seljuk Sultanate of Rum — palaces, pavilions, and such — have been destroyed, built as they were from perishable materials, even though their walls were decorated with a profusion of stuccowork and faience. In recent years, however, a program of research and excavation has begun to make these structures somewhat better known. One characteristic feature was the kiosk or pavilion, which is fundamentally a square structure with overhanging, or protruding, elements supported by corbels; one such was the kiosk in Konya of Sultan Kilich Arslan II (1156–92), destroyed in the first twenty years of this century. The pavilions at Qubadiyya and at Qubadabad — foundations of the most famous sovereign of Rum, Ala al-Din Kaykubad (1219–37) — demonstrate a preference for moderate, even small dimensions, scattered over rather wide spaces and in pleasant locales, suggesting some taste for life in the open air. Retained from the Iranian model was the *iwan,* which to our knowledge was not used symmetrically in the palace architecture of the Seljuks of Rum. However, the classical four-*iwan* design was not unknown in the palace architecture of an adjoining area, the Turkish part of Upper Mesopotamia, as is borne out by an Artuchid palace in Diyarbekir (dated between 1201 and 1222); notable in the court are the mosaic floors and a basin fed by a fountain gushing from the back of an *iwan.*

The exteriors of the edifices of the Seljuk Turks are generally quite sober and measured; their aesthetic effect was entrusted primarily to the neat cutting of the stone. The decoration was centered on the great portals in the Iranian tradition, but it also tended to spread out over the facades. In some cases, the work of Syrian artists is prominent, such as in that of the portal of the Ala al-Din mosque and in that of the *madrassa* of Karatay at Konya, particularly in the complex joints of the masonry and in the sober polychromy of the marble. To be traced back to Iranian influences is the use of great decorative inscriptions — although now

Konya (Turkey): A section of the portal of the Inje Minareli *Madrassa* (1258), one of the most famous and opulent works of architectural decoration in Seljuk Turkey. The plan of the edifice is similar to that of the Karatay *Madrassa.*

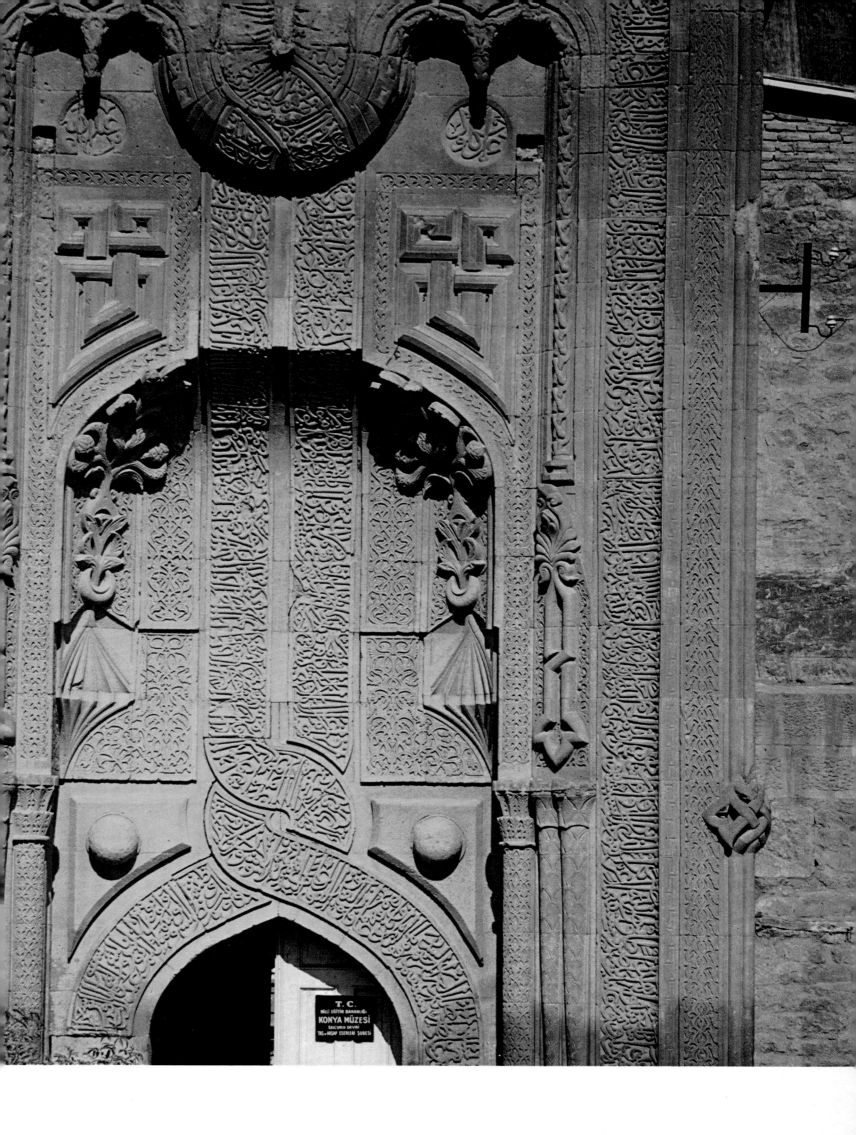

Kufic was being replaced by an elegant form of the *nashki,* known as *thuluth* — which, for example, adorn the rich, boldly colored portal of the Inje Minareli of Konya, creating a decidedly baroque effect with its tapestry-like motifs. In general, however, decorations in the structures of the Rum Sultanate's own territories of the "classical" period — that is, up to 1242 — were always restrained and subordinate to the architectural lines. The decorations in the eastern area, on the other hand, were highly elaborate, as is to be seen at Divrighi, where in the portal of the Great Mosque we have an exuberant and fanciful interpretation of stucco patterns being used on stone. The decorative repertory in the Divrighi complex is the classical one of Islam: geometric designs, arabesques, *muqarnas,* and inscriptions, but widespread use was also made of naturalistic animals and imaginary fauna, and on tombstones even human figures were carved.

Another important feature of the architectural decoration that can only be glanced at here is that of glazed tiles and similar ceramics; these enjoyed a particular vogue in Anatolia, perhaps in part nourished by the diaspora of the Iranian artisans fleeing before the Mongolian invasion. All indications are that it was in Anatolia that this type of decoration was first used consistently and on a wide scale, producing outstanding results, both with interiors — see the celebrated dome of the Karatay Madrassa of Konya — and with exteriors. Glazed tile painted with the Iranian metal luster technique, or in the more complex polychrome technique, adorned the palaces and pavilions of the sultans, often decorated with figured motifs. All this was in the Iranian tradition, although from the standpoint of their style they seem to evoke the ceramics of Raqqa, Iraq, while at the same time suggesting, by certain cadences, a kinship with more ancient Fatimid ceramics. No less developed, at least in interiors, was stuccowork decoration, in which figured motifs still abounded.

Erzurum (Turkey): The Cifte Minare *Madrassa* **(1253), a view of the court. This** *madrassa* **was erected by Khand Khatun, daughter of the Sultan Ala al-Din Kaykubad. It is a particularly striking monument, owing to the intense expressiveness and originality of its architecture.**

Erzurum (Turkey): Plan of the Cifte Minare Madrassa. *Note, on the axis with the entrance, the round mausoleum.*

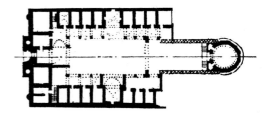

THE SYRIAN-EGYPTIAN REGION UNDER THE AYYUBIDS AND THE MAMLUKS

Salahaddin Yusuf ben Ayyus, "the Saladin," sent by the Zenghid ruler Nur al-Din to Egypt in 1169, put an end to the caliphate of the Fatimids. At the death of his own master in 1175, he brought the land under his own sway, winning the recognition of the caliph of Baghdad, extending his dominions through virtually all of Syria as well as Egypt, reaching as far as the Tigris River, and thereby founding the Ayyubid dynasty. Following in the footsteps of his former patron, Nur al-Din — instigator of the holy war against the Crusaders, champion of the moral unity of Islam, and the mainstay of orthodoxy — Saladin is remembered in history and legend as a just, chivalrous sovereign, victor over the Crusaders at the battle of Hittin, and conqueror of Jerusalem in 1187. Upon his death in 1193, his state broke up into three parts with their capitals — Cairo, Damascus, and Aleppo — closely linked to one another. The substantial reunification of Syria and Egypt brought about under Saladin generated a new prosperity in these regions, particularly after his death, when the war against the Crusader states was marked by a certain weariness. The new situation gave rise to what might be called "peaceful coexistence," which was a great incentive for the development of trade. It was in this period, in fact, that Western merchants began to penetrate this region's interior, and beginning in 1207 the Venetians were authorized to open a commercial establishment in Damascus, and later in Aleppo.

The architecture of the Ayyubid era followed the traditions that had already taken shape: the essentially stone structures took on three-dimensional forms, studied but limpid, with a carefully controlled taste for the technical or decorative detail inserted into a severe context. It was a moment of happy marriage between local traditions and Iranian teachings, along with the adoption of certain experiences of the best Crusader architecture. This latter was a component that took on particular prominence in military architecture, in which the most excellent result was the citadel of Aleppo, rebuilt in its basic parts under al-Malik al-Zahir between 1209 and 1212. The citadel's main portal is a masterpiece. The main section, set into the walls, is a bare, essential block cut in sharp angles, its surface broken by a series of machicolations supported by sturdy corbels, while the entrance is an immense barrel vault that connects by a viaduct to the forward section.

In harmony with the religious spirit of Saladin, numerous religious foundations flourished in the Ayyubid period; these included the *madrassas*, with no particular type predominating, although the *iwan* was used virtually always and everywhere. In the Aleppo region, one characteristic was the prayer hall at the back of the court, which in later types — such as the al-Zahiriyya of 1219 and in that of Firdaus of 1235 — is covered by three domes, side by side. A constant in the Damascus area is the simple, double, or triple — or even quadruple — *iwan* design. Both these types were widely used in Cairo as well, where the oldest four-*iwan madrassa* appears to be the al-Salihiyya of 1243–44, joined with the founder's tomb; above the tomb rises a minaret, a model monumental complex destined to reap considerable success in Egypt. In the *mihrab* of the tomb at the al-Salihiyya, we also have one of the oldest examples of decoration in polychrome marble to be found in Egypt, a style developed particularly in the subsequent Mamluk period.

The model of the mausoleum that came into widest use was that with a cubic base of stone, joined by means of stalactite elements with the brick dome. This type was to be repeated, without substantial variants, for some three centuries. Belonging to this category is the sepulcher of Saladin at Damascus, built in 1195; that at Cairo erected in 1211 on the tomb

of the *imam*, al-Shaffi, who died in 820 (the founder of one of the four major schools of orthodoxy in Islam); or the mausoleum of the Abbasid caliphs (1242–43). The mosques, at least in Syria, follow the Damascus model, with a hall tending to be wider than it is deep. Meanwhile, the distinctive architectural feature of exteriors came to be the portal, which took on greater and greater importance, absorbing the bulk of the exterior decoration. The facades were often enlivened by niches, which were covered by the now ubiquitous *muqarnas* element. The polychromy of the exteriors, invariably obtained by placing together two stones of different colors, was adopted for the interiors, particularly for the *mihrab* area.

Mamluk Architecture

At the death of the last Ayyubid sultan in 1250, the Turkish slaves who had provided the nucleus of his power, known as Mamluks (from *mamluk*, "the possessed," "slave"), ended by taking the place of their former

Aleppo (Syria): The monumental entranceway of the citadel, a work in its basic parts of the Ayyubid sovereign al Malik al-Zahir, erected between 1209 and 1212. It is one of the masterworks of Islamic architecture, in which there was a happy merging of local Syrian traditions, Iranian teachings, and the experiments of the architecture of the Crusaders.

Cairo: View of the court dominated by the great *iwans* of the *madrassa* of Sultan Hassan (1356–63), one of the masterpieces of Mamluk architecture. Deserving particular appreciation is the serenity of the space.

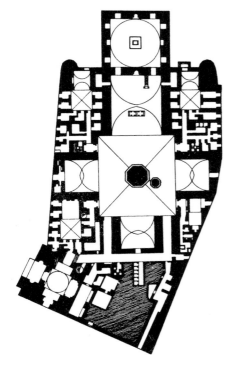

Cairo: Plan of the madrassa *of Sultan Hassan. The design is typical of one with four* iwans. *Behind the main* iwan *is the sepulcher of the founder, covered by a high dome. Situated at the four corners are the dwellings for the teachers and pupils of the orthodox schools–Hanafite, Shafiite, Hanbalite, and Malikite.*

masters. The Mamluks produced two dynasties, an initial one, that of the Bahrit Turks (named after their barracks on the island of Rhoda, in the Nile), and the succeeding one, from 1382, the Burjits, descendants of the Circassian slaves of Sultan Qalawun (1279–90); the latter dynasty held Egypt in its grip until the arrival of the Ottomans in 1517. The Mamluks deserve credit for having driven the Mongols out of Syria, defeating them in the battle of Ain-Jalut in 1260, led by their hero Beybars, sultan from 1261 to 1270, and for having wiped out in 1291, with the capture of Acri, the last Crusader stronghold in the Near East.

The Syrian-Egyptian region, particularly Egypt, enjoyed with the Mamluks one of their longest periods of political unity and relative calm; the frequent dynastic struggles that broke out affected the life of these regions only marginally. Both Syria and Egypt became increasingly important as centers of international trade, especially after the crisis of the Mongol empire in the fourteenth century, and with European economic expansion in full swing. The Mamluks profited tremendously from this, but unfortunately their rapacious fiscal policies, which forced all economic activity into the regime's monopoly — a system that in Egypt, to be sure, had come down through an unbroken line from the

time of the Pharaohs — reduced all commerce to the mere transit variety. The result was that there were no effective benefits for the economy of the nation, whose productive activities dropped to an ever lower level. The easy availability of money enjoyed by the ruling class, however, produced intensive building activity. But the architecture of Mamluk Egypt and Syria was without authentic creative qualities, although it revealed technical excellence. The same thing happened to Mamluk culture as a whole: it was highly productive but of an encyclopedic, erudite, and didactic nature.

Mamluk architecture was primarily based on the Syrian tradition, but it revealed a composite of other contributions that ranged from the Iranian to the Anatolian, from the Maghrebian to Romanesque-Gothic. The first mosque we might focus on is that of Beybars I in Cairo, built in 1266. It is of the Iranian type in its court and dome, but at the same time shows an influence from Christian architecture in the basilica-like tripartition of the main *iwan*, while its protruding portals are of the North African type. Related to this are the mosques of Qalawun, of 1318, and the al-Maridani, of 1334. Still, there was a tendency to reduce the mosque to no more than the prayer hall, as is the case with that of Argun Ismail, of 1347. There are also great numbers of charitable foundations, often organized into monumental complexes that join the *madrassa* and a hospital to the tomb of the founder, such as the celebrated one of Sultan Qalawun, which was begun in 1284 and finished by the sultan's son, al-Nasir. Here we have a great mausoleum influenced by the Syrian type in its central octagon inside a square ambulatory, a Syrian influence that is also revealed in the entrance portal, with its black-and-white stonework, the same bichromy that had been adopted at the Beybars mosque. Drawing on the same source is the three-nave arrangement, the one in the middle higher than the others, of the main *iwan* of the *madrassa*,

Cairo: A close-up of the great Kufic inscription adorning the main *iwan* (eastern) of the *Madrassa* of Sultan Hassan. This *iwan*, having been provided with a *mihrab*, also serves as a mosque.

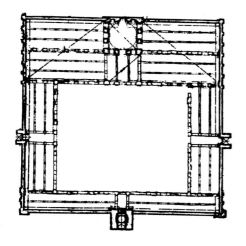

Cairo: Plan of the Mosque of Beybars I. The prayer hall is of the broad type, with naves cut by a typically Iranian feature–the domed hall with an iwan. *Also traceable to Iranian models are the* iwans *on the court.*

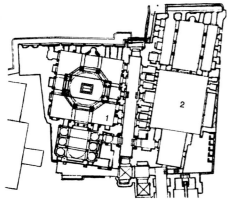

Cairo: Plan of the great architectural complex of Sultan Qalawun.
1 Mausoleum
2 Madrassa
*A hospital (*maristan*) was also included in the complex.*

which has two *iwans* placed opposite each other. The outer facades reveal an arrangement typical of Mamluk art, stemming from the Romanesque-Gothic architecture already introduced into Ayyubid architecture, with flat niches and others closed with a pointed arch.

The four-*iwan* type of *madrassa* was widespread at this time, and that of Sultan Hassan (1356–63), which follows this model, is without doubt the masterwork of all Mamluk architecture. Evidently the work of a Syrian architect, it is a creation of extreme elegance, sober and harmonious in its various parts. One enters it through a majestic portal, some 85 feet high, with a stalactite hood calling to mind Anatolian models. In the middle of the court, under a dome, was a basin. From the *qibla iwan,* adorned with a fine Kufic inscription of stucco, one enters the mausoleum; originally it seems to have been covered by a bulbous dome similar to those becoming popular in Iran. Still standing is one of its two towering minarets that originally stood at both sides of the mausoleum. The four corners between the branches formed by the *iwans* were intended to house one of the four great orthodox law schools each, complete with lodgings for teachers and students. The design of the *madrassa* also supplied a model for the *khanaqah* (monasteries), such as that of Beybars II that dates from 1309–10, and a great many mosques.

In the period of the Mamluk Burjits (1382–1517), the orientations that had taken shape with the Bahrits were carried forward. Mosques with a court were rare, although they were still being built — the Muayyadi of 1423–24 is one example — but even greater preference was given to the model of the *madrassa,* with a tendency to reduce the size of the court, which in some cases disappeared altogether, its space being covered by a wooden skylight. We can find a first-rate example of this latter in the Qaitbay mosque in the "cemetery of the caliphs" in Cairo; it dates from 1475 and has four *iwans.* The Mamluk minaret, meanwhile, assumed a characteristic appearance, with its shaft made up of a number of opulently decorated segments. In the older types, an octagonal shaft was erected atop a square base; its last segment, cylindrical in form and connected to the rest by a stalactite cornice, was covered by a ribbed cap. In the more recent types, the base section was octagonal and, to the advantage of the two upper sections, smaller in size. It ended with a tiny pavilion, while at the same time the stalactite-connecting elements were incorporated into balconies. The innovations in mausoleums regard primarily the aspect of the domes; by this time, they were of stone and decorated even on the outer surface with elements in geometric or arabesque relief.

In the Mamluk period, as already indicated, much importance was given to the treatment of the facades, which were handled with great care. Niches or panels were adapted to the facades' special needs, and they were dominated by monumental portals. Particularly extensive use was also made of *muqarnas* work, which by now, however, was often no longer part of the structure but merely decorative, fashioned of wood or stucco. An intensive feeling for polychromy emerged; on exteriors, use was made of the two-colored stonework of the northern Syrian type. But in keeping with the Iranian fashion, use was also made, beginning with the fourteenth century, of faience tiles. A significant development was the introduction on a wide scale of marble worked into geometric patterns, especially in the interiors for walls and floors; this technique may be traced back to both Italian–Romanesque and Byzantine influences.

In the long run, Mamluk architecture, which happens to be among the best documented of Islam, leaves one rather cold, justifying the rather severe view of Monneret de Villard: "Mamluk architecture never reaches a high artistic level: it is capable, sumptuous in its means, and to all appearances accurate in technique; but in reality it neither copes with nor resolves with creative genius any major new architectural problems."

THE MONGOL INVASION AND THE ILKHANID EMPIRE

The eastern territories of Islam were still in the throes of the collapse of the Seljuk empire when they were stricken with another invasion, this one accompanied by savage ruin: that of the Mongol hordes of Genghis Khan. Moving out of the Gobi Desert in the early thirteenth century, he quickly established an immense empire from China to Asia Minor before he died in 1227. As early as 1295, however, that empire had broken up into four great "khanates" — China, southern Russia, Iran, and Turkey — which recognized themselves, at least in theory, as subordinate to the Great Khan. The Iranian territories — including Azerbaijan (which became the chosen region of the new masters, owing to the excellence of its pasturelands), Georgia, Armenia, and part of Asia Minor — were placed under the authority of Hulagu, a grandson of Genghis Khan, who in 1261 was given the tile of Il-khan, or tribal-local khan, subordinate to the Great Khan. This has given rise to what is known as the Ilkhanid dynasty, essentially the name for the period when the Mongols were based in Iran. It was with Hulagu, too, that the Moslems' conquests of new territories came to an end. In 1258, Baghdad was taken and sacked, thus putting an end to the last remaining relic of the Abbasid caliphate. The Mamluks alone, as mentioned, succeeded in 1260 in containing the Mongols' drive toward the west, so that the Euphrates became the western boundary of the Mongol empire.

The regime established by the nomad-pastoral Mongol conquerors was a decisive episode in Iranian history. In fact, as Bausani has expressed it, "The Mongol invasion, with its 'external' catastrophe characteristics, rather than leading Ghaznavid and Seljuk feudalism into a consistent development, broke the evolutionary process to pieces, going so far as to reintroduce and strengthen elements of pastoral feudalism and a slave economy, creating or accentuating institutions extraneous to even the oldest period of the Moslem Middle Ages and outside Islamic law (for instance, serfdom, commercial usury, etc.) and delaying still further the possibility of the emergence of new forms within Islamic society." For several decades, the northern strip of the Iranian area in particular was reduced to a mass of ruins, and the land was subjected to a ferocious, pitiless impoverishment. The ancient landed aristocracy was wiped out, and the countryside, left to the mercy of bands of Mongols, was deserted en masse by the peasants. The artisans and their offspring were reduced to slavery in state-owned workshops. Thanks to the Mongols' spirit of religious and racial tolerance, the Christian and Jewish minorities and the "mandarin" class of Iranian functionaries fared somewhat better. These Iranians, in fact, allied themselves with their new masters, supplying them with administrative cadres. Although only sluggishly and amid uncertainties, a great deal of reconstruction got under way, so that by the end of the thirteenth century there actually began a period of exceptional prosperity in Iran. But the damage caused by the invasion, particularly that affecting agriculture, was never to be remedied.

Among the fundamental factors behind the prosperity of the Ilkhanid state centered in Iran was the reactivation of traffic of all kinds. In spite of all its upheavals, in fact, the Mongol conquest led to a political order that gave Asia a period of relative peace that lasted some fifty years — the *Pax Mongolica* — during which direct land communications were set up between the Mediterranean and the Far East. The movement of men and ideas that occurred had a truly international significance, the best known witness being Marco Polo. Iran under the Ilkhanids enjoyed particular benefits from its situation, now finding itself on the main trade routes of the Middle East, the conflicts between Mongols and Mamluks having sharply reduced the practicality of the classic trade route through the

TIE DOWN NO MAN'S HEART

Tie down no heart of friend, to any motherland, for ample are the earth and sea and men are many.
City dogs are ever beaten and ill-used because, unlike hunting dogs, they are never the first to leap upon others.
In the world there is not just the flower of the cheek and the plumage of the lip: all the trees are green, the garden is in flower!
How long will you, like a chicken, suffer torment within the house?
Why do you not instead travel away like a flying dove?
Pass like a nightingale from one tree to another.
Why, like a sad heron, do you bury your head in your breast?
The earth is kicked by oxen and asses, and this is so because it is fixed and, unlike the heavens, cannot move.
Even though a thousand beauties unheard of pass before you, you should look and pass on, and lend your heart to none.
Mingle with all; so that you can laugh happily with all; remain not chained to one alone, later to weep and lament!
Whyever should I be sad, and he happy? He sleep peacefully and I, thinking of him, lie awake? . . .
Happy is he who at night holds in his arms his lady friend, and at dawn drives her far away! . . .
When tasty and sweet fruit falls into my hands, why should I plant roots that bear none but bitter fruit?
The necks of noblemen and the noose of love may be compared to a foot soldier, caught by the rope of a knight; but I need a friend to lighten my burden, not a master whose weight I must bear? . . .
If my friend is cruel to me and says harsh words to me, what difference ever will there be between friend and ferocious enemy?
But even if he kissed the earth and swore himself dust beneath your feet, be not deceived: the trickster wants to play with you!
If he gives you the greeting of peace, beware: he's a hunter preparing a lure!
And if he falls down in adoration before you, beware: the thief is cutting your purse!

SAADI (1184–1291)

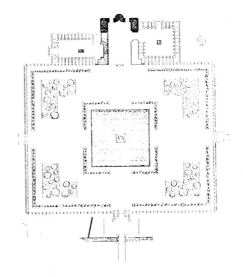

Tabriz (Iran): Plan of the reconstruction of the Masjid-i Jami. This mosque was a gigantic example of the simple iwan type facing onto an open court; its design is typical of Iranian architecture.

Sultaniya (Iran): The mausoleum of Uljaitu (1309–13). This city—whose name means "the sultans' " or "imperial" city — was founded by the Mongol sovereign Arghun in 1290 and later became the capital of the Ilkhanid state. The photograph shows the rear of the mausoleum, with the funerary mosque protruding. Characteristic is the division of the facade by thin pilaster strips to lighten and thin out the masses. The dome and the area of the drum gallery were originally decorated in glazed blue faience.

Page 93:
Isfahan (Iran): A close-up of the great *mihrab* in the Masjid-i Juma, a work done under Uljaitu and dated to 1310, shortly after the conversion of the great Mongol sovereign to the Shiite sect. The *mihrab* is a magnificent sculpture in stucco in which Seljuk arabesque decorative motifs were employed. Of particularly high quality are the inscriptions in Nashki characters and the great horizontal strip in Kufic characters.

Fertile Crescent, shifting its axis farther north, so that its pivot was no longer at Baghdad but at Tabriz, Azerbaijan, where the Mongol conquerors had set up their center of power.

The Mongols, professing Buddhism for the most part but with some sympathies for Nestorian Christianity — a heresy named after a patriarch of Constantinople — were highly tolerant as far as religion was concerned. But it was pure political expediency that induced the Mongol sovereign Ghazan Khan (1295–1304) to become converted, along with his people, to Islam; this conversion, in fact, marked the complete assimilation of the masters of this empire, who because of changed political conditions were beginning to lack fresh support from the populations of Central Asia. The work of construction undertaken primarily by Ghazan Khan continued with his brother Uljaitu (1304–17) and with Abu Said (1317–35). At the death of the latter, the kingdom broke up into a number of principalities: that of the Jalairids of Baghdad, who extended their dominion to Azerbaijan; that of the Karts at Herat; and that of the Muzaffarids in southern Iran, who in turn were to be swept aside by the invasion of Tamerlane.

The cultural significance of the Mongol rule was extraordinarily far-reaching, for it widened the gap between the pro-Arab elements of Islam and those associated with the Persian language. The rift had already become evident with the Seljuks, who had acted, so to speak, as a catalytic agent in the process of establishing the characteristic Iranian culture. From this time on, the Iranian tradition was to become ever more fully developed and explicit, although never overstepping the traditional framework of Islam. The thirteenth and fourteenth centuries, moreover, are considered the "golden age" of Persian letters, which had its voices in Sadi, Jalahuddin, Rumi, and Hafez. The mystic tone of their verses, which reach extraordinarily high summits, particularly with Rumi, unquestionably reflect the miserable conditions of the times, and the profound moral unease that the Moslems experienced while being subjected, en masse and for the first time, to infidel sovereigns.

The Mongol rulers, however, once engaged in the work of reconstructing the territories they had conquered, brought in artists, artisans, and literati from every imaginable region and culture, thus promoting a climate of intellectual cosmopolitanism. In particular, the Mongols' links with the Far East introduced major new influences into Ilkhanid work in such fields as miniature painting and pottery. In place of the ornamental spirit and graphic line of the Iranians, there now appeared a pictorial design and impressionistic tendency of the great Sung and Yuan traditions of China.

Maragha and Tabriz, in Azerbaijan, both of which served as capitals of the Ilkhanid rulers, became important centers of knowledge, particularly in the natural sciences and history. Founded around 1300 at Tabriz by the famous prime minister of Ghazan Khan and Uljaitu, the great historian and art patron Rashid al-Din, was the Rus-i Rashidi quarter, which unfortunately no longer exists; the quarter included schools, libraries, and a number of celebrated copying workshops that were, as had been intended by Rashid al-Din, a center of art and culture for Islam. Another of the great Ilkhanid achievements also lost to us is the settlement that Ghazan Khan erected some two miles from Tabriz, where in addition to the tomb of the founder there arose palaces, libraries, a mosque, monasteries, an observatory, an edifice for public administration, gardens, and fountains. Uljaitu moved the capital farther south to Sultaniya, where his great mausoleum still stands. Flowing toward Sultaniya by this time was the traffic from Central Asia, by the Khurasan route, and that from the Mediterranean and the Black Sea, as well as merchandise from the Indian Ocean.

Aesthetically, Ilkhanid architecture does not represent a new development in Iranian architecture; in general, it may be considered an extension of Seljuk architecture, from which it inherits the basic designs and technical solutions. Its distinctive characteristics are an accentuation of the vertical elements of structures and a lightening of the non-supporting elements through the use of false windows, the articulation of surfaces with niches, panels and pillar strips, and the concentration of the masses on a relatively few stress points. These technical procedures do not always assure a coherent stylistic expression, since it often happened that everything disappeared under a blanket of decorations, which were the architects' chief preoccupation. The verticality of the edifice was frequently accentuated, particularly in the interiors, by means of artifice — for instance, the use of unusually slender corner columns. And the height of the dome was increased; the older dome-type was used, but preference was given to a more pronounced oval shape, which foreshadowed the bulbous type that was to become the favorite in the Timurid period, while the double-shaft type became popular at the time of the Ilkhanids. Characteristic was the vault made up of a series of massive transversal arches joined by tiny vaults, either continuous or, more often, broken by steps up to the keystone. Coming into popularity at this time was the decorative feature of the segmented arch, which was almost completely unknown in Seljuk structures. The *iwan* received a special emphasis, being increased in height and virtually always flanked by two minarets. The ornamental motif of the *muqaurnas* spread far and wide, assuming highly complex forms. Unbaked brick remained the favorite material for the core of structures, but it was generally lined by

baked brick, while vaults and domes used this latter material exclusively. Stone and marble were seldom used, except in Azerbaijan.

As usual, religious and funerary architecture provides the most abundant testimony. Still used in the mosque was the simple domed tetrapylon, as in the Masjid-i Bab Abd Allah at Nayin, of 1300; also used was the domed hall preceded by an *iwan* and a court, as in the three mosques of Dashti, Kaj, and Aziram, all in the Isfahan area and all dating to about 1325. Seemingly made up of one sole *iwan* facing a court is the gigantic Masjid-i Jami of Tabriz, built between 1310 and 1320 by Taj al-Din Ali Shah Jilian Tabrizi, great patron of the arts and prime minister of Uljaitu and then of Abu Said. The measurements of the *iwan* are impressive: 210 feet long and 110 feet wide; the vault begins some 80 feet from the ground; the walls are 30 feet thick. Its overall appearance is particularly noble, with the exterior providing the greatest enjoyment; here one sees a mass of bare brickwork, its texture flawlessly homogeneous, its edges rounded and enlivened by a great buttress, aligned with the *mihrab* and an ample window on either side.

To the east, the ancient Khurasan formula, calling for two *iwans* opposite each other, was continued in the Forumad mosque, believed to have been built in 1320. The only good example of a four-*iwan* mosque of the Ilkhanid period that has survived is the Masjid-i Jami at Varamin, near Teheran, erected between 1322 and 1326, under the reign of Abu Said. Harmonious in its proportions, it represents a meditated, mature development of Seljuk principles. It was built with extreme care and boasts of a rich decorative mantle of tile in various shades of blue, enhanced by terra-cotta and stucco work, which never intrudes on the architectural lines but gently follows them, helping to accentuate them. Erected in the Muzaffarid period (1349) was another fine example of a four-*iwan* mosque, the Jami of Kirman, although its *iwan* at the *qibla* is not followed by a domed pavilion. Of exceptional interest in this mosque is the entrance portal, because of the particular articulation of its design and its monumentality, foreshadowing a feature that was to become fashionable in later eras. Evident in the decorative elements are the direct antecedents of Timurid architectural decoration. Features of a different sort are to be seen, on the other hand, in the Jami of Natanz, another four-*iwan* mosque forming part of a complex made up of a mausoleum and a monastery, erected between 1304 and 1325.

A number of other famous sanctuaries date back to this same period, including that of Pir-i Bakran (1303–13) at Linjan, consisting chiefly of a deep massive *iwan* adorned in the *mihrab* with sumptuous stuccos. Another complex, built on a much larger scale, is the one at Bistam, around the tomb of Bayazed, a celebrated holy man who died about 875; featuring towers with spurs, and covered by a dome hidden by a second roof, this tomb harks back to a widely used type. An example is the lovely Mil-i Radkan (about 1280–1300) to the east, with an outer curtain of semicylindrical bricks decorated with geometric designs and joined at the roof by a fringe of tiny continuous arches, in all likelihood modeled after tents. Another example, found at Maragha, Azerbaijan, consists of a square tomb-tower known as the Gumbat-i Gharfariya, dated to about 1328. A place all their own is occupied by a group of mausoleums at Qum, probably built between 1278 and the end of the fourteenth century; in design and elevation, they appear to have stemmed from the more ancient architecture of Azerbaijan. They are polygonal in shape, with a dome hidden by a pyramidal roof and largely supported by an extended drum. Characteristic is their tapered profile on the outside, which accentuates the monuments' verticality, together with an extensive

Varamin (Iran): The entrance of the Masjid-i Jami, erected under the Ilkhanid sultan Abu Said between 1322 and 1326. In it one can appreciate two distinctive characteristics of Ilkhanid architecture: accentuation of the structures in a vertical sense, and widescale use of glazed faience ornamentation.

use of niches and panels, typical of the repertory of Ilkhanid Iran, as in the Imamzada Ali ibn Jafar (1300) and the Gumbat-i Sabz (1330–65).

Another type of funerary monument, although less representative, is that with the square or polygonal base covered by a visible oval dome. The most illustrious example is the mausoleum of Uljaitu at Sultaniya, which the French scholar André Godard calls "without question the finest known example of Mongol architecture and one of the most expert and typical products of Islamic Persia, while perhaps the most interesting from a technical standpoint." Later, this monument was to become one of the main sources of inspiration for Iranian and Indian architecture. This mausoleum, built between 1309 and 1313, was situated amid a complex of buildings (since destroyed) and was the focal point of the new capital. It was a monumental structure on an octagonal base, crowned by a dome some 80 feet in diameter. The base section, with the burial chamber extending from its south side, supports a gallery that functions as the drum and is furnished with three arched windows on each side. This gallery ends in a cornice with stalactites, rising over which is the ovoid-section dome, its thickness diminishing from the base to the keystone through its successive setbacks. This technique, which is left visible in the dome of the Masjid-i Jami at Varamin, is here hidden by a thin mantle of bricks supported by a series of tiny arches. Each corner of the octagon is surmounted by a small minaret. Executed with particular finesse on the exterior were the east, west, and north facades, which were enlivened by panels and shallow blind niches. This structure may be considered the happy outcome of experiments that took their salient form in the mausoleum of Ismail at Bukhara and in that of Sultan Sanjar at Merv. The enormous mass rests on only a few points of support, so that the mausoleum, articulated by galleries, false windows, and niches, creates a striking impression of lightness, which must have been evident even when its mantle of light and dark blue tiles, which alternated with the brickwork sections, was still intact.

Still closer to the model of the tomb of Sultan Sanjar is the so-called Haruniya of Tus, which can be dated back to the early years of the fourteenth century, in which the facades are divided by thin pillar strips, providing the compact volume of the base with a rhythm leading the eye upward. Also to be remembered in this connection is the mausoleum of Garladan, composed of an *iwan* covered by transverse arches joined by diminutive vaults. As we have indicated, this type of roof was widespread in the Ilkhanid period and had illustrious antecedents in the Sassanid era; it offered the advantage of providing large rooms with sufficient light, an illumination that was more rational in that it came both from the side and from the top. We have some estimable examples of this variety of roof in the Khan Orthma of Baghdad, in the oratories annexed to the Jami of Yazd, to the mosque at Abarquh, and to that of the Great Mosque of Isfahan. This last-named oratory, added in the Ilkhanid or Muzaffarid period, contains a *mihrab* built by Uljaitu, a stunning example of stucco decoration still clinging to the Seljuk tradition.

We have only the scantiest knowledge of secular Ilkhanid architecture. For the most part, especially in the initial phase, the Ilkhanid palaces must have been built of perishable materials, because the Mongol court was exceedingly slow in giving up their atavastic habits of living in mobile tent communities. We know of only a few fragments of a great palace partly built by Abaq (1265–81) at Takht-i Sulayman: pillars of an enormous *iwan*, perhaps the palace's throne room, its facade decorated with a series of superimposed niches and a canopy of stalactites. Also worthy of consideration are a number of caravansaries with the design customary for such edifices, such as those at Marand (1330–35) and Sarcham (1332–33) along the Azerbaijan road; these reveal, in the combined use of stone and brick, influences from Syria, particularly clear in the marble and sandstone portal of the one at Sarcham. Lastly, there is the caravansary of Sin, on the road leading north from Isfahan, believed to have been built about 1330; in addition to the usual portal, this caravansary presents the peculiarity of a hexagonal vestibule jutting into the court.

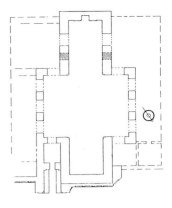

Forumad (Iran): Plan of the mosque. The two-iwan design for mosques was widely used in Khurasan, where it was preferred to the four-iwan variety. This latter, however, was typical in secular architecture (as in palaces and dwellings) and in that of the madrassas.

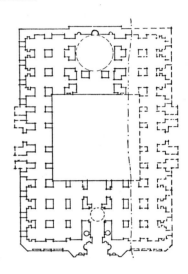

Varamin (Iran): Plan of the Masjid-i Jami, perfect example of the four-iwan mosque.

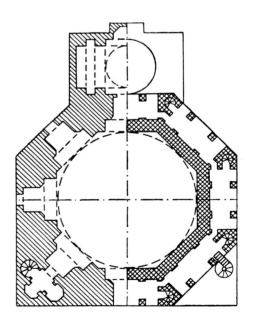

Sultaniya (Iran): Plan of the mausoleum of Uljaitu. The left half of the drawing represents the edifice just above the foundation, with the deep niches making up the sides of the octagon in the interior; the right side represents the structure at the level of the upper gallery.

Tabriz (Iran): Rear view of the *iwan* of the
**Masjid-i Jami, erected between 1310 and 1320
by Taj al-Din Ali Shah Jilan Tabrizi, prime
minister of Uljaitu and then of Abu Said.**

RISE UP, CUPBEARER

Rise up, cupbearer, and offer the bowl,
For love, which seemed at first so easy, has now
brought trouble to my soul.
   With yearning for the pod's aroma, which
by the East that lock shall spread
   From that crisp curl of musky odor, how
plenteously our hearts have bled!
   Stain with the tinge of wine thy prayer-
mat, if thus the aged Magi bid,
   For from the traveler of the Pathway, no
stage nor usage can be hid.
   Shall my Beloved One's house delight me,
when issues ever and anon,
From the relentless bell the mandate: " 'Tis
time to bring thy litters on?"
   The waves are wild, the whirlpool dread-
ful, the shadow of the night steals o'er:
   How can my fate excite compassion, in the
light-burdened of the shore?
   Each action of my forward spirit has won
me an opprobrious name: Can anyone conceal
the secret which the crowds proclaim?
            HAFIZ (d. 1388, is considered
                the greatest Persian poet)

As for decoration, the Ilkhanid period marks a decisive moment in the
history of Iranian architecture. While stucco remained the main element
in the interiors — variably employed, whether smooth, molded,
sculptured, engraved, or painted — exterior decoration with open-face
bricks, one of the distinctive elements of Seljuk architecture, without being completely set aside in the Ilkhanid period, came instead to play a part
in the color effects. This was achieved by exploiting the various colors of
the brickwork, but especially by an increasingly extensive use of glazed
tiles. These latter were employed to line broad surfaces, with decorative
compositions obtained either by using tiles and prefabricated elements or
genuine mosaics with either geometric, floral, or epigraphic motifs. The
first wide-scale experiments in tile decorations over broad surfaces appear to have been conducted during the thirteenth century in the Sultanate of Rum, under the promptings of Iranian artisans who had fled
there from the Mongols. This artistic practice is believed to have later
been re-imported from this region back into Iranian territories, and the
Uljaitu mausoleum is held to be the first monument on which this dazzling form of ornamentation was employed. The palette was initially
confined to only four colors — dark and light blues, white, and black. But
toward the middle of the fourteenth century, the coloration was enriched
in the Isfahan area by the addition of green and brown. In the subsequent Timurid and Safavid periods, tile decoration was to attain its
greatest splendors.

ARCHITECTURE IN THE EMPIRE OF TAMERLANE

Moslem Asia was thrown into upheaval in the closing part of the fourteenth century by another catastrophe: the invasion of Tamerlane. (His real name being Timur, followed by *lang*, "the lame," in reference to his disability.) This invasion, like that of the Mongols before, was carried out by nomadic-pastoralists, whose lightning-like plundering often led to the annihilation of agricultural and handicraft resources in the subjected territories, particularly those of Iran and Afghanistan. Tamerlane himself, a Turk-Mongol born at Kesh (now Shahr-i Sabz) in Transoxiana, in 1336, was a figure typical of the ferocious adventurer and military leader of that era. A fanatical Moslem, he yet fought almost entirely against adherents of his own religion, in the name of a more severe orthodoxy and with the aim of restoring the unity of Islam. Even then, it is not easy to find a well-thought-out program behind the succession of victories that saw him rush from one end of Asia to the other along roads marked by the notorious pyramids of heads of the defeated. In 1380 Tamerlane began his conquest of Iran, defeating the Golden Horde on the Volga in 1391–92; between 1392–95, he reconquered Iran and sacked Baghdad. Passing through the Caucasus he once again struck a powerful blow at the Golden Horde, which had become an ally of the Mamluks, and laid waste to the Crimea, dislocating the rich trade route between Europe and Asia. In 1395–96 he burned Asterabad and Saray on the Volga. In 1398 he pounced on Delhi, rushing back to the north to put down one of innumerable revolts, ravaging with sword and fire Georgia and Syria. He unleashed an attack on the Ottomans and in the battle of Ankara (1402) took prisoner the Ottoman Sultan Beyazed II, thus delaying by half a century the fall of Constantinople. In 1404 he returned to his capital Samarkand and while preparing to invade China died at seventy years of age in 1405.

Tamerlane was much more harmful to Asia, especially the Iranian territories, than was Genghis Khan. (Without doubt, his invasion bears responsibility, together with previous Turkish-Mongol invasions, for the present backwardness of these regions as far as their agricultural productivity is concerned.) Tamerlane was without the gifts of a statesman, and most of his enterprises had to be reworked. But although the typical nomad, his exploits reveal a fundamental streak of sedentary culture; unlike the nomads who went before him, he did not locate his capital in any of the conquered lands but he treated them as sources of artists, artisans, and wealth for his native land, the center of which he established at Samarkand.

The far-flung empire running from Russia to China therefore turned out to be an exceedingly fragile creation, although it found in Tamerlane's son, Shah Rukh (1409–47), a peace- and art-loving prince, a balanced successor who assured a period of tranquillity, at least in the eastern parts of the state, which by then had its capital at Herat. Upon the death of Shah Rukh, decadence came quickly. The reign of his son, Ulugh Beg — he, too, an artist, man of letters, and astronomer — was laid waste by wars that broke the territory up into a group of minor principalities, while the effective power of the ruling house narrowed down to Samarkand, Bukhara, and Herat. In the second half of the fifteenth century, Central Asia fell before other Turks, the Uzbek Sheibanids. Western Iran was at the same time tormented by the struggles of two rival Turkoman confederations, known by their tribal insignias as that of the Qara Qoyunlu ("Black Ram") and the Aq Qoyunlu ("White Ram"), whose best known figure in the West was the Aq Qoyunlu, Huzun Hassan (died in 1478), because of his relations with Venice, undertaken in a vain attempt to perfect a plan to wipe out the common Ottoman enemy. Meanwhile, at Ardebil, in Azerbaijan, toward the end of the White Ram dynasty, a new dynasty began to emerge, it, too, of Turkish origin but of the Shiite faith — that of the Safavids. Another

Preceding pages:
Herat (Afghanistan): Mausoleum of Gauhar Shad, wife of Shah Rukh, a son of Tamerlane (1432). With its dazzling lining of glazed faience, the dome supported by stalactite-type corbels is one of the most characteristic Timurid monuments.

Left:
Herat (Afghanistan): A part of the interior of the mausoleum of Gauhar Shad, showing the supporting structure of the dome. The interlocking arches permitted a lowering of the center of gravity to create a more elastic construction that was more resistant to earthquakes.

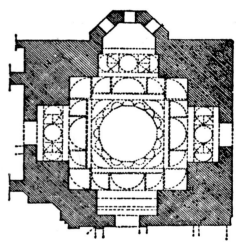

Herat (Afghanistan): Plan of the mausoleum of Gauhar Shad, located inside the madrassa *founded by this empress.*

contemporary military leader was Babur, who boasted that he descended from Genghis Khan *and* Tamerlane, and carved out a small realm at Kabul, Afghanistan, from which he was to launch the conquest of India, laying the basis of another great empire, that of the Moguls.

But despite the seemingly endless tale of destruction, this was a period of considerable interest for the arts, which found patrons in all the Timurid princes (as descendants of Tamerlane, or Timur, are known). It had begun with Tamerlane himself, who gathered all the artists, artisans, literati, and scientists he could from the lands he had subjected and assigned them the job of making Samarkand a worthy capital for his gigantic dominions. The greatest and most lasting results were obtained, amid the general excellence of artistic production in this period, in the art of book making and illustration. Outstanding patrons were Prince Baysunghur (died in 1433), Sultan Husayn Bayqara (1469–1506), and his vizier Mir Ali Shir Nevai, who in their court at Herat encouraged a school of painting that had in the famous Bihzad (1455–1533) the most significant artistic personality of medieval Islamic painting. It was at Herat, a true center of culture, that the last of the classical Persian poets, Jami, lived, and that the Turkish Chaghataic school of poetry flourished.

Great builders, the Timurids left a considerable number of monu-

Samarkand (U.S.S.R.): Plan of the mausoleum of Tamerlane, the structure also known as the Gur-i Mir.
1   *Tamerlane's sepulcher*
2   *Courtyard*
3   *Khanaqah (monastery)*
4   *Madrassa*
5   *Gallery of 1424*
6   *South annex*
7   *Domed room*

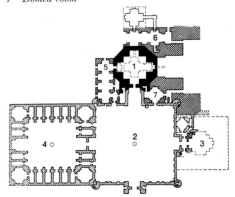

Samarkand (U.S.S.R.): The mausoleum of Tamerlane, known as the Gur-i Mir ("tomb of the emir"), seen from the north. The oldest part is that in the center, with the great external ribbed dome, its slightly bulbous profile resting on a towering drum. The inner dome begins at the bottom of the drum supporting this visible dome.

ments, most of which are to be found in the east, particularly in Transoxiana — at Samarkand and Bukhara — and in Khurasan — at Herat, Meshad, Balkh, and Mazar-i Sharif. Only little, on the other hand, is known of the architecture in central and western Iran, although this includes one superb edifice, the Blue Mosque of Tabriz, the work of a Turkoman sovereign of the Qara Qoyunlu dynasty. Timurid architecture did not produce new or original works but followed the Iranian tradition established earlier in the Ilkhanid period, and particularly in the Jalairid and Muzaffarid elaborations, but with Timurid variations that include an obvious Central Asian component. It was first and foremost the art of an empire, speaking a monumental language and flaunting its wealth with a sumptuous decorative mantle, although this art was never vulgar and was free of clumsy improvisation. In fact, one always senses a keen sensibility behind the harmonious quest for proportional relationships that presuppose careful study by the architects. Altogether exceptional was the interest devoted to urban planning, substantial traces of which remain in a number of monumental groupings, such as in the famous Righistan square of Samarkand.

One notes in the designs, for instance, greater effort to make use of internal spaces, particularly appreciable in the structures erected after the middle of the fifteenth century. The portal began taking on proportions that were often gigantic, becoming a distinctive element, together with the dome, which became the object of attention. Tireless experimentation led to the invention of a bulbous-type dome atop a high drum. But while this variety strengthened the dome's symbolic significance, it no longer had a real relation to the inner space, in that for reasons of statics, it demanded a low, flat internal dome invisible from the outside. The most elegant example is without doubt that of Gur-i Mir ("tomb of the emir"), the sepulcher of Tamerlane himself; the exterior has cylindrical ribs resting on stalactite corbels, splendid in its surface of glazed ceramic tiles. The evolution of the dome and its giganticism had certain limitations in the design of the base; it used corner piers that discharged stress exclusively onto the corner areas, which thus required a considerable robustness. Furthermore, the elevation of the dome by means of the drum raised the building's center of gravity, most inauspicious in a region that often suffered from earthquakes. In the area between Khurasan and Transoxiana, a new structural system was worked out to distribute along all the walls the weight of the high roof by means of a system of intersecting transverse arches connected by a network of ribs — a technique that has been called the most significant triumph of engineering in Central Asia of the fifteenth century. The new system made it possible to lighten the weight of the dome considerably without compromising the internal space; in fact, it led to a reduction of the inert wall masses in the corner areas, permitting a better distribution and a greater development of the rooms. It also permitted a lowering of the building's center of gravity, creating an elastic system of construction more resistant to earthquakes. For example, the system was used in 1432 in the mausoleum of Gauhar Shad (Shah Rukh's wife) at Herat, and it saw one of its most complete applications in the Ishrat-Khana mausoleum at Samarkand, initiated in 1464. The decorative qualities typical of this construction technique spread the fashion throughout the Islamic east, soon reducing it to a purely ornamental formula.

The taste for the magnificent and the sumptuous found its flawless expression in the decoration of the structures; it made wide use of polychrome ceramics, realized both with sculptured and glazed terracotta elements or, more frequently, with a special kind of small brick. Predominant on large surfaces was ornamentation with a geometric design, and an important part was also played by Kufic inscriptions. At the same time, wide use was made of full-blown faience mosaics and minute elements for decorations of a floral variety and with cursive inscriptions in *thuluth* characters, a lavish technique that as early as the fifteenth century was gradually replaced by more economical tiles, generally square and with their decoration painted with the so-called dry-cord technique. The dominant colors were turquoise and blue (lapis lazuli or cobalt), but there was no lack either of purple, green, or yellow.

The ceramic polychromy tended to enfold the structures completely like a gorgeous garment, but in the finest examples it never forced the architectural lines. Particularly in the works of the first half of the fifteenth century, an ever more harmonious balance was achieved between structural volumes and the chromatic "urge," and the latter came

THE CASKET OF PEARLS

Mine eye hath lost the substance of sight, and like a child winking destiny deceived me with tricks of glass; and pearls of words once scattered from the gateway of sound when I had hidden thirty-two pearls in the casket; but hard it is now to scatter pearls, for impious, cruel Heaven has sacked my casket of pearls!

JAMI (1414–92, the last great Persian classical poet)

LOVE LAMENT

O heart, come now, let us set our eyes together on a handsome young man, let us seek a person as slender as a cypress tree, let's set our eyes on cheeks as shiny as silver!

Since he who was dear to us has set his sights on another friend, we too have eyes, indeed; let's set them on another friend!

Since others lighten their eyes with the dust raised by his steed, let's not languish, but go and set eyes upon another horseman!

Let's wander the countryside and round the gardens in search of a friend. Let our eyes wander in the countryside, let our eyes wander in the gardens!

Even if we don't find another calamity like him, full of his tricks, disturber of the city, let's set our eyes on some poor lad who will console our woes, affectionately!

And even if we don't succeed, may the desire go on! as far as we can, let's set our sights among nobles and plebeians!

Oh Navai, yet nonetheless you cannot do without him. Come let's be patient and calm and wait for him to join us!

ALI SHER NAVAI (1441–1501, the most refined Turkish poet and outstanding exponent of Timurid culture)

Samarkand (U.S.S.R.): Plan of the Righistan.
1   Madrassa *of Ulugh Beg*
2   *Shir-dar* Madrassa
3   *Tiliya-kari Mosque-*Madrassa
4   Chaharsu *(crossroads), the center of the bazaar.*

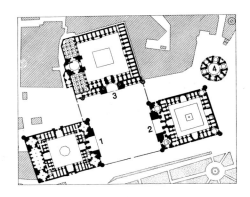

to be concentrated on the focal points such as portals and domes, while relaxing into slower and more spacious rhythms on the walls. This was a manifestation of barbarian pomp, which came under the rule of the typically Iranian moderation. It was a rule that conceded nothing to mannerism and rendered its own use natural, even in defensive structures, as can be seen in some of the surviving towers of the Herat citadel. Stucco was used extensively, especially for the interiors, and the various palaces were adorned with paintings. A number of landscapes are still to be seen here and there, even in mausoleums, although purely ornamental motifs are more common in this type of edifice.

Today all we know of Tamerlane's great secular structures are the remains of the towering portal, flanked by two minarets, of the Aq Saray, the palace Tamerlane had built for himself at Shar-i Sabz, where he had considered building his capital as an alternative to Samarkand. An enthusiastic description of it has been left by Clavijo, the Spanish ambassador to the Timur court, who saw it in 1404, before it was completed. It was a palace of the Iranian type; its main *iwan*, according to Babur, was larger than that of the Taq-i Kisra at Ctesiphon, and there are indications that it was flanked by two minor *iwans*. Still to be found at Samarkand are the immense ruins of the congregational mosque that Tamerlane had built. Begun in 1399 and known by the name of Bibi Khanum, it was of the four-*iwan* variety, into which the multiple minarets feature was introduced: four at the corners and a pair each for the entrance portal and for the main *iwan*, which stands in front of the domed prayer hall. Small domes on pillars appear to have covered the wings, in line with the criterion already adopted in the Seljuk period in the Masjid-i Juma at Isfahan. In the *madrassa* of Ulugh Beg of 1417–20, in the Righistan square of Samarkand, we find the design of the four domed halls at the building's corners. Another four-*iwan* mosque is that founded at Meshad by Gauhar Shad, wife of Shah Rukh, between 1405 and 1418, the work of a great architect of Shiraz, Qivam al-Din, who in 1417 began work for the same empress on the *musallah* (an open sanctuary) of Herat, of which only two corner minarets remain. This edifice has the peculiarity of possessing a double shrine comprising two domed halls, one following the other behind the *iwan*. This architectural formula was used for the first time in the mosque of Khvaja Afmad Yasavi, in Turkestan, dated to 1394–95, the work of another architect from Shiraz, Haji Husayn. The edifice, of exceptional beauty thanks to the compactness of its forms, is a complex including in addition to the mosque — which is of a rather rare type, without a court — a mausoleum, a monastery, and a library.

Perhaps also to be traced back to Qivam al-Din is the *madrassa* of Gauhar Shad at Herat, the remains of which, aside from the minaret, are limited to the sepulcher finished in 1432. It was placed in the western corner — as described in connection with the new Timurid system — to support the dome by means of intersecting arches. We find the same support system in another structure, the *madrassa* of Kharghird, which was begun by Qivam al-Din but finished in 1444 by another Shiraz architect, Ghiyath al-Din. To be noted in connection with this latter edifice, in addition to the importance given to the vestibular area, is the outside projection on the back wall of the main *iwan*, and two sorts of apses with five windows that articulate the two domed corner rooms. This design is also to be seen in the *madrassa* of Gauhar Shad at Herat, which presents analogies with Anatolian architecture. Apparently to be assigned to the school of Qivam al-Din is the reconstruction, ordered in 1428 by Shah Rukh, of the Khvaja Abd Allah Ansari sanctuary near Herat. Of the four-*iwan* type with an extended court, its decoration shows one of the most ambitious repertories in Timurid architecture, particularly fascinating in its kaleidoscopic effects. The four-*iwan* type of edifice had by this time taken hold once and for all. It was to be generalized and carried forward, with only a few variants, even in the Uzbek period, as in the constructions to be seen near the *madrassa* of Ulugh Beg at Righistan in Samarkand. It would also replace previous Timurid structures, such as the reconstruction of the Shir-dar *madrassa* (1619–36) and the Tiliya-kari *madrassa*-mosque (1660), and at Bukhara the Masjid-i Kalan (1514) and

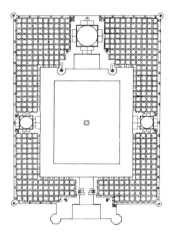

Samarkand (U.S.S.R.): Reconstruction of the plan of the Bibi Khanum Mosque.

Turkestan (U.S.S.R.): Plan of the mosque-monastery of Khvaja Ahmad Yasavi.

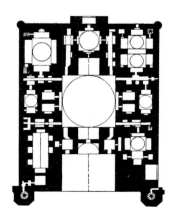

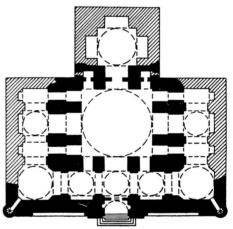

Tabriz (Iran): Plan of the Blue Mosque. Of the type without a courtyard, this is probably to be traced to Anatolian sources.

the Mir-i Arab *madrassa* (1530–36) and that of Abdulaziz Khan (1652).

For the most part, the sepulchral edifices of this period were not isolated but parts of larger complexes, whether through being joined to religious foundations — as is the case with the Khvaja Ahmad Yasavi complex and the mausoleum of Gauhar Shad — or by being arranged in groups, although even then the tombs maintain their individuality. An instance of the latter are those built in Samarkand for Shah Zinde ("the living king," a name given to Qasim ibn Abbas, who was believed to have introduced Islam into Samarkand). The necropolis in question is a small one, stretching along the road reached through a portal built by Ulugh Beg. The tombs belong to one of the most widespread types, that with a square base topped by a dome. Their interest lies in the fact that they reveal a development of the Timurid style from its antecedents in the mosque-tomb of Qasim ibn Abbas, built in 1334, up to the period of Ulugh Beg (second half of the fifteenth century). Of outstanding im-

Right:
Balkh (Afghanistan): The mausoleum of Khvaja Abu Nasr Parsa (1460–61). Although polygonal, it has rounded corners broken by two tiers of niches. The facade, in keeping with Timurid design, was immense, and flanked by two grandiose tower-minarets (now largely destroyed).

Above:
Bukhara (U.S.S.R.): The Chahar Bagh Mosque, built in the middle of the sixteenth century.

Below:
Ghazni (Afghanistan): The mausoleum of Abdurrazaq (1507), a good example of late

Timurid provincial architecture. Characteristic are the massive corner towers, elements stemming from the civil architecture of Transoxiana; and the gigantic portals looming up on each facade, accentuating "staccato" rhythms typical of Timurid architecture, a style that was taken up again in the Safavid period.

ADMONITION TO THE KING

The royal palace where the banquet is laid out is adorned like Paradise itself:
    Its drapes are woven with the souls of the people, blood of the people are rubies and cinnabar.
    Its friezes are gilded with the substance of the people, and the crusted gems are the pearls and rubies (the tears, and tears of blood) of the people.
    Bricks were brought by demolishing mosques, stones were found by taking them from the tombs of the people.

    ALI SHER NAVAI (1441–1501)

CONTEMPLATIVE REPOSE

An apple branch was loaded with ripe fruit. On each twig there remained four or five leaves so well arranged that even a painter, if he wished to produce a similar copy, could not have done so precisely.

On the slopes grew flowers of all kinds and colors. Once I had them counted, and there turned out to be thirty-three or thirty-four different sorts. One of these had a scent somewhat like that of red roses; I called it the "rose-scented tulip."

The trees loaded with ripe fruit were extremely beautiful. As they admired them, the wine-lovers began to yearn for their favorite drink. Though we had already taken drugs, since the sight was too beautiful, we drank, seated under the trees with their ripe fruit. We stayed there talking till sunset.

    BABUR (1483–1530, from *Vaqai-i-Babur, The Adventures of Babur*)

FROM THE TURCOMAN PAGEANT

The horse
Your dear brow is like an open arena,
Your dear eyes like two carbuncles,
Your dear mane as soft as silk,
Your dear ears are twin brothers
Your dear back bears the warrior to his goal
I call you not horse, but brother;
You are better than a brother.

Infidel dogs!
O infidel dog, you bay like a dog, avid as a circassian, banqueting
on the flesh of little pigs
You lie on a sack of straw
You have half a brick as a pillow
As a god you have a bit of carved wood!

I, Qazan, the hero
If from the high and misty mountains there rolled down a boulder, I, Qazan, was the hero who stopped it with my strong heel or hip . . .
    When the high mountains were covered with mist and the black vapors raged, when you could not see the ears of my black charger, when travelers without guides lost their way I, Qazan the hero, went out without a guide!
    Nor even then did I boast or vaunt my prowess as hero and leader. Never do I love the vainglorious. O infidel, since I have fallen into your hands kill me, put me to death! I shall not deny my origins, my lineage!

    [From the *Kitab-i-Dedem Qorqud* (*Book of the Ancestor Qorqud*), a Turkish anthology of tales on epic and chivalrous subjects]

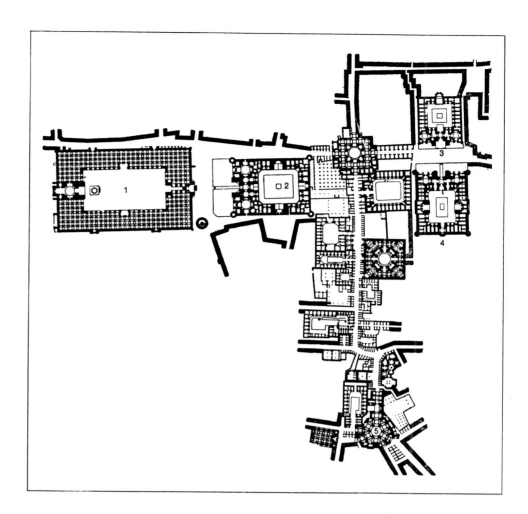

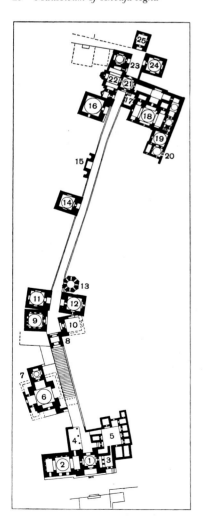

portance are the tombs of a number of Tamerlane's relatives, including several of his sisters and nephews, datable after 1371, and that of the astronomer Ghazi-Zade Rumi of 1437. The octagonal design was used in one of the smaller tombs as well as in the most famous and loveliest of the Timurid tombs, the aforementioned Gur-i Mir (of 1405) of Tamerlane (which is set somewhat apart from the necropolis of Shah Zinde); the octagonal form of this latter was subsequently surrounded by a complex of great proportions. We come across the polygonal model again in a fantastic, even turgid, context — the mausoleum of Khvaja Abu Nasr Parsa at Balkh, dated to 1460–61.

The late provincial structures include a number that are interesting for the particular design of the inner rooms, as in the Ghazni mosque of 1507. Built for Abdurrazaq, a Timurid epigone, it again employed four massive corner towers, a design typical of the architecture of Transoxiana, originally based in secular architecture. Resulting from a different architectural tradition, one in which strong Anatolian influences are to be found, is an important survivor of the Timurid period in western Iran: the Blue Mosque of Tabriz, built by a ruler of the Qara Qoyunlu dynasty in 1462–65. It is a courtless mosque, made up of a great central dome surrounded by seven smaller ones. The decoration of many-colored tiles, although consistent with the general Timurid style, shows characteristics of the art of central-western Iran.

This brief survey of Timurid architecture cannot close without a few words about that of the Timurid gardens, of which, to be sure, nothing is left except certain memories. The gardens were of the Chahar Bagh type, with geometric layouts and surrounded by high walls; this much is known from those of later periods, planned in the same manner as their forerunners. Timurid gardens were credited as being the Islamic world's most exquisite creations, a fabled interpretation of nature in a hostile environment: land enhanced by water, and all conjured up by a lively, decorative imagination.

SAFAVID IRAN

The rise of a "Turkicized" dynasty on the Iranian horizon toward the end of the fifteenth century, the Safavid dynasty (which ruled from 1501 to 1736) — natives of Ardebil, in northwest Iran — was a development of major historical importance. Not only did a group of territories inhabited chiefly by Iranians rise up in arms still another time, with the advent of Shah Ismail (1501–24), but the basis of modern Iran was laid. In fact, the Safavids, at the outset a mystic confraternity as much as a dynasty, managed to make their subjects accept their Shiite doctrine, although only gradually and by force. The result was that, with this dynasty, Iran began to take on the characteristics that to this day distinguishes it from all other bordering states, all of which are officially Sunnite. "With the religious unification, even though effected by force," Bausani has written, "the Persians at least became 'a people' in the only way possible in this Islamic context, adding to a union under common dogmas and laws, an isolation from neighbors." It goes without saying that, in the shaping of Iran, a major role was also played by the endless clashes with the Ottoman empire to the west and with the Uzebks to the northeast, as well as with the Moguls of India, with whom the Iranians long disputed for the possession of what is today Afghanistan. In fact, it was precisely the Afghan invasion of the eighteenth century, to all intents and purposes putting an end to the Safavid state, that was a key agent in reviving the ties among the Persian people. From a cultural point of view, it was only with the eighteenth century that eastern Islam lost its substantial unity, breaking up, broadly speaking, into three parts: Iran, Central Asia, and Mogul India.

With Shah Abbas the Great (1588–1629) — the "Great Sophy" of the West, roughly a contemporary of Philip II of Spain, Queen Elizabeth, Ivan the Terrible, and the Mogul emperor Akbar — the Safavid empire reached its apogee. Power remained strongly centralized, resting on a series of sage administrative provisions, which were constantly aimed at enriching the productive forces of the nation. An attempt was made to lighten the fiscal burden, handicrafts were developed, and a stimulus was given to domestic and foreign commerce by providing a first-rate system of roads equipped with a "chain" of caravansaries. Because of its anti-Ottoman position, the Safavid empire also attracted the sympathies of the European powers, with which friendly relations were established. (An exception were the Portuguese, who disrupted trade in the Persian Gulf, which after the opening of the Cape route had become accessible, irrespective of the attitude of the Ottomans.)

Particularly strengthened was the production of both raw and processed silk; together with carpets, which in the seventeenth century reached their utmost technical perfection, silk was the key item in Iran's international trade, earmarked chiefly for Europe. The network of trade relations reached far and wide. The great seventeenth-century traveler Chardin tells us that Iranian commercial agents were active even in the most distant lands, such as Sweden and China. But it must be said that these far-flung business operations were substantially in the hands of either the Armenian minority or the most powerful European trading firms — British, Dutch, French — which drained Iran's outbound commerce, particularly that using the sea routes. The era of great international trade conducted by land routes had now reached an end, and together with the technological competition of Europe and the tremendous damage done to agriculture by centuries of invasions and insensate exploitation, this spelled the ultimate crisis not only of Iran but of the Islamic world in general. At the death of Shah Abbas II (1642–67), the Safavid state began heading toward decadence, which in fact soon came with the Afghan wars of 1722–38, wars that brought fresh, awesome destruction. In the region of Isfahan alone, more than a thousand villages were wiped out — two-thirds of the total.

Isfahan (Iran): The Masjid-i Shah (1611–16), a mosque erected by Shah Abbas the Great (1588–1629). This is a view of the north *iwan* from the inner court. Entrance from the Maydan-i Shah, or great square (see pages 116–17), is through the mammoth portal flanked by the two minarets. Angled entryway is dictated by the *qibla's* orientation.

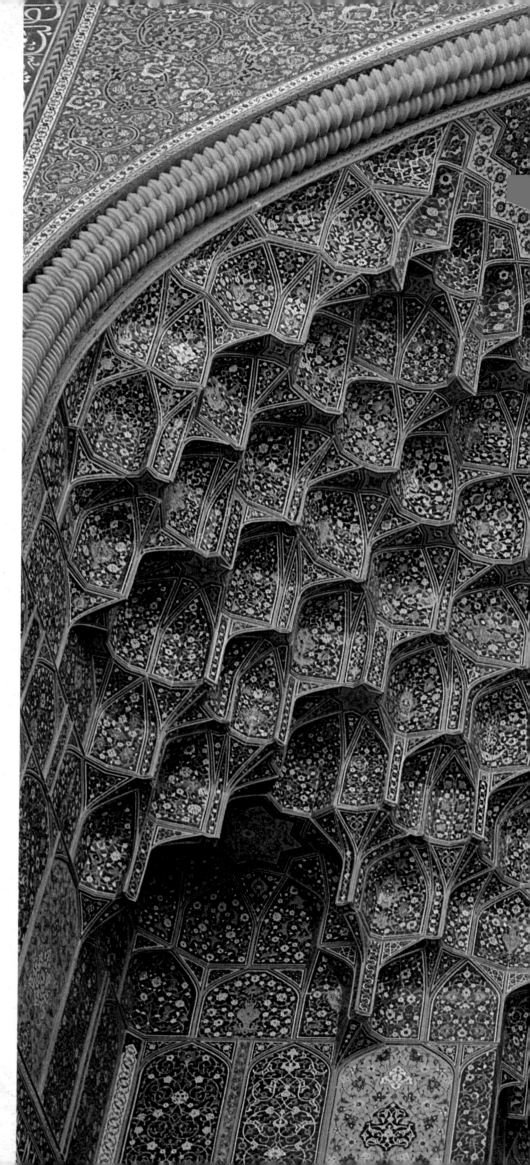

Isfahan (Iran): A close-up of the stalactite hood of the great entrance *iwan* of the Masjid-i Shah. As in the Timurid period, the access areas are largely monumental. The ornamentation is of enameled faience mosaics.

MYSTICAL RAPTURE

Yesterday, overcome by love, drunken with desire, stupefied I wandered everywhere,
and at last the longing to see Thee turned my horse's head toward the convent of the Magi;
and there I saw a secret meeting (let the evil eye keep away) lit by light of True and not by fire of hell,
and throughout that place I saw burning that fire first seen on Sinai by Moses, son of 'Emran.
An old Master celebrated there the worship of fire and in veneration the young Magi surrounded him,
all with cheeks of silver, with rose-like faces, with sweet tongues and slender mouths,
lutes and harps and flutes and tambourines and rebecs, candles and sweetmeats and flowers and wines and aromas,
a moon-faced cup-bearer whose locks were scented with musk, a light-spoken minstrel whose harmonies were sweet,
Magi and sons of Magi, all with their thighs bound in the service of God.
and I, ashamed that I was a Moslem, hid in a dark corner.
When the Master asked "Who is this?" they replied to him: "He is a lover, overcome and without peace."
Then said he "Give him a cup of purest wine, though he be an uninvited guest!"
And the fire-worshipping cup-bearer with his hand of fire, poured burning fire into my cup;
and when I had drunk of it I was without mind or thought, that flame within me burnt both doubt and faith,
and I fell into a stupor; and in that deep stupor a voice (in a powerful tongue that now cannot be told)
seemed to come from all my limbs right to the vein of my neck and the artery of my heart:
He is one and there is no other than He,
The Only One, there is no other God than He.

> HATEF (poet at Isfahan in the
> eighteenth century)

Isfahan (Iran): Plan of the Masjid-i Shah. The mosque is not on an axis with the Maydan-i Shah because of the necessary orientation of the qibla wall.

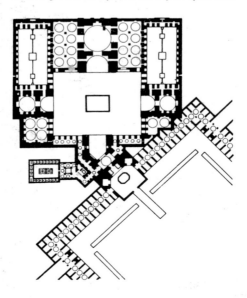

MAKE GLORIOUS MINE ANCESTORS

Make glorious mine ancestors through my hand! Were I to flee, shorten my life an it were long. Let it be that through mine hand mine ancestors put the envious to shame. Let it not be that any man shall spit upon my face, but rather upon my corpse. Make of mine adversaries thirty thousand heroes, each one of which shall be a Rustam [*hero of Iranian sagas*]!

When that I shall wish to go out upon the field, and they shall come, I shall fight against them alone!

All of them shall I put to the sword. They shall not be able either to concert their force or to attack.

Do heroes perhaps worry over death? Shall I not cause a sack of chaff to rot?

SHAH ISMAIL (founder of the Safavid dynasty)

O FAITHLESS GIRL

O thou whose face is like a rose, thou of the rose-colored tunic, thou whose legs are dressed in red.

Having put on clothes of fire thou hast made us burn amongst the flames!

The sun and moon, for what concerneth beauty, bow down before thy face.

Amongst human creatures none is born like thee, o faithless girl!

One would think thou wert born from the shining moon and sun!

FUZULI (d. 1555, considered one of the great Turko-Islamic poets)

All things considered, however, the Safavid period witnessed a flourishing of artistic culture, in spite of the fact that the literature — to be fair, not yet sufficiently studied — appears to be rather arid. At the same time, this literature released popular elements heretofore ignored by the aristocratic and decorative traditions of Persian poetry, and it generated a flower of refinement: the lyrics of the "Indian style," so named in that it was preferred by the Indian connoisseurs of Persian culture. All fields of the minor arts also attained excellence. Mention has been made of the textile arts, but attention should also be called to the pottery of the period, which received a strong impetus from an imitation of blue-and-white Chinese porcelain. The result was a new decorative style, the so-called international Chinese of Persian stamp, particularly fashionable in Turkey. The taste for porcelain, no longer intended for use but for decorative purposes, encouraged the assembling of collections and gave rise to an architectural decoration feature: the wall with vasiform niches, in which precious Chinese porcelains or their Iranian imitations were placed. Miniatures as well knew a period of great splendor. In this field, a particular fame was enjoyed by the "Tabriz school," named after the first Safavid capital, built up around Bihzad and his disciples, whose mastery had far-reaching effects throughout Turkey and also in India, where he inspired the great Mogul school of painting. A lively impetus was also given to the art of book-making, thanks to Shah Tahmasp (1524–76), who moved the capital to Qazvin. And when Isfa-

han regained its role as capital in 1598, with Shah Abbas the Great, it produced one artist of genius in Riza-i-Abbasi; fortunately, European painting — Dutch and Italian in particular — never exerted the influence on him that was to prove harmful for so much of the Persian painting of the following period.

Once again, architecture represented one of the most significant aspects of Iranian artistic culture, despite the fact that it generally failed to renew its patterns. Thought out in grandiose terms in line with the imperial aims of the dynasty, these patterns had received their magniloquent formulation, as we have seen, in the Timurid period. But in Safavid Iran, the architectural discourse chose a mode of its own in quest for structural rhythms that were less exalted: variations on a theme, highly studied and well chiseled, suitable to meet the needs for refined luxury of an aristocracy that was still thoroughly medieval and whose artistic ideal was decorative and abstract, with flashes of intellectual pithiness in which *how* something was said was more important than *what* was said. It was precisely the failure to consider this particular aspect that made many a modern critic judge Safavid architecture severely. There has been much talk of a "decorative crust" in connection with its profusion of colors. When the crust crumbled away, it was said, one saw the poverty of the structure beneath. And it is true that the materials used were often of inferior quality, and this, together with the extreme rapidity with which edifices were often erected, condemned them to swift ruin. Nevertheless, a more careful study of the Safavid monuments astonishes us by the wealth of technical solutions, which were often daring and original, revealing in full the vitality and creative possibilities of Iranian architects. This does not mean that Iranian architecture was lacking in candor, but only that the visualization of structural factors in stylistic terms nearly always took place through a process of intellectual projection. The emergence of structural factors at the surface is bound up with their possibilities of becoming stylized, of qualifying decoratively, and of respecting the conventions of a language whose aesthetics was theologically conditioned by the principle, unfailingly found in every Moslem artist, that all is changeable, transient. From this it follows that the ambiguity to be seen in the relationship between the "wrapping" of a monument and provides a yardstick to judge the quality of the architecture of Iran and of the Islamic world, in general.

The most numerous and conspicuous testimonials of Safavid architecture are those provided by the Isfahan of Shah Abbas. In discussing the activities of this sovereign, we should first mention his urban planning, conceived in terms of imperial opulence, of the new Isfahan, which was built some distance south of the ancient urban nucleus. The main axis is the great Chahar Bagh ("the four gardens") avenue, made up of three separate streets — the one in the middle, which included a canal, was intended as a promenade — bordered by double rows of plane trees and poplars and adorned with colorful flowerbeds. Ranged alongside the Chahar Bagh were the gardens of the homes of aristocrats, who were granted land on the condition that they build on it. Another focal point of the city is the towering Maydan-i Shah ("royal plaza"), intended for polo games, parades, or just strolling. The north side is reached by passing through a gigantic portal at the bazaar, which is matched on the opposite side by the mammoth Masjid-i Shah. Standing on the east and west sides of the square, one opposite the other, are the small mosque of Shaykh Lutf Allah and the Ali Kapu, the portal-pavilion serving as an entrance to the gardens of Chehel Sutun, which reached as far as the Chahar Bagh. The Maydan-i Shah itself, is so vast — measuring some 1600 by 500 feet — that the edifices described above and their connecting wall, with its two tiers of arcades, fail to hold together as a unified urban space, so that the square remains irremediably vacant.

The Masjid-i Shah (1611–16) — which because of the obligatory orientation of its *qibla* is not parallel with the square's main axis — connects by means of an elbow corridor with the great portal, flanked by two minarets, that is parallel to the south side of the Maydan-i Shah. The interior has four *iwans*, each of which — in accordance with the type

launched in Transoxiana in the Timurid mosque of Bibi Khanum — is followed by a dome, that of the *mihrab* standing on an octagonal drum with arches. The sanctuary proper is located between two pillar-type naves, covered by small domes leading toward two *madrassas*. It should be noted that the structures of the four *iwans* are connected with one another only around the bottom, thus revealing a process of unshackling

Isfahan (Iran): The *Madrassa* of Madar-i Shah (1706–14), a name meaning "the *madrassa* of the Shah's mother." The dome is over the prayer hall. Built alongside the *madrassa* was a caravansary, Khan-i Madar-i Shah; its profits guaranteed the maintenance of the teachers and students in this adjacent school.

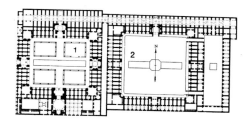

Isfahan (Iran): Plan of the Madrassa of Madar-i Shah (1) *and the caravansary (2).*

Meshad (Iran): Plan of the mausoleum of Khvaja Rabi. The edifice stands over the tomb of an old-time comrade of Ali, the fourth of the original caliphs. The plan is a square with rounded corners, inside which deep niches have been built. The ornamentation of glazed faience that lines the work is of excellent quality.

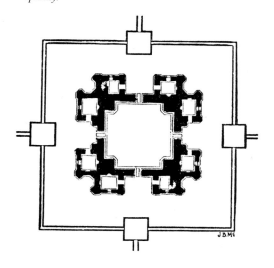

from the more traditional structures, in line with a tendency already found in Timurid architecture. The edifice's proportions are grandiose and its balance flawless, although a certain staccato tendency is to be seen in its volumes, which are joined in a sumptuous mantle of glazed ceramics. The mantle reveals an exceptionally wide use of tiles, with the most costly mosaics being left for the areas of crucial importance. Dominating on the outside are various shades of blue, which endow the architectural mass with an airiness, while the covered interiors disclose a play of whites and yellows.

Dating to approximately the same time is the small mosque of Shaykh Lutf Allah (1603–17), situated on the east side of the Maydan-i Shah, erected there by Shah Abbas in honor of his father-in-law. Like the Masjid-i Shah, this mosque is not on an axis with the plaza, and as a result the prayer hall is entered ingeniously by means of a long elbow corridor. Built without a court, the mosque consists of a square hall with corner piers, and a dome resting on the hall itself, supported by a drum with blind windows. The dome's profile has a somewhat crushed appearance, echoing older Seljuk models. The outside is lined with enameled tiles, with green or blue arabesque decorations surrounded by black on a cream background. Shades of blue predominate inside, the pattern calling carpets to mind. The inscriptions adorning the drum are exceptionally elegant. The harmony of its proportions, the decorative syntax of the embellishments, the palette choices — all make the small mosque of Shaykh Lutf Allah one of the masterpieces of Persian architecture.

Outstanding among the achievements of Shah Abbas are his added touches in the Shiite shrine of the *imam* Riza at Meshad, and the embellishing and enlarging of another great sanctuary at Mahan, near Kirman (although this latter was extensively altered later). A work of various Safavid sultans is the fascinating complex that took shape around the tomb of the dynasty's founder, Shaykh Ishaq Safi, at Ardebil. Nor should we forget the interventions that the Safavids made in the older Masjid-i Juma of Isfahan, including the bulk of the faience decorations and the positioning of the stalactites of the *iwan* (although this has been partly redone, more or less faithfully, in modern times). To be ascribed to the reign of Suleiman Shah (1667–94) is the *musallah* of Meshad; with its towering *iwan* flanked by two domes, this sanctuary follows the Timurid models established in Transoxiana. The last great Safavid achievement in Isfahan is the *madrassa* Madar-i Shah, on the Chahar Bagh, begun in 1706. Here we find joined together a mosque, a *madrassa*, and a caravansary, a work of quiet appeal in the relaxed rhythms of its great courts and in its harmonious architectural lines.

Funerary architecture shows a preference for the domed structure on a square or polygonal base. Prominent among those erected at the outset of the dynasty is the highly elegant portal of the mausoleum of Harun-i Vilaya of 1512 at Isfahan. Its decoration is still of the Timurid type in its western version, of which the most faithful example is the Blue Mosque of Tabriz. The mausoleum of Bibi Dukhtaran at Shiraz is square with a cruciform hall, making use of the deep-niche design on three facades. To be singled out from the time of Shah Abbas is the original pentagonal design of the mausoleum of Baba Rukh al-Din. But the most widespread variety is octagonal in shape, with deep niches in its sides, such as that of Khvaja Rabi at Meshad, built in 1622, and the sanctuary if Qadam-gah, built by Shah Suleiman in 1643.

The architecture of palatial structures is known to us beginning with the time of Shah Abbas. Rather than great coherent complexes, these structures are relatively modest, even small in size. Built in verdant surroundings, they bring out a typically Iranian taste, dating back at least to the Achaemenids of the ancient world, that had received frequent graftings from Central Asian nomadic traditions, as is to be seen in the fact that the pavilions were placed amid the geometric patterns of the formal gardens. These architectural works took the form of free, capricious, and refined interpretations of ancient types that had evidently remained alive in the framework of private Persian architecture: for example, those of the *talar*, the terraced veranda with a flat roof sup-

Isfahan (Iran): **Portal of the** *Madrassa* **of Madar-i Shah (1706–14). This is a highly elegant work of the late Safavid period, with particularly harmonious proportions.**

Isfahan (Iran): Plan of the Chehel Sutun.

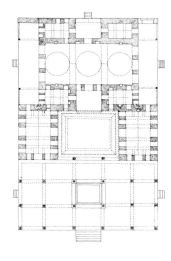

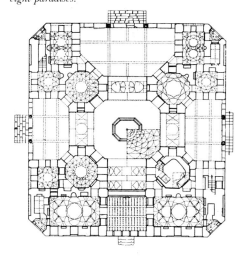

Isfahan (Iran): Plan of the palace of Shah Suleiman, known by the name of Hasht Bihisht, "the eight paradises."

ported by towering wooden columns, among which tents were erected. The *talar* became one of the typical designs of Safavid palatial architecture. An outstanding example is the *talar* forming the second floor of the Ali Kapu, which looks out on the Maydan-i Shah. The Ali Kapu ("the great gate"), an edifice of several stories and a complex construction, is in effect the entrance to a great garden located behind it, the Naqsh-i Jahan — "image of the world." But its ground floor also housed various administrative offices, while the upper floors were set aside for the sovereign, who often used them for audiences with foreign ambassadors. Ali Kapu, like the Ottoman's "Sublime Porte," was used at one and the same time as the sovereign's residence and as a symbol of power.

In what remains of the great Naqsh-i Jahan gardens is the famous Chehel Sutun, "the forty columns" — in reality there are twenty, the name referring to the reflection in the waters of a basin that extends from it. Its *talar* serves as a veranda for an *iwan* placed between two wings of small rooms, which preceded a spacious tripartite salon with transverse arches. Large segments of the original painted decoration remain intact (and others have been added by modern restorers); some reveal a European influence, particularly Dutch. The ceiling of the *talar* is a magnificent example of the cabinet-maker's art. A three-part *iwan* design, this too with ample windowless walls, is the Ashraf *talar* of the time of Shah Abbas II (1642–67), covered by highly complicated vault systems. Remaining as one of the masterpieces of this type of architecture is the small palace of Hasht Bihisht, "the eight paradises" of Suleiman Shah (1667–94); this is a two-story edifice with a square design but rounded corners, which conforms with the vintage type of cruciform hall and the resulting corner rooms, a form still productive in far-flung areas of contemporary Iran. In the Hasht Bihisht, this design is extraordinarily articulated, distributed over two floors, with extensive open sections facing outward by means of three great *talars*. Still existing in its essential lines near Isfahan is the garden of Farabad, "the sojurn of happiness," the summer residence of Shah Sultan Husein, built in 1700; this is a flawless example of a garden with a geometric layout, enlivened by an ingenious system for the distribution of water.

We can only refer in passing here to the highly varied programs that Shah Abbas sponsored to develop commerce; in addition to the municipal bazaars, he also concentrated on a series of imposing caravansaries, in which a rational system for access to stables was developed. Of the various bridges that were strengthened or completely rebuilt in the Safavid period, the most interesting are doubtless the two most celebrated of Isfahan, both crossing the Zayahde Rud: the Allahverdi Khan, named after the general of Shah Abbas who built it; and the Pul-i Khvaju, built in the time of Shah Abbas II. Both are two-story bridge-dams, in the Sassanid tradition; they contain rooms and pavilions, once adorned with paintings, in which travelers could linger to rest and to enjoy the cool air from the river.

The tragedy of the Afghan invasion (1722–38) put an end to the already languishing Safavid dynasty and triggered a rush on Iran by the Ottoman enemy. It was once again a Turk who restored Iran to its rightful borders, a general of the Afshar tribe, who in making himself king took on the name Nadir Shah. He succeeded in driving out the enemy, and even in sacking Lahore (now in Pakistan), in the heart of the dominion of the Moguls, the theoretical lords of the Afghans. Nadir Shah's fiscal policies and oppression, however, soon alienated the Iranian people, and he was assassinated in 1747. In Fars, meanwhile, after more than one thousand years, an Iranian dynasty took hold, that of the Zends, who became masters of all Iran, except Khurasan; with Karim Khan Zend, Iran enjoyed some thirty years of good government (1750–82). Under his guidance, the area of the new capital, Shiraz, made a strong economic recovery and a considerable cultural revival; this was manifested in a series of monuments, not without praiseworthy qualities, Karim Khan Zend built in the section of Shiraz he himself founded. Standing out among them is the Masjid-i Vakil ("mosque of the regent," the title assumed by Karim Khan), which incorporates quite unexpectedly

Above:
Isfahan (Iran): The Ali Kapu, a high pavilion that serves as the entrance to the great park known as "the image of the world." This building also functioned as a government palace and was used to receive ambassadors.

Below:
Isfahan (Iran): The Chehel Sutun, or pavilion of the "forty columns," built for Shah Abbas the Great (1588–1629).

Isfahan (Iran): The *talar* ceiling in the Ali Kapu, an exceptional achievement in wood and metal, supported by three rows of tall wooden columns with stalactite capitals. On the terrace of the pavilion is a marble basin with three jets fed by hydraulic machinery.

Following pages:
Isfahan (Iran): Pul-i Khvaju, the Khvaju Bridge, over the Zayande River, which supplies the great oasis that supports Isfahan. Built under Shah Abbas II (1642–67), it is a bridge-dam along the road to Shiraz. Iranians still love to linger under the arcades and in the pavilions and to enjoy the cool breezes off the river. The same is true of Isfahan's other famous bridge, the Allahverdi Khan, named after its builder, a famous general of Shah Abbas I.

a "long hall" type design, with a roof of small domes resting on marble columns of the characteristic spiral variety.

The strife that followed the death of Karim Khan brought the emergence of still another dynasty, that of the Qajars (1794–1925), which accentuated the culture isolation of Iran from the rest of Islam. In this period, the art of the region took on special characteristics marked by a nostalgia for the past, from the Achaemenids to the Safavids. It was a neo-archaic vision that nevertheless allowed certain plebeian elements, which before this time had little role in Iranian art. It was also open to Western influences; although more supinely accepted than interpreted, particularly in their Russian–Central Asian versions, these proved capable of contributing to the production of a number of quite tasteful Iranian works. But still it must be said that the last great epoch of Iranian art was under the seventeenth-century Safavids. It fully justifies the admiration it aroused in a great many European merchants, travelers, and artists — such as the Roman Pietro della Valle and the Frenchman Chardin — who in their attentive, curious observations of Persia anticipated our modern interest.

Isfahan (Iran): Plan of the city of Shah Abbas the Great.
1 Maydar-i Shah
2 Masjid-i Shah
3 Mosque of Shaykh Lutf Allah
4 Ali Kapu
5 Chehel Sutun
6 Entrance to the bazaar

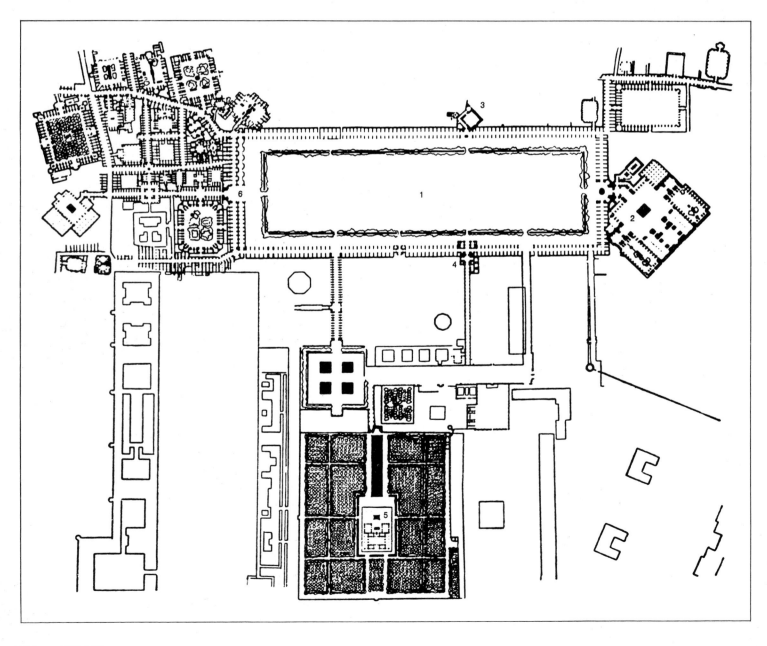

MOSLEM INDIA

It is difficult to imagine two worlds more completely different than those of the Hindus and of the Moslems. For the former, there was a broad religious flexibility — in which the highest goal was the realization of the self, and even a belief in God was to a certain extent secondary — and a social system rigidly locked into the laws of caste; yet despite the apparent discrepancy between the Hindu religious and social systems, they shared an extremely ancient and rich traditional legacy. And then there was Islam, with its monolithic monotheism and — at least theoretically — social progressiveness, joined together under the brotherhood of a common religion that also pretended to a universal political law. The Indian world, in its metaphysical adherence to a luxuriant, demoniac nature, which affords it the subject of its credo as well as its medium of expression, is matched against a myth-destroying, de-sanctifying Islam, practical in its aims but using an abstract language that recoils theologically from all naturalistic mimesis. The clash between these two civilizations, once they had come into contact with each other, was inevitable and dramatic, but the situation of endless conflict gave rise to an original and pregnant artistic culture, in which, while Islam ended by feeling the fascination of Hindu art, this latter became permeated with Islam, even drawing fecund stimuli from it. Indo-Islamic art, it is now widely recognized, is a luxuriant branch of Moslem art, but at the same time it is an essential facet of Indian art.

One should not lose sight of the fact, however, that many centuries before the advent of Islam, the Indian world was thrown into disarray by the Buddhist and Jain heterodoxies, which had found an avenue of penetration primarily among the mercantile classes. These heterodoxies appealed through their more or less universalistic character, or in any case a character that tended to break through the Hindu caste structure. And, indeed, the message of Islam would find its most receptive audience in India among the same mercantile classes who had earlier tried to break out of this caste structure via these new religions. Even at that, the penetration of Islam in India was slow and strongly opposed, so that as a rule we see none of the massive conversions to the new faith that was noticed elsewhere under Islamic conquest. "India, in fact," as Vacca has said, "is the only Asian country where Islamism enjoyed a virtually absolute political supremacy for centuries without ever bringing its religious conquest to completion." Up to the time of the 1857 Indian mutiny, Islam involved essentially only the elite — the class in power. It was a foreign faith or felt to be such, a faith of princes, soldiers, functionaries, and of that favorite class under Islam, the merchants — precisely those who played a crucial role in spreading Islamic power throughout the land. There was no lack of conversions among members of the upper castes, such as the great landowners of the north, although it should not be thought that this was customary. Only a few of the most disinherited fringes of the Hindu population became Moslem: those who had only recently become city-dwellers, those who had been uprooted, the caste-less, those who gravitated around the seats of power and commerce, all who in the religion of their new masters saw a possibility of social promotion. A fair amount of proselytizing was carried on by the sufis, those Moslem mystics who were organized into confraternities that, although religiously orthodox, could bring to bear a signal spiritual message by means of a certain similarity in their living style to that of Indian society.

The overwhelming mass of the Indian population, however, was made up chiefly of peasants, living in a closed village economy in which no money and little else changed hands. As a rule, cultivated land was left to the administration of local princes, who in exchange for a certain independence became responsible for the collecting of the extremely high taxes and supervising the intermediaries of power. In such a situation, India's static agrarian society could scarcely be swayed by the theoretical egalitarianism of Islam, with which it had few opportunities to come into contact, and from which it would not have known how, in any case, to draw any particular advantage. Furthermore, in practice Islam was discriminatory; it often exempted the Brahman caste from the payment of taxes but demanded them from the new Moslems. The fact remains, however, that although never to attract more than a minority, albeit an influential one, Islam gave India the forms of a state and infused the dislocated Hindu world with a desire for renewal. The areas that experienced the most intensive Islamization correspond roughly to the present-day Pakistan and Bangladesh, in the northwest and northeast parts of the subcontinent. This phenomenon is to be explained by the fact that the Punjab region, with the valleys of the Indus, because of its geographical nearness to the Iranian world, was the region most continuously subjected to Islamic pressure. In addition, it was a region of intense commercial traffic, where Buddhism had flourished and Hinduism was less firmly rooted. In Bangladesh, to the east, however, the widespread success of Islam may have been the result of the great vacuum left by Buddhism, which Hinduism had ferociously persecuted in the twelfth century.

The political vicissitudes of Moslem India were highly complex, and in a work such as this we can only outline them briefly. By and large the conquest can be divided into three different periods. As far back as the Umayyad period (in the eighth century), Islam established itself solidly at Sind (part of today's Pakistan). It was only with the end of the tenth century and the beginning of the eleventh, under Mahmud of Ghazni, however, that Islam moved down the classic road of the invaders from the north through the Khyber Pass and lunged at India's riches, under the ideological shield of a holy war. The result of these wide-scale raids, the chief aim of which was the capture of booty, was a conquest confined to the basin of the Indus; but the effect was more far-reaching, for it upset the precarious balance of the already divided and inconsistent Indian subcontinent.

The Ghorids, who replaced the Ghaznavids, were the protagonists of the next phase. With the battle of Tarain of 1192, which was decisive for the history of Hindu India, they imposed the hegemony of Islam on India's northern territories, a hegemony that reached out as far as Bengal. The Ghorid Shibab ud-Din Muhammad, having died without heirs in 1206, one of his "slave-generals, the Turk Qutb ud-Din Aibak, took up his Indian legacy, giving rise to what was to become known as the Sultanate of Delhi; this also established the first Islamic dynasty of India, the Mamluks (1206–90), so called like the Egyptian dynasty because of the slave origins of one of its chief representatives. The founder's successor, Iltutmish (1211–36), took steps to consolidate the empire and in particular to bolster the frontiers on the northwest against the ever-present Mongol threat, a development that was to slow down Islam's expansion toward India's southern regions. The expansion was successfully resumed by the Turk–Afghan Khalji, Ala ud-Din (1296–1320), who conquered virtually all the subcontinent, thus concluding the third phase of the advance of the Islamic armies across India. Ala ud-Din, who rated himself on his own coins as "the second Alexander the Great," was without doubt the most outstanding Moslem sovereign of India prior to the great Mogul emperors. With him, Islam in India began to shake off the characteristics of a mere military occupation force to take on those of an Indian state ruled by native-born Moslems. The rapid growth of the empire, made up of heterogeneous peoples, posed tremendous problems of state organization, which were tackled with energy and ruthless firmness by Ala ud-Din; in the end, though, the achievements based on his own personal despotism did not survive him.

In 1320 a Turk with an Indian mother, Ghiyas ud-Din Tughlaq, mounted the throne of Delhi, founding the Tughlaq dynasty (1320–1414). This dynasty helped spread Islam more widely among the local population and at the same time led to a progressive "Indianization" of the Moslem leadership class. The Tughlaqs set about to reorganize the state, creating a more complex system of taxation and tributes, but this

TO THE LOVED ONE

In my head I no longer have order or sense; in my heart a pain for which there is no balm.

My life hath forgotten all trace of day, for there covereth me a night that endeth never.

A Kingdom do I possess, O Sovereign of the beautiful, that hath no subjects but for ruined hearts.

And, to await Thee, an eye that hath no more dreams, not even confused dreams.

If Khusrav is thus miserable, turn not away Thy face from him if life he hath no more, it is an Image that enters into dreams!

AMIR-I-KHOSRAU (1235–1325, lyric poet)

EVEN THE DESTINATION HAS TAKEN TO THE ROAD

O how many men with shining Hearts have, out of the shining independences given by Passion, have brushed the black earth like a ray of sunshine!

And how many mirrors because of whose rusty vestment, a gathering of most beautiful Yusufs has fallen into the solitude of the well!

They have kept secret from the unaware the profound sense of the fortune of Poverty, otherwise they would see that in every dust many sublime Riches are fallen.

Wherever a dust-grinder prepares collyrium for the eye, no ignorant man passes that way, but that on that dust falls a regal crown.

From atom to Sun all is a manifestation of consciousness, but to what end? Eyes of ignorant men know not where to look.

There stirs a world that bears Illusion on its back; who is there that comprehends that even the destination has taken to the road?

MIRZA BEDIL (1644–1721, a leading figure of the "Indian style")

succeeded only in dividing the two categories of subjects still further: the privileged one of the Moslems and the category without rights, or hardly any, the Hindus. Discrimination became intolerable under Muhammad Tughlaq, who, though an intelligent and often talented sovereign, ended by embarking on a series of misguided initiatives that kindled popular uprisings and that, added to famines, fatally dislocated the state economy. At the death of Muhammad Tughlaq in 1351, the Sultanate of Delhi began to break up into a series of independent sultanates, but the Hindus failed to take advantage of the situation by attempting a return to power.

It was this politically splintered and militarily feeble world that was hit by the ruinous, lightning-like invasion of Tamerlane, which climaxed with the notorious sack of Delhi (1398). A Timurid governor of Punjab gave rise to an effete vassal dynasty, that of the Sayyids (1414–51), and they also seized the throne of Delhi, which had been reduced to a mere phantom whose authority went little beyond the city itself. The Sayyids were supplanted by the more vigorous Afghan Lodis (1451–1526), who made a new bid to unify the territories in the north. The disputes between the Afghan generals — who arose under the last of the Lodis — led to the emergence of Babur, a dispossessed lord of Ferghana. He started out from his "kingdom" at Kabul with a small but well-organized militia and seized the Delhi throne in 1526, giving rise to the most celebrated Moslem dynasty of India — that of the Moguls. (In fact, Babur was a Chaghatai Turk, and had Mongol blood only on his mother's side.) This new dynasty took upon itself to bring to completion one of the most ambitious historical enterprises — the political unification of this vast, heterogeneous subcontinent — an undertaking to which Babur gave a new lease while writing some of the most brilliant chapters in India's history.

Relatively rapid though it was, the Mogul conquest of India was not easy, beset by Rajput counterattacks and by the rebellion of the Afghan Sher Shah Sur, who in 1540 compelled Humayun (who had succeeded his father Babur, who died in 1530) to take refuge with the Safavids in Iran. The reign of Sher Shah (1540–45), though brief, was nonetheless highly beneficial to the organization of the state administration, which served as a basis and model for that of the later Moguls. It was only in 1555 that Humayun regained possession of his dominions, and he died a short time afterward, in 1556, leaving the throne to his son, Akbar, who was to become the most outstanding and complete figure of a Mogul emperor. Akbar was an enlightened ruler, an indefatigable organizer, a brilliant politician, and at the same time a deeply religious and tolerant spirit — and a great patron of the arts. He understood the fact that to govern India effectively the economic and social gap between the Moslem minority and the mass of Hindus had to be bridged. The result was that he put an end to fiscal discrimination and the feudal system. He achieved a strong centralization of power, and by means of personal contacts endeavored to set up close bonds with the Hindu aristocracy, especially the Rajputs', offering them some of the highest posts in the state. Convinced that if it was to be politically compact, India would first have to be united spiritually, as well, Akbar abandoned orthodox Islamism and founded a new, universal syncretist religion, which absorbed the most diverse religious exigencies. In the intentions of its creator, this religion was to have surmounted the irreconcilable positions of the Moslems and Hindus. But the religion turned out to be too cerebral, to all intents and purposes remaining confined to the court circles, and when Akbar died it disappeared.

Akbar's universalism, aimed at creating an Islamic–Hindu state, clashed with India's political realities and with Islam's traditions, and albeit Akbar's spirit of tolerance survived in part in his immediate successors — Jahanghir (1605–27) and Shah Jahan (1627–58) — with the advent of Aurangzeb (1658–1707), a rigid orthodoxy brand of Islamism was restored. The facts demonstrated, as Bausani says, that "an Islamic state, given the situation, was possible only as a unified Islamic state with Hindu 'subjects,' and that only an acceptance of the traditional supernational Islamic law could render governors equal." Aurangzeb, a tragic, gloomy figure, obstinate and energetic to the point of cruelty, religious to the point of fanaticism — he has been compared to Philip II of Spain — proclaimed himself the champion of Islam, and beginning in 1669 completely overturned the policies of Akbar, persecuting the bulk of his Hindu subjects, restoring the most hateful forms of discrimination, all with an intransigence that sparked bloody revolts. The wars undertaken in the south of India after 1680, with the aim of forcing it under the aegis of Islam, laid prostrate the organization of the Mogul state, which in turn led to the disintegration of the army and the collapse of the economy. At the same time, they paved the way to the terrible years of the eighteenth century, perhaps the most tragic in the entire history of India. The commerce that had represented one of the main sources of revenue for the Mogul treasury and which functioned as a redistributor of wealth, suffered shattering blows and moved into other channels. Along the coasts, which had never really interested the central powers, the Portuguese maritime domination was replaced by that of the East Indies companies of England, Holland, and then France, the first step toward the harsh colonial occupation of the subcontinent. The death of Aurangzeb (1707) marked the real end of the Moguls' power. But "while the second Mogul empire finished its historical mission in the eighteenth century and its state organization fell to pieces," Bussagli has said, "it continued up to 1833 to exist in name and to exert its sovereignty as the theoretical source of all political power on the subcontinent. And while the British government eliminated this dynasty, following the great uprising of 1857, this did not change the fact that in 1876, Queen Victoria — in adopting her imperial title — seemed to take a place, though from a distant world, in the long list of rulers initiated by Babur."

From a cultural standpoint, Islamic India was a tributary, although often an original one, of the Iranian world, at first through Afghanistan and Transoxiana, and then directly under the Moguls. Persian was the official language of the Delhi Sultanate, and it gave rise to an extremely rich literature that boasted of an intensive historical output and great poets such as Amir-i Khosrau (1253–1325). Poetry had quite original characteristics in the so-called Indian style that developed at the outset of the sixteenth century. Its fundamental precepts, according to Bausani, were the shattering of the law of formal harmony, de rigueur in the classical school of Persian poetry, and a substitution of the concrete for the abstract. It was a cerebral, contrived poetry, hard to appreciate for the average European taste and comprehensible only through labored commentaries; one of its most illustrious practitioners was Bedil (1644–1721). Another contribution of Islam to India was Urdu, the Hindustani language as spoken and modified by the Moslems; from the outset it served as a common tongue for all India, remaining in use up to the early years of the twentieth century, and now the official language of Pakistan. A mixed language with its Indian basis imbued with Arabic and Persian words, and written in Arabic characters, Urdu took shape in the north in the wake of the Moslem invasions — especially at the Delhi court — as a vehicle for communication between the invaders and the local populations. Its very name, in fact, calls attention to its military origins: in Turkish and Mongolian, *urdu* means "encampment," and thus refers to "the language of the imperial camp." The first literary manifestations of Urdu took place not at Delhi, however, but at Deccan, where Urdu had been introduced by the Khalji soldiers; this occurred both because of the propaganda of the sufis, who found in Urdu a means of easy communication, and because of the feelings of opposition at the Delhi court. It was only in the eighteenth century, with the advent of Vali, the major Deccanese poet, that the great period of Urdu poetry got under way in the north.

In the artistic culture of Moslem India, a front rank was occupied by miniatures, which the Mogul court greatly encouraged. This art developed at first under Iranian influence, owing to the activity of Safavid artists who came to the Delhi court in the entourage of Humayun, setting up great library workshops. But before long, with the advent of Akbar, a

NO MORE DO I ENTER

I am a presence of Unity, I enter only into the heart of an intimate confidant; I am the wine in the ampulla of Realization; I shall not enter into a humble receptacle.

What great riches — O Lord — the workshop of primordial indeterminacy possessed; which — like Breath — contains not even for a moment the Reign of the Heart?

In this desolate desert which possesses the dust of the Image of my folly, if Paradise became a mirror to me, it too, like Adam, could not contain me.

Now I set in motion a hundred heavens in the eye of an ant; now, in a hundred oceans I enter not the embrace of a drop of dew.

Now pales my heart so much that I hide my head in the breast of an atom, now of such Longing I boast that I enter not even into myself.

The subtlety of my spirit has thrown me, like a pearl, out of the sea; so far am I entered into the depths of myself that I no longer enter into the world.

MIRZA BEDIL (1644–1721)

DECREES

After my accession to the throne, the first order I gave was to fix the Chain of Justice so that an oppressed person, if treated unjustly by any man, could come to this chain and shake it so as to attract our attention with its noise. I therefore ordered that a chain be made of pure gold, 30 *gaz* [about 16 yards] in length, to which 60 bells were fixed, reaching a total weight of about 4 Indian *manns*. One end of it was fixed to the bastions of Shahburg of the fortress of Agra, and the other to a stone column on the river bank. I further pronounced twelve decrees to be followed as general rules of conduct throughout my dominions: 1) the abolition of local taxes such as *tamgha* and *mirbahri* and others imposed by the *giaghirdar* [feudal lords] for their own lucre; 2) the erection of hotels, mosques, and wells along those almost deserted roads that are most infested by bandits, at the expense of the local *giaghirdar*; 3) merchants' sacks and bales may be opened by no one along the road unless they are informed and their permission obtained; 4) the property of any man who dies within my dominions, be he Moslem or Hindu, is to be left to his legitimate heirs; 5) though I myself drink wine, having persisted in this habit from the age of 18 years until today, when I am 38, I prohibit the preparation of wine or intoxicating drink. When I first began to drink, I drank as many as 20 cups of wine a day; then, when I saw the harmful effect this had upon me, in seven years I reduced my drinking to five or six cups . . . After the age of 30 I drank only in the evening and now I drink only to digest my meals; 6) I forbid any man to take possession of another man's house; 7) I ban the custom of cutting off the nose or ears of any person and I myself have sworn by the Throne of God that I will never make use of this punishment; 8) the officers of the Crown and the *giaghirdar* must not sieze subjects' land forcing them to cultivate it for them; 9) tax collectors of the government and *giaghirdar* must not, without permission, marry women of the district in which they work; 10) hospitals are to be set up in the larger towns, with full-time doctors. The expenses will be paid by the Treasury; 11) the usage of slaying animals for a number of days corresponding to the years of my life starting from the 18th of rabi'u'l-avval (date of my birth) is abolished and it is furthermore forbidden to slay animals on Thursdays and Sundays.

JAHANGHIR (*Autobiography*, seventeenth century)

Delhi (India): The mausoleum of Iltutmish (about 1235) is of the *qubba* type, with walls barely broken up by extremely shallow niches. In the center is a great marble cenotaph, adorned with designs of continuous, polylobed arches on a background of arabesques, probably of Ghaznavid derivation. The walls are lined with a dense decoration sculptured with motifs both of the typically Islamic repertoire and of the more typically Indian variety. The mausoleum was a type of edifice unknown in the Hindu world, accustomed to cremating its dead; this explains why these monuments are basically of the Iranian type in their architecture.

school of painting with autonomous and original characteristics had taken shape, availing itself of a wide-scale participation of Hindu artists, who contributed a lively feeling for nature. The Mogul court miniature was sensitive to influences from European figurative arts, particularly of the Belgian and Flemish varieties, under Jahanghir and Shah Jahan, these having originally penetrated into India in the form of engravings. Particularly impressive was the portrait miniature, which has left us a considerable number of sensitive, refined works. Deserving special mention among the minor arts are the Persian-style textiles and carpets. In the end, though, it is the architecture that provides the most suggestive and profuse chapter of Moslem art in India, and perhaps it would not be going too far to say with Sir Mortimer Wheeler that "Indo–Islamic architecture constitutes the most fascinating episode in the entire history of architecture."

Indo-Islamic Architecture: The Early Phase

Indo-Islamic architecture, initiated under the Mamluk dynasty of Delhi, began taking form under the successive imperial dynasties, but a stylistic unity of its own was not to emerge until the time of the Moguls. Contemporaneous with the first "imperial" phase — from the twelfth to the sixteenth century — and characterized primarily by the monuments of Delhi and Ajmer (Rajastan), was the output of the provincial sultanates, which gained their independence with the fall of the Tughlaqs: Bengal, Gujarat, Jaunpur, Malwa, Deccan, Khandesh, Bijapur, and Kashmir. Jaunpur and Malwa were more closely dependent on the imperial style of Delhi; in the other areas, considerable differences are to be seen, resulting from the prevalence of strong local traditions (as in Gujarat) or particular environmental conditions (as in Kashmir and Bengal). In Deccan, on the other hand, the Bahmanid sultanate showed at the outset a strong Iranian influence, noticeable, among other ways, in the architecture of the sultanates that were linked to them (as in Bijapur and Golconda). Also easily discernible in the structures of these sultan-

Delhi (India): The Alai Darvaza (about 1305),
the entranceway for the enlargement of the
Quwwat al-Islam planned by Ala ud-Din
Khalji. It is a square pavilion covered by a
somewhat flattened dome. Its walls are enlivened by blind niches or false windows,
with marble grilles. The composition is
extremely well balanced, although with a
certain ostentation. The materials used were
red sandstone and white marble, with inlays
of black marble and blue schist, a detail that
reveals the hand of artisans from Gujarat.

*Delhi (India): The Quwwat al-Islam (in the re-
construction of Percy Brown).*
1 The first mosque of Qutb ud-Din Aibak
2 Qutb Minar
3 Enlargement of Iltutmish
4 The Mausoleum of Iltutmish
*5 Enlargement, realized only in part, of Ala ud-Din
Khalji*
*6 Alai Minar, the colossal minaret planned by Ala
ud-Din Khalji but never completed*
7 Mausoleum of Ala ud-Din Khalji
8 Madrassa of Ala ud-Din Khalji
9 The Alai Darvaza, entranceway

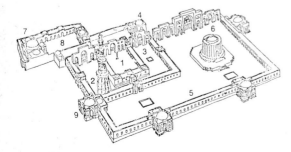

ates, beginning with the second half of the sixteenth century, is a powerful return of Hindu influences, while at Bijapur, in the seventeenth century, clear-cut Ottoman influences were at work.

Unlike Hindu architecture, which was almost exclusively religious, that of the Moslems in India is represented by a variety of edifices — many religious, to be sure (as mosques and tombs), but many secular, whether for public or private use (fortresses, royal palaces, bridges, pavilions, gardens, dwellings, etc.). In India, in fact, more of these secular buildings have come down to us than in other Islamic lands, partly as a result of the fact that the building material most frequently used — except in Bengal and Kashmir — was stone, a fine red sandstone, to which was added, primarily for decorative reasons, some white marble, to make windows and arches. The design of the various structures is fairly basic, although it was long in finding a common source of inspiration. The result was a progression from a vague Iranian influence, in harmony with the Iranian culture of the early Turkish-Afghan dynasties, to a more clear-cut Timurid-Central Asian influence (particularly at Jaunpur) and then a return to an Iranian inspiration with the Moguls. A key role was played in the shaping of Indo-Islamic taste, in fact, by the force of local tradition. In the Delhi sultanates, but especially in the provincial ones (Gujarat, Kashmir, Bengal), this often conditioned the choice of the decorative elements if not the structure's basic design. In the Mogul era, adherence to local aesthetic precepts was deliberate, like a conscious attempt to amalgamate the two worlds.

The first Moslem structures in the Sind, Punjab, and Lahore regions — this last named for many years the capital of the Ghaznavids — have been destroyed, with the exception of a number of mosques of the early Abbasid type, found amid the ruins of Mansura-Brahmanabad and at Tatta, in southern Sid, built of brick and teakwood. But enough is known to realize that the Ghaznavid and Ghorid architecture of Afghanistan supplied some of the prototypes of the Indo–Islamic monuments that have survived. Based on the Ghorid minaret at Jam, Afghanistan, for instance, was the celebrated Qutb Minar of Delhi. But also of great importance, especially in the decorative field, was the influence India brought to bear, at the time of the Ghorids, in a number of areas of Afghan; this is borne out by a large number of marble funerary structures at Ghazni. Clear evidence is also provided by a rare work of stone architecture, a small mosque discovered by Gianroberto Scarcia in southwestern Afghanistan; the mosque reveals a strongly marked influence from the art of Rajastan. The oldest mosque of Delhi, the Quwwat al-Islam, which served as a model for numerous Indian imperial and provincial mosques, has a complex design, the result of numerous rebuildings. It drew its inspiration from the type of mosque preceded by a court; built from materials taken from Hindu and Jain temples, its first phase can be dated to 1195. Added to the prayer hall in 1199 was a monumental facade with arches of Iranian inspiration, a facade that does not fit in, however, with the remainder of the edifice. It was built by local workmen, who used the false arch with jutting stones.

An almost identical design is to be found in the Arhai-din-ka-jhompra at Amir, erected between 1200 and 1235. In this edifice, the facade — the Iranian type, with a massive central *iwan* surmounted by two minarets — has no connection with the Hindu pillar structure. No variations in this design are to be found in the extensions of the Quwwat al-Islam: that undertaken by Iltutmish, completed in 1229, and the third gigantic one attempted by Ala ud-Din Khalji, which was to have included the mosques of his two predecessors. All that was actually realized of this mammoth project were the foundations, and only the southern part of the wall with an ambitious entrance pavilion, the Alai Darvaza (1305). This was a square pavilion covered by a "crushed" dome, with its walls enlivened by niches and blind windows and overlaid with a luxuriant sculptured decoration; this last-named is done in red sandstone and white marble, with inlays in black marble and blue schist, which in its polychromy reveals an influence from the art of Gujarat. The plans of Ala ud-Din also included a colossal minaret (of which only the base

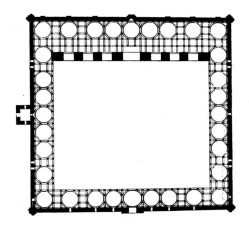

Ajmir (India): Plan of the Arhai-din-ka-jhompra. The edifice is of the wide-hall type with the roof supported by Hindu pillars, part in the inner section and part along the qibla wall, and by the pseudodome porticoes along three sides. Added to this mosque in front of the prayer hall, as with the Quwwat al-Islam, was a monumental facade of the Iranian type, with great pointed-arch iwans, which does not fit in with the original Hindu-style structure.

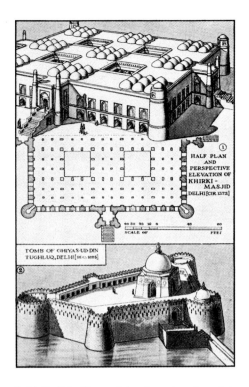

Delhi (India): Plans of the elevated section of the Khirki Masjid (upper) and the mausoleum of Ghiyas ud-Din Tughlaq (lower), in the reconstructions of Percy Brown.

Ahmadabad (India): Plan of the Jami Masjid (in the reconstruction of Percy Brown). This mosque was erected between 1411 and 1423 by Ahmad Shah, the founder of Ahmanabad, who made the city the capital of Gujarat. This is a typical monument of one of the most important provincial states. A particular development was given to the central part of the prayer hall, which was covered with domes supported by tall columns with superimposed shafts in the Hindu style, creating a succession of roofs decreasing in size and with broad slopes. In these roofs, the curvilinear architecture of Iranian derivation, also to be seen in the broad iwan, draws closer to Hindu tradition.

element ever was completed), which was to have been almost three times the size of the already mammoth Qutb Minar. This latter minaret, annexed to the first mosque of Delhi, had been started in 1199 by Aibak to "throw the shadow of God on the East and West," as is stated in one of its inscriptions. It was completed and reworked by Iltutmish, by Firoz Shah Tughlaq, and by the last Mogul emperor, Akbar II, in 1828. At present it stands some 240 feet high and is made up of five superimposed tapered shafts, but only three of them — polygonal in shape and channeled — are the originals. These shafts are divided by small balconies that protrude over the fine *muqarnas* elements, and are embellished by elegant bands with inscriptions further enriched with geometric and floral motifs. Originally it probably was topped by a small domed pavilion (*chhattri* such a structure is called in India) like its nearest model, the Ghorid minaret of Jam. Although one of the most significant monuments of the Indo-Islamic world, the Qutb Minar was rarely imitated. In India, the minaret was later to merge with the structure with which it was connected, and in any event it was never to see the development it underwent in the Iranian world and under the Ottomans.

The Tughlaq mosques, which like all the other structures of the time, reflect the militaristic ideals of the dynasty, have a somewhat different design, tending to be more closed-in and compact. Seen from the outside, the Khirki Masjid (about 1375) looks like a bastioned fortress, resting on a platform with arches, with portals jutting out over elegant stairways, and with four small quadrangular courts on the inside. The roof alternates flat areas with small multiple domes. A variant on this design is to be found in some of the mosques built later in Bengal (such as the Chota Sona Masjid of Gaur, 1493–1519), which are rectangular in shape with only a few narrow openings on the sides; they were essentially courtless halls covered by small domes and by a special kind of sloping roof, derived from the wooden huts traditional in the region. This design was to reap an exceptional success with the Mogul builders as well (as in the *bangaldar* pavilions in the fortresses of Lahore, Delhi, or Agra). In the oldest Bengalese mosques (Adina, 1364, for example), the design base on a court with a long hall was maintained, although the hall was cut by a broad transept with a barrel roof. All the Bengalese structures are characterized by a certain massiveness and heaviness, due to the use of large bricks in place of stone, in short supply in this region.

The transept, of conspicuous proportions in relation to those of the side naves, assumed a special importance in the mosques of Gujarat, the area where the Indian stone-working tradition was most deeply rooted. The mosques of Cambay (1325), Ahmadabad (1423), and Champanir (1523), cities that were later the capitals of local Moslem dynasties, present an engagingly picturesque juxtaposition of elements of Iranian curvilinear architecture with those of the traditional Hindu architecture. The manual ability of the Jain goldsmiths, who were located in numerous communities in this area, becomes evident in the openwork decorations of many of the marble windows of the mosque of Sidi Sayyia (Ahmadabad, 1515), a prelude to the splendid marble lacework of the Mogul palaces.

In the Sayyid and Lodi periods, no major congregational mosques were erected in Delhi, but only small private ones annexed to funerary complexes. These latter are highly interesting, however, in that they throw light on an independent evolution of the primitive Iranian-inspired local style, with vital graftings from Timurid architecture. The facade with massive arches, in fact, which in the Quwwat al-Islam remained a sort of independent element, now became an integral part of the edifice, which is given still greater emphasis by the eye-filling dome, slightly pointed at its keystone (as in the Motki Masjid, 1505). Of the same type are the more recent Jamala Masjid (1536) and the relatively small but splendid Qala-i Khona (1545), the primitive mosque of Sher Shah Sur at Delhi, where one also finds polychrome marble decorations, the type preferred by later Mogul builders. The rather crude expansion, in the monumental sense, of the massive *iwan*-type facade is found once again in the mosques of the tiny sultanate of Janupur (between about 1360 and 1480), where

Delhi (India): The mausoleum of Ghiyas ud-Din Tughlaq (1325), the founder of the Tughlaq dynasty (1320–1414). The heavy, severe lines of the structure were typical of this dynasty's style, which influenced among others that of the Sultanate of Malwa and of Deccan.

Right:
Agra (India): The Khass Mahal, a fortress of the time of Shah Jahan (1637). This is the main room of the women's quarters, flanked by two pavilions with a *bangaldar* roof. The pavilions were called *naulakki* — that is, "nine millions," a reference to the many small hiding places for jewels carved into the marble walls, each with an aperture just large enough to permit the entry of a feminine hand. A pool is located in front of the structure.

Delhi (India): The mausoleum of Humayun. Begun eight years after his death in 1556, it was completed in 1572. The edifice, situated in the center of a garden on a high terrace, was considerably influenced by Persian architecture. The architect was of Iranian origin, in fact, and his style was typified by an exceptional lightness and airiness, obtained through the lightening of the walls by means of niches and false windows. Note the *chhattris*, the little elevated dome-roofs, at the corners, built in conformity with Indian taste.

Page 142:
Fathepur Sikri (India): The Diwani-i Khas, a hall for private audiences (that for public audiences being the Diwan-i Am), dates from the time of Akbar (after 1568). It is one of the city's most engaging structures. Hindu art, especially that of Rajastan, played an important and regular part in the structures of Fathepur Sikri, in keeping with Akbar's ideal of universalism, which wanted to reconcile the Indian world with that of the Moslems.

Page 143:
Fathepur Sikri (India): The great *iwan* of the Jami Masjid, seen from the portico of the shrine of Shaykh Salim Chisti. It was built in the Akbar era (after 1568). Note the characteristic *chhattris* atop the mosque roof and the S-corbels (foreground) of the Rajastan type, supporting the Indian-style sloping roof.

the prayer halls are dominated by *iwans* of gigantic proportions, in line with the parallel evolution of the Timurid taste in Iran (as seen in the Atala Masjid of 1408 and the Jami Masjid of 1470).

A revival of the Tughlaq style may be encountered in the architecture of the sultanate of Malwa, a meeting point because of its geographical position for influences from Delhi, Gujarat, and Deccan. In the religious edifices of its capitals, Dhar and Mandu, we find all the elements characteristic of this region: high platforms accessible by stairways, sloping roofs, arches, and large round domes. The prayer halls are of the transept type, with pillars connected by arches. A local characteristic was the lively color of the decoration, most of which has disappeared, obtained by using colored marble and stones, including such semiprecious stones as agate, jasper, and carnelian. A special surface brilliance was given by the use of blue and yellow enameled tiles, arranged in borders and panels on the outside of the structure in keeping with a tradition that the local Moslems may have learned from Multan (Punjab), where it was widespread. A strong Tughlaq influence also characterized the regional architecture of Deccan which, however, owes much to Iranian and Central Asian forms. This resulted largely from the fact that the first independent dynasty that replaced the Tughlaq sultanate had originally come from Iran, with the result that there was a constant influx of artisans, merchants, and soldiers from the Iranian region.

The mosques of Gulbarga, Bidar, and Golconda — this last-named being the capital of the state from 1347 to 1687 — show Iranian forms in

their design and construction; they also exhibit great bulbous domes in the Timurid fashion and minarets ending in small swollen domes. At Gulbarga, in 1367, an architect from Qazvin built a congregational mosque without a court but with a perimetral arcaded wall and with large domes resting on windowless drums. The interior, equally original, is made up of a series of great arches with an especially low base. The arches create a particularly pleasant effect, later imitated in the Tughlaq mosques of Kali and Khirki, built a bit later (1370 and 1375) at Delhi. Another unusual edifice is the *madrassa* of Mahmoud Gawan at Bidar (1481), which closely resembles a Timurid structure, primarily because of the monumentality of its elevation, spread over several floors, and because of the vivacity of the ornamentation in enameled tiles.

A typically local imprint is found in the religious edifices of Kashmir, built mainly of wood in keeping with the oldest native traditions. The designs of the mosques, usually with four *iwans* laid out in the form of a cross, maintain many Indo-Kashmirian elements in the pointed crowns of the portals, based on Buddhist or Hindu pagodas. The interiors, which are exceptionally high, exploit the various properties of wood through the use of high, elegant columns, often grouped together to support broad festooned archways and sloping ceilings. The building of mausoleums was something new for India, which was accustomed to cremating its dead and scattering the ashes in sacred rivers. If Hindu tradition had played a role in influencing the design of the mosques, the form of the monumental tombs was wholly imported from Iranian territories. But this did not prevent local builders, often indigenous workmen in the service of Moslem lords, from stamping their taste on a number of key details of the decoration, such as the addition of the small domes supported by thin pillars (the *chhattri* first referred to at the Qutb Minar of Delhi), placed around the central dome on the roof; or the stylized inverted lotus flowers crowning the domes. As was the case with the mosques, the structures of the mausoleums reveal an evolution from the more rigid, severe forms of the first examples (the mausoleums of

Above:

Agra (India): The Taj Mahal, "crown of the palace," (1632-48) was built for Mumtaz Mahal, the favorite wife of Shah Jahan (1628–58). This is considered the greatest masterpiece of Indo-Islamic architecture.

Left:

Sikandra (India): The mausoleum of Akbar (1555–1605), near Agra. Planned during the lifetime of the great emperor, it was not completed until 1613, under his son Jahanghir, and it incorporates changes in the original plans. It is a grandiose sandstone structure with five diminishing floors. The last floor is of marble and contains a cenotaph in the open air, this latter being unusual for monumental Moslem funerary architecture in India. According to Fergusson, the edifice was to have been completed with a dome that was never built. The terraced structure of the mausoleum appears to have been influenced by Buddhist architecture.

Following page:

Agra (India): The mausoleum of Itimad ad-Daula (1628), the father of Nur Jahan, the powerful and cultivated wife of Jahanghir.

Iltutmish and Ala ud-Din Khalji at Delhi), stemming from the *qubba* type, to the "military" type of the Tughlaqs — with the great mass of red sandstone and sloping surfaces softened by the dome and decorations in white stone — to the more elaborate Sayyid and Lodi mausoleums, in which the dome appears to rest directly on a polygonal platform with large arches.

The striving for monumental effects is accentuated still more in the Suri funerary edifices (the tombs of Hassan Khan, about 1535, and of Sher Shah, 1540, at Sasaram), with the use of platforms with steps and the addition of high drums, often devoid of windows at the base of the domes and surrounded by appealing *chhattris*. The resultant design, exceptionally airy and elegant, was to be taken up again in several large-scale Mogul tombs. The type of mausoleum used in the provincial sultanates, for the most part stemming from models devised in the Tughlaq–Lodi worlds, was from time to time modified in keeping with local taste. Covered with Hindu adornments, in fact, closely resembling those of the *mihrab* of the Adina mosque at Pandua, is the mausoleum of Jalal ud-Din Muhammad (1414–31), in the same locality. In the great funeral complexes of Gujarat, especially in the tombs of the queens of Ahmadabad, the Indian taste for delicate ornamentation over all architectural elements became preponderant. In spite of the presence of minarets, miniature arches, and Islamic domes, these edifices appear in no way different from the Hindu ones. Of unusual interest in Malwa is the tomb of Hoshang (about the fifteenth century), not so much because of its structure — a square, surmounted by a dome on a drum, which is almost identical to that of the early Indo-Islamic mausoleums — as for the fact that it is the first example of this type built entirely of white marble. In 1659 it was visited by the Mogul architects of the Taj Mahal, who engraved an inscription on it.

A wide type range is represented by the tombs of Deccan; these are sumptuous like the contemporary mosques, placed on high platforms with arcades and covered by elaborate bulbous domes, which appear to blossom from open lotus flowers (as at the Ibrahim Rauza tomb, in Bijapur, 1615). On some occasions (Gol Gumbaz, 1666), the tombs maintain the square design, but they are enhanced at the corners by original minarets of several stories, opening out in arcades and ending in domes narrowed down at their bases. At Khandesh, the tombs of the Faruqi dynasty (fifteenth century) follow the polygonal design of numerous Iranian mausoleums, but they are covered with a dense Hindu-style decoration, hewn from stone. A remembrance, although greatly modified, of the Seljuk tower-tombs, or *gumbats*, is the mausoleum of Sultan Jamshid at Golconda — polygonal in design and open on every side with doors, with two tiers divided by terraces supported by Hindu-style corbels. The uppermost floor is marked at the corners by miniature domes, while the whole edifice is crowned by a bulbous dome resting on a low platform. Another remembrance of Iranian mausoleums, this too modified by local taste, is found in the Kashmir mausoleum of Srinagar, dedicated to the mother of Zain ud-Abidin (1417–67), whose great entrance *iwan* is surmounted by domes arranged in such a way as to form a rounded pyramid.

Mogul Architecture

The territorial unification of India under the Moguls coincided with the spread of more cohesive aesthetic characteristics throughout the land. The true initiator of Mogul architecture was Akbar, since his predecessors, too busy with their conquests, were unable to dedicate themselves to artistic activity. (This remains true despite the fact that Humayun, on returning from the Safavid court of Shah Tahmasp, managed to found an Imperial Library, with the help of the celebrated Persian painters and calligraphers, Mir Sayyid Ali and Abd us-Samad, who provided the chief impetus for the creation in India of a great Islamic miniature tradition.) In order to foster in a tangible way his policies of reconciliation with all his subjects, Akbar attempted to give the art of his immense empire a common mode of expression, in which all tendencies could converge, whether Moslem or Hindu, which up to this time had manifested themselves only in the most diverse areas. As a result, Akbar gave rise to the so-called eclectic style, to be seen in his numerous religious and secular structures — at Agra, Allahabad, Lahore, Ajmir, and Nagarcain — and superbly exemplified by the edifices at his citadel at Fathepur Sikri, which Wheeler has called "an orgy of Hindu imagination in an Iranian form." In fact, while the general design of the palaces was based on the simplicity of Iranian types — already revised to accord with the taste of the Khaljis, the Shaqis of Jaunpur, the Lodis, and the Suris — their ornamentation (pillars, corbels, architraves, *chhattris*, sloping eaves, and balconies, combined in the most unexpected and ingenious manners) is thoroughly Hindu. Also included in this composite, opulent taste were semi-natural decorations of twining vine leaves, flowers, pomegranates, figured reliefs, and murals, in which there was fusion of Iranian, Rajput, and Chinese artistic tendencies.

The other residence-fortresses of Akbar were built, like those of the Tughlaqs (for instance, the Kotila-i Firzshah) in a strategic location, between a river and the city itself, and each dominated the entire area, although remaining independent of it. The private palaces were situated on the river bank, while the city quarter had the offices, the mosque, the barracks, the bazaar, and the audience court. High brick walls covered with slabs of sandstone fortified the entire complex, accessible from the outside by means of four gates protected by bastions and often flanked by statues of elephants. The "eclectic style" of Akbar was also found in the constructions of his son, Jahanghir, and even in some of the buildings of his grandson, Shah Jahan (*e.g.*, the palace-garden on Lake Ana Sagar at Ajmir, 1637), and thus can be said to have stamped Indian architecture with a new style. However, a relative independence from the style was shown by the construction of mausoleums. There was, for example, that of Humayun at Delhi, finished in 1572, in which the Iranian influence was predominant; yet even this mausoleum already revealed the Mogul tendency to broaden the basic Iranian nucleus by forming a more complex pavilion in which there was an increase in the number of arcaded floors and the *chhattris* around the central dome.

The abandonment of the eclectic Indo-Islamic style coincided with the campaign for the restoration of Moslem orthodoxy after the death of Akbar. This was not achieved, however, with the adoption of thoroughly Iranian forms because of the political rivalries then dividing the two countries, but by using the Indo-Islamic motifs of Deccan and Bengal to replace those of Gujarat and the north. The most evident characteristic was a preference for white marble in the main structures, while red sandstone was used for foundations and for minor buildings. The linear design of the various constructions was enhanced by pillars and by capitals in the form of the lotus flower, by polylobed and pointed arches, asymmetrical floral corbels, *bangaldar* roofs, and slabs with flower reliefs — all drawing their inspiration from Kashmir, which had become the summer residence of the emperors. For that matter, there was no lack of European influences, such as rounded arches, baroque curls, or Florentine hardstone mosaics. Initiated by Nur Jahan, the Persian wife of Jahanghir, this style reached its most complete and sumptuous expression in the marble buildings of the fortresses of Lahore, Agra, Delhi, Ajmir — all built by Shah Jahan — and in the famous mausoleums of Jahanghir at Lahore, of Itamid ad-Daula, and of Mumtaz Mahal (the Taj Mahal) at Agra, as well as in the great public or private mosques of the same region. Usually arranged around courts, or situated inside gardens, the various buildings are of an exceedingly simple design (pavilion style with sloping roofs) enhanced by varied decorative elements: pillars and arcades of the most elaborate forms, marble slabs ably pierced by goldsmiths, and floral or geometric ornaments of diverse types.

Built in conformance with a refined yet magnificent simplicity was the world-renowned Taj Mahal, the mausoleum of Mumtaz Mahal, the favorite wife of Shah Jahan, erected at Agra between 1632 and 1648. An articulated octagonal in plan, topped by a bulbous dome, and crowned by *chhattris* and small minarets, the Taj Mahal looms atop a platform with minarets at its corners, the usual Mogul design already used to advantage by the Suris. Preceded by a wide basin, it is located in a huge garden and flanked by a pavilion mosque and by another symmetrical building intended as a reception hall for visitors, these latter two edifices of red sandstone. The Taj Mahal itself, made with the warm, luminous marble of Makrana, shows Iranian influences. Its extraordinarily pure architectural forms are in the closest imaginable relation with the highly elegant network of inlay decorations. But its deepest and most lasting appeal unquestionably lies in the flawless way its architecture blends in with the landscape, along the banks of the Jumna River, engendering an ineffable atmosphere of serene melancholy. This masterpiece, one of the great works of architecture of all times and cultures, was the mature and unparalleled fruit of Indo-Islamic civilization. It was the loftiest moment of a laboriously sought synthesis, the realization of the desire for limpid harmony that the refined Iranian sensibility of Babur had sought in vain in the exuberant, dislocated India with which he came into contact in his marches of conquest.

The great imperial mosques of Delhi (1648) and Agra represent the taste of Shah Jahan. Erected on platforms, they have a court enclosed by low colonnades serving as the foundation, on the Central Asian model, for the prayer hall, preceded by a giant *iwan* and covered by three large bulbous domes of white marble. In Delhi, the domes are set off by strips of black marble; at Agra, they had joints of red sandstone. Marble panels with inlaid colored stones adorn the facades on the court, the great entrance pavilions, and the *mihrabs*. Mosques reduced to the prayer hall alone, covered by three small bulbous domes, are the tiny, refined Moti Masjids ("pearl mosques") in the fortresses of Agra and Delhi; or that

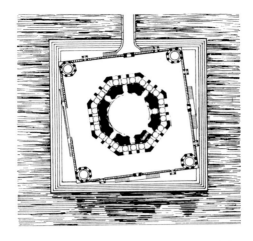

Sasaram (India): Plan of the tomb of Sher Shah Sur. The tomb rests on an artificial islet in a sheet of water, the tomb proper standing on a square platform with four corner pavilions. The mausoleum is octagonal and surrounded by a gallery of small domes, looming up from the rear of which is the drum supporting the dome. Chhattris are located at each corner.

Delhi (India): Plan of the mausoleum of Humayun, richly designed in accordance with an architectural experiment initiated in the Iranian environment of the Timurid period.

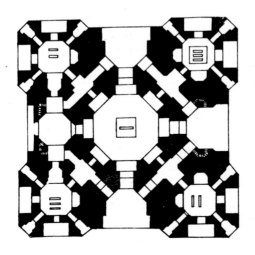

Agra (India): One of the corner towers of the tomb of Itimad ad-Daula, showing the delicate inlay work in hard stone, typical of great imperial Mogul architecture. In the background is one of the various structures enriching the garden, in the center of which the mausoleum stands.

Agra (India): Plan of the garden and mausoleum of the Taj Mahal. One approaches the mausoleum, situated on the banks of the Jumna River, by passing through a great Persian-style formal garden. The tomb, entirely of white marble with inlays of hard stones, stood on a low platform with four corner minarets and surrounded by open space. It is flanked by two pavilions in red sandstone, a mosque, and lodgings for visitors; each pavilion is made up of a broad hall divided into three chambers covered by a dome. The design of the tomb (see enlarged plan, lower square), derived from Iranian types. The great bulbous dome rests on a high drum hiding the lower internal dome, in keeping with a widely used system of Timurid architecture.

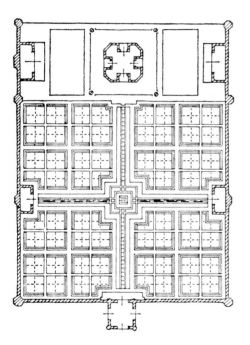

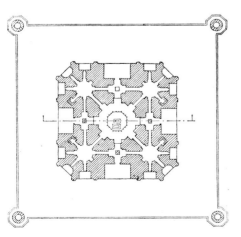

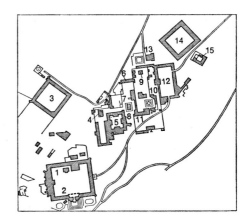

Agra (India): The Moti Masjid, "the pearl mosque," in the fort of Agra. It dates from 1646 to 1653, and was erected by Shah Jahan. This view shows the bulbous domes over the prayer hall and several *chhattris*.

Fathepur Sakri (India): Plan of the "victory city," the citadel, some 20 miles from Agra, founded by Akbar in 1568 to celebrate the conquest of Gujarat. It is near the village of Sikri, where the hermitage of Salim Chisti was located, Salim Chisti having been an ascetic to whose intercession the emperor attributed the birth of his heir, the future emperor, Jahanghir. Seventeen years afterward, in 1585, Akbar shifted the capital to Lahore, and Fathepur Sakri was abandoned, in part because it was difficult to supply the city with water.

1 *Tomb of Shaykh Salim Chisti*
2 *Great Mosque*
3 *Caravansary*
4 *House of Raja Birbal*
5 *Palace of Jodh Bai*
6 *Hospital*
7 *Panch Mahal (five-story palace)*
8 *Palace of Maryam al-Zamani, the Rajasta princess who was the wife of Akbar and the mother of Jahanghir*
9 *Diwan-i Khas (hall for private audiences)*
10 *Girls' school*
11 *Daftar Khan (archives)*
12 *Diwan-i Am (hall for public audiences)*
13 *Baths*
14 *Mint*
15 *Treasury*

erected by Shah Jahan in 1640, in the vicinity of Kabul, following the conquest of Balkh and Badakhshan, not far from the modest tomb of his great forerunner, Babur.

With the ascension of Aurangzeb to the throne in 1658, Mogul architecture swiftly fell into decay. While the systematic destruction of Hindu temples was matched by an equally systematic building of mosques and edifices for public functions, the materials used for these became more and more of the perishable variety — in tribute to the most rigorous Moslem orthodoxy. Rough stone and used bricks took the place of marble and sandstone, while decorations were executed in embellished and painted stucco, producing a rather miserable effect, and the style became overburdened and uncertain. The finest works of this period include the mausoleum of Bibi-ka Rauza, one of the wives of Aurangzeb, in the new capital of Aurangabad, Deccan, built in imitation of the Taj Mahal; although without the splendid grandeur of the latter, it is not devoid of its own fascinating simplicity.

With the last of the Moguls, there was an attempt to make up for the lack of originality in the various structures by an opulence, often in bad taste, in the decorations. The only heirs of the great imperial tradition were the Nawabs of Audh, the Nizam of Hyderabad, and the Rajput princes. But rather than take leave of the Moguls at their architectural nadir, we might better recall one of their more refined legacies to India — formal gardens. Based on Iranian formal gardens, these were introduced into India by Babur, who felt an overwhelming desire for the green fields and streams of water of the land of his youth, Ferghana. A man with an extraordinarily keen, although certainly not literary, sense of nature, Babur made an effort wherever possible to provide himself with green oases for the refreshment of body and spirit. The joy he expresses in his *Memoirs* is touching, as when he recounts his success in establishing a garden near Agra: "And so it was that in India, this land devoid of grace and harmony, such well-laid-out, neat gardens arose. Pleasant lawns were to be seen on every side and in the midst of each were rose bushes and narcissuses, all arranged in a precise, flawless manner," We should retain this Mogul gift to Islamic India as our final impression.

Agra (India): View of the Moti Masjid's prayer hall. This is a most limpid example of Mogul architecture. The festooned arches are characteristic. Note the *mihrab* designs on the floor, indicating the position of the individual faithful during prayer.

Delhi (India): The Jami Masjid (1644–58), erected by Shah Jahan, the largest Mogul mosque. The front of the prayer hall is here seen from within the great courtyard. Framed by two minarets, the prayer hall is dominated by the great *iwan* and three bulbous domes, in keeping with its Timurid models. The mosque rises above the high terrace, served by three stairways that lead through three doors into the great court, enclosed in low arcades.

THE OTTOMAN EMPIRE

"Sultan Mahomet Dei gratia totius Asie et Grece Imperator" — this was the significant form of address used in a number of documents issued in 1480 by Venice for Muhammad Fatih ("The Conqueror"), who had sealed the end of the Roman Empire of the East in 1453 when he seized its last stronghold, Constantinople, and brought to a close a century-and-a-half struggle between the Byzantines and the Ottomans. This last of the great medieval Mediterranean empires had originated shortly before 1300 in one of the Turkish principalities that had once made up the Anatolia of the Rum Seljuks. The Ottoman state, deriving its name from that of its founder, Othman (or Osman) who died in 1326, was initially confined to a small area between Phrygia and Bithynia, in western Asia Minor. It set up its first stable capital at Bursa (or Brusa), which was conquered in 1326, and gradually began taking an ever more important place among the Anatolian principalities. Taking advantage of the anarchic situation in the Balkans, the Ottomans laid seige to Gallipoli in 1354, and driven by the spirit of the *jihad*, or holy war, and with a well-organized army, they entered Europe to stay, capturing Thrace and Macedonia. The Ottoman state suffered a grave setback in its expansion drive in 1402, however, when the Timurid army emerged victorious at Ankara; the Ottoman sultan, Beyazed II Yildirim ("the thunderbolt") was himself taken prisoner by Tamerlane. While a large part of the Anatolian territories was lost, the Ottomans still retained those in Europe, where they reorganized their state quite rapidly. Half a century later, they reconquered Anatolia, and in 1453 took Constantinople; from this point on, this historic city became known as Istanbul and remained Turkish.

The period running from the fall of Constantinople to the death of Suleiman the Magnificent (1566) was what may be considered "the golden age" of the Ottoman-Turkish Empire. Its confines in Europe reached out as far as the Danube and into the Crimea. The entire Middle East was under its scepter: Syria, Mesopotamia, the Arabian Peninsula, Egypt, and North Africa except for Morocco. The Ottoman Empire was the most enduring and complex creation of the Turkish world, although it remained within the frame of Islam. It was a state built with farsightedness and energy, which availed itself of a well-organized army, an administration of a special type, and a well-devised system of social equilibrium that, although on the whole medieval, unquestionably had vital, modern aspects as well. Its leaders were not without open-mindedness: Islamic religious law, the *sharia*, was accompanied by a secular code (*qanun*), which worked especially efficiently under Suleiman. In the Middle East, in fact, Suleiman was known as "the legislator"; it is the West that knows him as "the Magnificent." The secular code made it possible to cope with the practical necessities of the state, a topic that the *sharia*, otherwise replete with details on the behavior of the individual Moslem, dismissed with relatively few words.

Thanks to its tolerant policies, the Ottoman state succeeded in guaranteeing itself domestic tranquillity on religious matters, originally absorbing the ancient Islamic institution of *dhimma* ("protection") afforded to defeated peoples. These latter were organized into *millets* that assured regular taxation revenues and whose fundamental obligation was allegiance to the sovereign. In the Ottoman state, all the *millets* theoretically had the same status, although a Moslem one was obviously favored, since it was the one to which the leaders belonged. Although society was divided into two fundamental classes — that of the rulers, the Ottomans, and that of the subjects, "the protected flock" — the division was not rigid but based on the merit system, a fact that guaranteed considerable social mobility. The genuine lack of an ethnic consciousness — the result of the prevailing notion of Islamic ecumenism — paved the way for the spread of a strongly assimilative Turkish culture, suitable for a composite society. Conversions to Islam were never forced. However, the shift to Islamism was a social factor, one that radiated from the cities, as well as a reaction

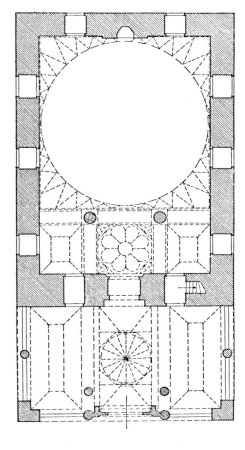

Isnik (Turkey): Plan of the Yeshil Jami, "the green mosque." This is a highly elegant example of a mosque with a single ambulatory, covered by a dome on triangular connecting units, typical of the first Ottoman period. The three-arch portico is probably due to Byzantine influence.

Following page:
Istanbul (Turkey): The fortress of Rumelihisar, situated on the European banks of the Bosphorus. It was erected by Muhammad the Conqueror in four months, in 1452, opposite that of Anadoluhisar (1394–95) on the Asiatic coast, and is one of the most superb military structures of the Islamic world. The plan is said to have been traced out by the Conqueror himself, who also took part in the actual building operations; he supervised in particular the erection of the curtain of walls, while he entrusted the three great towers to as many of his ministers.

to special ethnic or religious situations, such as the widespread spontaneous conversions in Bosnia, Erzegovina, Serbia, and Macedonia. An exception was the original Ottoman institution known as the *devshirme:* that is, the groups of Christian adolescents — particularly of Balkan peasants — who, having been "converted" to Islam, were sent to Anatolia to learn the language and customs of the Turks; drawn from the ranks of the *devshirme* were the components of the efficient military group known as the Janissaries, as well as individuals for government service. While the *devshirme* was execrated in Christian Europe, locally it met with some favor, to the point that it was often urged to be used as an instrument of reconciliation between the victors and the defeated — which it occasionally did with some success. Contributing to this success was the fact that the Janissaries were affiliated with the widespread Islamic fraternity of the Bektashis, a Dervish order that had formed in Anatolia, with strong Christian overtones. In the Ottoman Empire, however, Sunnite orthodoxy essentially remain unchallenged, and Shiism was persecuted and stamped out — in part because it represented an expression of the power of the Ottomans' Safavid rivals. The heretical ferments of sufism, meanwhile, found their outlet inside the religious confraternities that, controlled directly by the sultan, were unswervingly loyal to him.

With the conquest of the Mamluk sultanate of Syria and Egypt, Selim I (1512–20) proclaimed himself protector of Islam's Holy Places, thus enjoying an unbounded prestige among all the Arab and Islamic peoples. And the successes reaped by Ottoman arms legitimized to a certain extent his assumption of the title of caliph, restoring an energetic guidance to the Islamic community at large. The conquest of the Arab world reinforced the Arab component of the empire and Ottoman culture moved entirely within the framework of traditional Islam. Cooperation with the Western world, meanwhile, remained confined to the so-called practical disciplines. Despite certain undertakings of Muhammad II, such as his recall of the Greek population to Istanbul — which earned him the title of "The Philhellene" from the historian Cristobulus — and the presence at his court of Gentile Bellini, who left a celebrated portrait of the Conqueror, or Beyazed's suggestion that Michelangelo build a bridge between Istanbul and Galata, we must not assume that the Ottomans played a direct part in the European Renaissance. One development of great importance, however, was that the doors of the *madrassas* were opened to secular subjects. Culture, although essentially encyclopedic, like that of the late Islamic period, was rich and fervid, and Istanbul became one of Islam's major centers of knowledge where great libraries were collected. Alongside Arabic and Persian, Turkish became the third major Islamic literary language.

In Istanbul, enormous riches were concentrated, the result of the booty and taxes of the immense empire, which took on the role of a world power. Suleiman became the arbiter of the clashes between Charles V and Francis I. The Ottoman empire had made a cohesive state out of the Islamic world, which had long been broken up into a number of restless and often ephemeral political entities. Hardly extraneous — in fact, probably decisive in the plans and conquests of the Ottoman Empire — were commercial interests. Under Selim I, a new proposal was made to build a canal across the Isthmus of Suez, a project that was to be vigorously championed again in 1580. Toward the end of the sixteenth century, a Don-Volga canal was proposed; by crossing the vassal territories of the Crimean Tartars, such a waterway would have paved the way to efficient reactivation of the northern route to Asia. But, as Bombaci puts it, "while the Turkish Ottomans hungered after the envisioned profits, they never acquired the necessary spirit nor made an all-out effort." Their great navy was first and foremost a war fleet, and while for some time they enjoyed supremacy in the Mediterranean, their merchant marine was really negligible. In the Indian Ocean, in addition to the Ottomans' rivalry with the Persians, new competitors came to the fore. This was the era of the great geographical discoveries, and the Ottomans proved themselves to be well informed: the map of Admiral Piri Reis, drawn up in 1513, already included the coasts of America. The world had

suddenly become larger, and the "Isthmus zone" of the Near East began to lose its importance. At the very time of the Ottoman conquest, the Cape route was opened up, and the Portuguese navy was to become the ruthless enemy of that of the Moslems. As time went by, the types of merchandise changed as well. Shipments no longer consisted of small quantities of spices, luxury fabrics, gems, etc., but of large cargoes of raw materials, which obviously preferred the sea routes to those across land, which were slower and more expensive.

Following the reign of Suleiman the Magnificent (1520–66), the Ottoman Empire, although only gradually, entered the phase of "decadence," triggered by a number of internal and external factors. A key role was played by the grave worldwide economic crisis caused by the dumping of American silver onto European markets, which began between 1550 and 1580. The dumping led to an increase in the value of gold, while at the same time the expenses of the state grew by leaps and bounds and there was a drop in revenues. Agriculture fell into a period of serious disarray, and far-reaching social phenomena emerged: a powerful increase in the population, and a flight from farmlands, as well as a widescale outbreak of both isolated and organized banditry. But it was only toward the end of the seventeenth century that the Ottoman Empire plunged into its full-blown phase of decadence. This was when the structure of the state, which had remained essentially medieval, failed to meet the needs of the new Western dynamics. The lack of technological updating, the economic colonization of its resources by the great European commercial firms protected by the famous "unequal treaties," the maritime "asphyxia," to which was added the increasingly violent pressure from Russia beginning in 1700, all led to the long collapse of the Ottoman Empire that World War I merely brought to a conclusion. Nevertheless, that terrible conflict did leave a Turkey of the Turks, which thus became the sole Islamic nation of the Near East to have escaped

Bursa (Turkey): The Yeshil Turbe ("green mausoleum"), on the left, the sepulcher of Chelebi Mehmed (1421), with its distinctive lining of green-blue tiles. On the right is the Yeshil Cami, also of 1421.

Bursa (Turkey): Plan of the Yeshil Cami. The inverted-T design stems from the four-iwan Seljuk madrassas, a plan that was long to remain in use in Ottoman architecture.

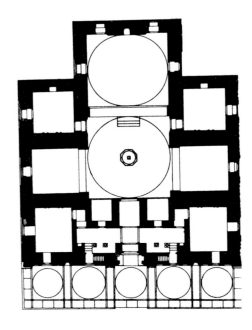

Istanbul (Turkey): A view of the Suleiman Mosque, erected by Suleiman the Magnificent between 1550 and 1557. It was designed by the famous imperial architect, Sinan.

MY COLORED POETRY

I am that master, maker of words, whose poems cultivated men of all the world inscribe upon pages of souls.

I am that poet-magician whose genius at times, with mysterious power, threads not concepts, but pearls on the thread of expression.

I would steal a hair from the locks of Venus shining in the sky if I wanted to thread upon it the regal pearls of my verse.

Thousands of inspirations are ready to be set down upon the heart, as soon as the agile pen touches my fingers.

While I write, the form of the face of my virgin ideas, with its excess of chastity, veils with wonder the eye of painters.

My colored poetry enfolds virgin ideas as a veil of scarlet silk the visage of a beloved bride.

If my thought, like an archer, sets hand to bow and arrows, it strikes as of a target the center, the heart of cherubs.

NEFI (born in Erzurum, condemned to death in 1635)

foreign domination — and also, ironically, the constraints of Islam.

In its common experience, Europe had long, narrow-mindedly, and in the end falsely, represented Turkey — first in the light of the fear inspired by the sultans' powerful, well-disciplined armies, and then in the nineteenth century with annoyance at a "sick man" whom the political-diplomatic game sought to make survive. But it should not be forgotten that the Ottoman Empire was a gigantic creation that existed for no less than six centuries, and which enjoyed moments of true greatness. Istanbul, the meeting place of Europe and Asia, resumed with the Ottomans its role as a "polar" city, upon which the wealth of the entire state converged. In little time, it became the center of a civilization of an imperial stamp, promoting handicrafts and artistic activities appropriate to the needs of a court and an ostentatious aristocracy. Standing out among the luxury arts were those of textiles, with the famous satins and silk brocades of Bursa, Istanbul, Amasya, Mardin, Damascus, and Chios, exemplified chiefly by the wardrobes of the sultans. There were also the carpets of the imperial workshops, the arms, jewels, and excellent polychrome pottery of Iznik (Nicaea), whose ateliers produced, in addition to a lovely variety of vases, some characteristic tiles intended for use as wall decorations. At the same time, a far-reaching impetus was given to the art of the book — calligraphy in particular was cultivated — and a place of foremost importance was assumed by miniatures. Although these latter never reached the splendors of the Persian school, they possessed originality; this was especially true of some of their realistic qualities and their choice of subjects, such as those treating historical or daily events. These latter provided an extraordinarily rich source, though as yet relatively little explored, for our knowledge of the usages and customs of Ottoman society.

Edirne (Turkey): A view of the interior of the *mihrab* of the Great Mosque of Sultan Selim, the masterwork of the celebrated architect, Sinan (begun in 1569, finished in 1575). It was erected by Sultan Selim II to celebrate the conquest of Cyprus.

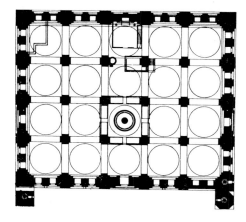

Bursa (Turkey): Plan of the Ulu Cami ("great mosque") begun by Murad I and finished by Beyazid I (1394–99). This is the type of mosque with a wide hall covered by a series of small domes resting by means of pendentives on pillars. A court is lacking, but it is nevertheless symbolized by a fountain for ablutions placed under a dome.

Edirne (Turkey): Plan of the Uch Sherefeli Mosque, erected by Murad II between 1437 and 1447. This represents the first approximation to the architectural realization of the imperial Ottoman mosque.

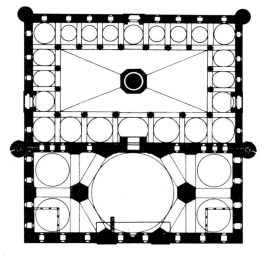

Page 160:
Istanbul (Turkey): View of the left side of the entrance section of the Mosque of Suleiman. Note the little tower that serves as a stabilizer.

Page 161:
Istanbul (Turkey): View of the main dome on its spherical pendentives, one of the semidomes, and an exedra of the Suleiman Mosque.

Ottoman Architecture

The Ottoman era was one of the most profuse in architectural inventiveness. Traditions were not set aside, but a liberal use was made of them, and with an open mind toward all. The Byzantine, Armenian, and Seljuk experiences were broadly and originally exploited, renovated by constant experimenting by a group of architects who were to produce their major representative in the prolific, brilliant Sinan. Even in the period of decadence, although the energy for large-scale works was lacking, the Ottomans' style came under the influence of European baroque in the eighteenth century, thus displaying an exceptional creative verve that blended its original angular syntax with new curvilinear geometry.

The origins of Ottoman architecture are to be sought in that of the Rum Seljuks and that of the emirates that had emerged after the Sultanate of Rum broke up. Especially influential among these latter were the Karamanids, the Germians, the Sarukhanids, the Aydinids, and the Mentesheids, whom we can only mention in passing in such a work as this. But the first phase of the Ottomans was marked by a reduction in the size of the monumental portal, which was redesigned to meet the needs of the facade with its windows removed. Primary attention was focused on the dome, which became the dominant element of the mosque. The wide, or hypostyle, type of prayer hall was to remain in use for some time. We have an example of this in the mosque of Isa Bey at Ephesus, the work of a Damascus architect, where we find the reintroduction of the court design, which in the Seljuk era had tended to disappear. Further use was made of the wide hall in the Great Mosque (Ulu Cami) at Bursa, which has no court and is covered by a series of small domes resting on great pillars that break up the space into so many cellular units. Taking hold, meanwhile, was the type of mosque with one hall covered by a dome, such as the Alaaddin Mosque at Bursa (1326) and the lovely Yeshil Jami ("Green Mosque") of Iznik (1378). These mosques are preceded by a three-arch colonnade, covered by miniature domes on vaults, which display a Byzantine influence. Especially in the Iznik and Bursa edifices, of the early Ottoman period, this influence is also revealed in the texture of the walls, composed alternately of stone and brick (whereas later more use was made of marble).

The Seljuk four-*iwan madrassa* model gave rise to an edifice with a design that has the appearance of an inverted T; often made up of two stories, the edifice was used not only as a prayer hall but also as a school, a monastery, a home for the aged, and a refectory. This type of building — examples of which are the mosques of Orkhan (1340), of Murad (1363), and the Yeshil Cami of Bursa (1421) — represents a finished, formal expression of complex functional needs, which are not absorbed by a single wall surface but must be indicated from the exterior as well. The architectural feature of the main *iwan* jutting out over the perimeter like an apse, and often fitted out with blind windows, was not improbably a result of Byzantine influence. The room corresponding with the court, a few steps lower than the others that face it, is covered by a dome with an "eye" (that is, a glass block) at the keystone. As a rule, the main *iwan* as well is covered by a dome, which is often connected with the ambulatory walls by means of the characteristic Turkish-type passages. In the inverted-T edifice, in fact, in which two contiguous domed halls make their appearance, the Seljuk tendency toward a type of hall longer than it is wide is continued. But, as Monneret de Villard has said, "All these solutions, interesting though they are, led to a breaking up of the architectural space and to a lack of unity and of a basic motif, with all its development, that is considered the aesthetic aim of Ottoman architects. With the second half of the fifteenth century, it may be said that these architects concerned themselves only with the testing of various solutions for a mosque with one principal dome, to which all the others, of much smaller proportions, would have to be subordinate."

The goal of the great imperial Ottoman mosque, which focused the expressive and architectural problems on the dome, was to be fully realized, however, only after the capture of Constantinople, when the Ottomans found in Ayia Sophia an inspirational model and produced the architect, Sinan, as an interpretive genius. An approximation of this architectural goal is represented by the Uch Sherefeli Jami of Edirne, built by Murad II between 1437 and 1447, in which the prayer hall, preceded by a colonnaded court, is made up of a massive dome on an octagonal base, flanked by two small naves covered by two miniature domes (a type still bound up with Anatolian antecedents, such as the Ulu Jami of Manisa, erected by the Sarukhanid Ishak Bey in 1374). The mosque founded by Muhammad the Conqueror in 1462–63 on the site of the Justinian church of the Holy Apostles has unfortunately been destroyed. But we know from descriptions, drawings, and from a copy Selim I had erected at Konya, that its dominant element was a great dome (83 feet in diameter), spreading out on the *qibla* side into a semi-dome, the whole included between two side naves covered by three smaller domes. This was the first large-scale attempt by an Ottoman architect, under the stimulus of imperial Byzantine architecture, to give the prayer hall a large unified space, although this had been tested on a minor scale in the mosque of Yashid Bey at Tire in 1446. Belonging to the initial phase of the mosque of The Conqueror (rebuilt in 1767–71, after a fire had destroyed it) was the colonnaded court covered by small domes, of the type

used in the Uch Sherefeli of Edirne and which was to become classic for the imperial Ottoman mosques. A more direct influence was brought to bear by Ayia Sophia on the mosque of Beyazed II at Istanbul (1501–6), in which the central dome was extended by two semi-domes, while the side naves are covered by three miniature domes. On the exterior, the volumes are sufficiently well coordinated, but the interior remains rather cold and empty.

An original interpreter of the lesson of Ayia Sophia was Sinan Agha, who was born near Kayseri in central Anatolia about 1490; although of a Christian family (from which he was drawn into the *devshirme* of 1512) Sinan early became Turkish–Moslem in training and spirit. He is the first

Left:
Istanbul (Turkey): The Mosque of Sultan Ahmed, the work of the imperial architect, Mehmed. Built between 1609 and 1617 for Sultan Ahmed I (1603–17), it was to have rivaled, in the intentions of the sovereign, Ayia Sophia. The only Istanbul mosque with six minarets, it follows the Seyzade Mosque in its architectural design: essentially a dome surrounded by four apses.

authentic individual architect who emerges from Moslem medieval anonymity, and he was without question one of the great builders of all times. Ascribed to him are more than three hundred and fifty works, and a mastery that greatly conditioned the generations of architects that followed him. Three works in particular stand out in his artistic biography, two belonging to his maturity and one to his vigorous old age: the Seyzade Mosque (1544–48) and the Suleiman Mosque (1550–57), both in Istanbul; and the Great Mosque of Selim II (1569–75) at Edirne. In the first of these, Sinan tackled the problem of an edifice with a central design, developing in monumental form a theme that had already been tried a quarter of a century earlier in the mosque of Fatih Pasha at

Diyarbakir. The Seyzade Mosque is covered by a dome some 60 feet in diameter, with the drum amply provided with false windows and resting on four large arches placed atop as many octagonal pillars and buttressed by four semi-domes, each of which broadens out into two exedras. Four small domes occupy the corners. The main dome turns out to be unusually light, forming a contrast with the exterior, which is rather massive, although its line is excellent, characterized by four small stabilizing towers anchored to octagonal pillars. Particularly elegant are the two "needle minarets," of a kind typical in the Ottoman world, a refined offshoot of the Seljuk model.

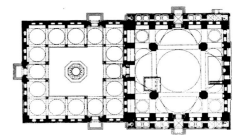

Istanbul (Turkey): Plan of the Seyzade Mosque, an early work of Sinan. The problem of the central plan structure was faced by Sinan by countering the force of the dome with four apses that extend into exedras.

In the Suleiman Mosque, founded by Suleiman the Magnificent, Sinan resumed the spatial discourse begun by Ayia Sophia one thousand years earlier, reinterpreting it for Islam in the concrete sense, creating what in many ways may be considered his masterpiece. In order to increase its monumental nature, the mosque was placed atop Istanbul's highest hill. It has been well described by Monneret de Villard: "The nave is completely symmetrical at its two ends, each of which has a semi-dome joined at the corners by exedras. The two side arches of the central dome are divided into three parts by two columns . . . so as to constitute three unequal arches, a larger one at the center flanked by two smaller ones. The side naves are covered by five domes, three larger ones and two smaller. The upper galleries, such as those to be seen at Ayia Sophia, disappear. The four large arches that hold up the central dome are well accentuated, whereas they disappear in the Byzantine prototype, with the result that a clear stress is laid on the structure's framework. Tied in with the aperture differences of the side arcades, this eliminates the sense of the nave given by the multiplicity and sameness of the side arches in Ayia Sophia, more effectively stressing the predominant value of the dome and placing it, as far as dimensions are concerned, with those of the rest of the edifice, whereas the architects of Justinian had exploited the partitioning of the side walls to create the illusory impression that the dome was larger than it actually was . . . . The lack of an apse in the center of the semi-dome on the south [*qibla*], an apse demanded by a Christian church but useless in a mosque, compelled Sinan to resolve the continuity and the union with two side exedras with the construction of an arch closed by a wall: this is the only weak point of his creation."

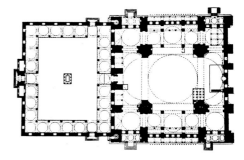

Istanbul (Turkey): Plan of the Mosque of Suleiman.

Sinan considered his Seyzade mosque as the work of an apprentice. In this mosque, the lightness of the dome was betrayed on the outside by the overhanging structures and the view of the *mihrab* was not guaranteed from every part of the prayer hall. Sinan, however, considered the Suleiman mosque a work of his maturity. With good reason, moreover, he felt that the Great Mosque of Selim II at Edirne, initiated in 1569 when he was 80 years old and completed in 1575, was his masterpiece. The edifice dominates the city from atop a hill with its harmonious profile stressed by four slender minarets. In this mosque, which Selim II had erected to celebrate the capture of Cyprus, Sinan once again took up in decidedly monumental forms the problem of the central design edifice and perhaps achieved his loftiest aesthetic result as far as the spatial effects of architecture are concerned. The dome rests on eight arches that distribute the weight onto as many pillars, lightened by sober panel-work; opening out from these arches, beyond the perimeter of the dome, are four exedras covered by semi-domes alternating with rectangular niches. The one in front of the entrance, containing the *mihrab*, deeper than the others, is covered with a canopy on a much lower level than the semicircular exedras. The prayer hall is within the octagon under the immense dome, which rises up lightly by means of ascensional dynamics stemming from the proportional harmony given to the mass of pillars. The extensive areas without windows assure a "solid" light, which reveals the splendid organization of the internal space. In a mixture of elegance and sincerity, the outside appearance bears witness in its wondrous expressive unity to the glory of the interior. The work of this consummate artist has been compared to the great architecture of the Italian Renaissance and reasonably so, although such analogies are difficult to prove. What is beyond question, however, is that the cult of

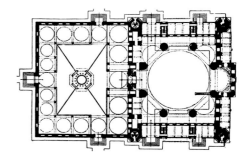

Edirne (Turkey): Plan of the Great Mosque of Sultan Selim II.

As I see the blandishments of an agile cypress tree, as shadow, I fall down at its feet. Starlike tears flow down my face whenever I see a lunar cheek . . .

If the All-Pitying will weigh me and my sins on the field of the Last Judgment, the scales will break.

If all my faults must be examined, the others' turn will never come . . . .

Today thou destined me to the fire of separation; interpose not tomorrow the flames of Hell . . .

Today I was not allowed that cypress-tall person, allow me tomorrow the tree of Paradise, Touba!

Since on this earth I was not allowed the ruby lips of my lover, tomorrow there let me drink the waters of river Kevser!

MESIHI (d. 1512, a poet of the classic Ottoman period)

harmony, which in architecture consists of geometric perfection, a devotion to symbolism in the circles and in the dome, as well as an almost puritan attitude toward decoration, characteristics that permeated the works of Sinan, also evoke the figure of such great Renaissance architects as Giovanni Battista Alberti.

The teachings of Sinan exerted an extraordinary influence on Ottoman architects for a long time to come. Nevertheless, these architects did not continue along the road indicated by their master in the Selim and Suleiman mosques; they preferred the model of the Seyzade, as in the Yeni Valide, designed by the architect Davud Agha in 1597 (but not finished until 1663), and in the mosque of Sultan Ahmed I, a work of the imperial architect Mehmed Agha, built between 1609 and 1617. This mosque, which in the intentions of Sultan Ahmed I (1603–17) was to have rivaled that of Ayia Sophia, was the last great mosque of the Ottoman classical period. Erected near the Hippodrome, it offers the best of itself in its highly balanced and imposing exterior, particularly if seen from the sea. Characteristic is its profile, with its six minarets standing out against the sky. The interior is rather weak, however, the spatial tension is minimal, and one gets the impression of a dissipation of energies. The enormous round pillars turn out to be far too massive for the dome, which does not appear to be especially elegant; its keystone is some 140 feet from the floor and its diameter is 75 feet. Three-quarters of the interior is lined with ceramics from the workshops of Iznik, whose production on an edict from the sovereign in 1613 was monopolized for this edifice; predominating are shades of blue, which have given it the familiar name, the Blue Mosque.

Ottoman Secular Works

The presence of the imperial state manifested itself by including these mosques in grandiose complexes of charitable and cultural institutions, with *madrassas*, hospitals, refectories for the poor — a typically Ottoman innovation — markets, caravansaries, and often even the tomb of the founder. The use of the Seljuk type was continued in the mausoleums, the sole change being that the dome covering was left in evidence. At this time, many thermal baths were also constructed, scores of which remain intact, many of them still in use. With only a few variants, the design falls into the following pattern: a spacious domed hall, square in shape, serving as a dressing room and meeting room, then a *frigidarium*, and lastly a *calidarium*. The tops of the domes are "eyes" made of colored glass imported from Venice. Two examples among the many available are the baths of Mahmud Pasha, finished in 1466, the first Ottoman *hamman* built in Istanbul; and the double baths of Haseki Hurrem, divided horizontally into two symmetrical parts, one for men and one for women, a work of Sinan in 1556.

The gorgeously opulent imperial palaces adopted the principle of construction aggregates, with courts or tile pavilions distributed within other courts or gardens. The palace in Bursa has disappeared and that of Edirne has been reduced to only a few fragments. But we still have the most famous one, the Topkapi Palace, built on the site of the ancient acropolis of Byzantium. It was begun in 1462 by Muhammad the Conqueror and completed ten years later. It was only then that Istanbul really became the seat of the imperial government. The history of the complex, which was a lively center of culture in addition to the residence of the sultan, identifies with that of the empire and includes a wide range of examples of Ottoman architecture. The various structures, built in different periods, are arranged around four great courts. Among the oldest ones is the Cinili Koshk, the "majolica pavilion" (1472), with its ceramic decorations vividly evoking Timurid models. The various rooms are located at the four corners and are served by a cruciform corridor surmounted in the center by a dome. The front is preceded by a col-

Istanbul (Turkey): Plan of the Topkapi Palace.

1 *First court, where the Cinili Koshk is located (but not represented here)*
2 *Middle door*
3 *Second court*
4 *Kitchens*
5 *Treasury*
6 *Hospital*
7 *Third court*
8 *Library of Ahmed III*
9 *Harem*
10 *Fourth court*
11 *Revan Koshk*
12 *Baghdad Koshk*

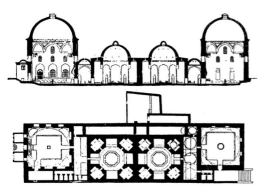

Istanbul (Turkey): Plan of the Haseki Hurrem double baths, the work of Sinan. One section was intended for men and the other for women. This type of bathing establishment derived from Roman-Eastern models; the baths that used thermal waters, called kapleji, *had a similar design.*

Istanbul (Turkey): Plan of the Cinili Koshk, "the majolica pavilion," so called because of its glazed faïence lining. Located on the outermost court of the Topkapi Palace, it is also one of the oldest structures of the celebrated complex. It has a cruciform design, domed in the center, with rooms distributed at the four corners; it is preceded in front by a veranda on talar-*type columns.*

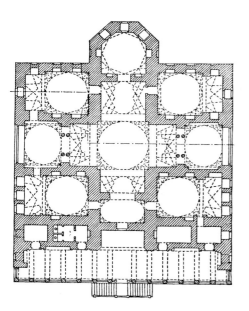

onnaded veranda (a *talar*) of a type familiar from its place of origin, Iranian-Central Asia, and which was long used in the architecture of private Ottoman structures.

Although the basis of the Ottoman state was agriculture, its economic dynamics remained tied to commerce. The entire territory was covered — thanks to interventions particularly on the part of the central authority — by an exceptionally well-organized network of caravansaries, the oldest of which, according to the most reliable dating, was from the time of Beyazed I (1394) in Bithynia; it was based on Seljuk models. The interior was enhanced by two enormous chimneys, a comfort not especially common in such structures and which appears to be alluded to by the name given to the building, the Issiz Han, "the smokeless caravansary." At the same time, a number of commercial structures were taking shape, such as covered markets — which in the beginning were intended for selling fabrics — the profits from which were usually used for the expenses of charitable and cultural works. The celebrated bazaar of Istanbul was built up around such a market, originally of wood, that Muhammad the Conqueror had built in 1461.

Aside from the building of the mosque of Ahmed I and the completion of the Yeni Valide, the seventeenth century saw the erection of no large-scale Islamic edifices. As a rule, the buildings were of rather modest proportions, and a certain tendency toward the miniaturization became evident, a development that also coincided in this same century with a new and more precise measuring unit, thus permitting more accurate designing. Outstanding buildings of the period are the Revan Koshk of 1635 and the Baghdad Koshk of 1638, both situated in the fourth court of the Topkapi Palace, their design a variant of that of the Cinili Koshk.

The opening decades of the eighteenth century represent a brief but particularly fine period for Ottoman culture, which gave signs of a lively renewal and of a clear-cut receptivity to reforms. Founded at Istanbul in these years was the first Turkish printing shop, and work began on Turkish versions of ancient and modern European texts. This period is known as the "Tulip era (*lale*), after the flower that became the typical element of this happy and winsome moment in Turkish culture. The tulip, which grows wild in the East, had been taken to the court of Vienna by Busbeck, the ambassador of Ferdinand I (1503–64) to the Sublime Porte, and had then spread throughout Europe, finding passionate cultivators in Holland, from where the fashion spread to Turkey, which became a fanatical importer and cultivator of the tulip on all social levels.

Architecture produced a series of monuments of no exceptional size but of excellent quality. Outstanding were the dwellings and pavilions, particularly those of wood (*yali*) on the shores of the Bosphorus. Among the finest structures were the fountains that in such numbers — in the eighteenth century there were more than one thousand — supplied Istanbul with water. They were of two types: wall fountains (*sebil*), which apparently made their appearance on the walls of the Anatolian mosques in the Seljuk period; and *chesmes*, the typical free-standing fountains of the great Ottoman cities. One of the loveliest examples is the fountain of Ahmed III, built in 1728 behind Ayia Sophia. It was of a square design, with protruding rounded corners, covered by a characteristic pyramidal roof extending out on all sides, and surmounted by five miniature towers. Particular attention was paid to the profiles and cornices with their sensitive lines, thus displaying a spontaneous willingness to profit from the baroque style arriving from France. Even though Western baroque and rococo influenced the decorations more than the basic structures, it was possible to note a positive effort to adapt and interpret the eighteenth-century French architectural language even in the plans, as for example in the Nuruosman Mosque, begun by Mahmud I and completed by Osman III in 1755, where the prayer hall, although conventionally square and covered by a dome, is preceded by a curvilinear court. An authentic little baroque jewel is the Kuchuk Efendi complex of 1825, also in Istanbul, with its oval hall serving among other things as a hall for the ritual dances of the Dervishes of the adjoining monastery. Compared to the sobriety of the classical period, the late-Ottoman architectural dec-

Istanbul (Turkey): The Fountain of Sultan Ahmed III (1728). It is one of the most representative structures of the so-called tulip period, when lessons from the European baroque were being spontaneously and sensitively absorbed by Ottoman architecture.

SCARLET MANTLE

A calamity with castanets between his fingers
has pierced my breast;
    Rose cheeks, scarlet mantle veined with
violet dark!
    My master has wound about his locks a
turban with lace and broidery.
    Bistre at his eyes, the lashes perfumed
with essence of geranium.
    I suppose by now he's fifteen years old.
    Rose cheeks, scarlet mantle veined with
violet dark!
    Ornament of roof-gardens, jewel of
embraces.
    His nurse had left him but a year ago.
    My love, joy of mine heart, wealth of my
life.
    Rose cheeks, scarlet mantle, veined with
violet dark!
    His ways, his manners, his smiles are
incomparable.
    His throat is scattered with beauty-spots,
his eyes are marvelous.
    Curly blond hair, silver neck, tidy
forelock, slender thigh,
    Rose cheeks, scarlet mantle, veined with
violet dark!
    Let me not speak of the suffering inflicted
by that fairy face!
    Let me not speak of the sighs and laments
of Nedim sick for love.
    Though I have said no ill of him, yet will I
not reveal his name!
    Rose cheeks, scarlet mantle, veined with
violet dark!

AHMED NEDIM (d. 1730,
the classic poet of the "Tulip Era")

oration is certainly more abundant, but it remains rather restrained and academic. The interiors, progressively abandoning luminous polychrome faience for stuccowork, ended with overloaded and capricious effects.

We cannot do better in concluding this brief look at Ottoman monuments than to use the words of Monneret de Villard, who, in stressing the fervor and tenacity with which Turkish architecture had pursued its aesthetic experiments, said: "For the first time in the Islamic world, we see an uninterrupted series of great architects conceive construction as a work of art and not as the repetition or elaboration of a given type of edifice. The Turkish architects had the courage to reject all traditional data: the prayer hall as a wide hall, its nave-structure, a particular axial layout, and so on. They conceived the edifice as a work of art with which they wished to test a spatial concept all their own, space being the only true architectural problem. This Turkish school, usually neglected or pushed into the background, must be reassessed in its rightful importance by all those who would have an exact concept of the nature of architecture and the nature of art."

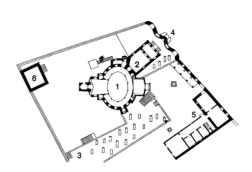

Istanbul (Turkey): Plan of the Kuchuk Efendi.
1 Oval hall for the ritual dances of the dervishes (lodged in nearby monastery)
2 Oratory
3 Cemetery
4 Fountain
5 Cells
6 Water tank

ISLAM'S FAR WEST: NORTH AFRICA AND SPAIN

Marrakesh (Morocco): Minaret of the Qutubiyya ("booksellers") Mosque, begun by the Caliph Abd al-Mumin and completed in 1196 by Caliph Yaqub al-Mansur. Excavations have brought to light a particularly interesting detail, comfirmed by an anonymous chronicle of the time: the presence in front of the *mihrab* of eight ditches on the ground of the oratory, from which the wooden panels of the *maqsura* — the enclosure set aside for the sovereign — were made to emerge. Remains of the mechanism used for this operation were also found.

Within the Islamic macrocosm, the Maghreb (North Africa) and Andalusia (Spain) represent a cultural unit with characteristics very much its own. These characteristics began to take shape primarily in the second half of the eleventh century when the area, already largely Islamic but turbulent and politically divided, was for the most part united in the name of a return to a purity of religion by a dynasty of recently converted Berber nomads. In Islam's far west, this dynasty, the Almoravids, was to play its role at virtually the same time as that of the Seljuk Turks in the eastern part of the *dar al-Islam*. With the collapse of the Umayyad caliphate of Spain in the first half of the eleventh century, numerous emirates contended for the territory of Andalusia, giving rise to large numbers of principalities, one always fighting with the other but all rich in a vital, refined cultural life, which had as centers not only Cordova with its famous library but also Seville, Granada, Toledo, Malaga, Saragossa, Valencia, Denia, and still others. This turbulent period — known in Spain as that of the *Reyes de Taifas*, from the Arabic *muluk al-Tawaif*, "king of factions" — saw the spread, through those parts of Spain that had remained Christian, of the spirit of the *Reconquista*, against which politically splintered Andalusia was unable to mount an effective resistance. In the end, the king of Castille, Alfonso VI, succeeded in gaining permanent control of Toledo, and in order to check the Christians' advance the Moslem rulers of Andalusia were compelled to turn to the powerful Almoravids, who had already asserted their authority over virtually the entire Maghreb.

The Almoravids — from *al-murabitum*, "people of the ribats" — were nomadic Berbers who had fought a holy war in the ribats, or fortresses, along the frontiers of the western Sahara. Under the guidance of their chief, Ibn Tashfin, they organized themselves into a vigorous state that adopted the aim of leading the Maghreb back to the proper religion; to this end, they founded Marrakesh in southern Morocco in 1061 as their capital. Meanwhile, the western Maghreb was overrun by the Banu Hilal, Arab nomads stirred up by the Fatimids of Egypt against their rebel vassals; although the invasion was to cause the region much additional bloodshed and suffering, it also had the effect of making the use of the Arab language more widespread. It was following this, the situation having become critical in Spain, that the Almoravids were called upon to save Islam by the Emir of Seville, *al-Matami* (who was also a fine poet). Except for the fact that they shared the same faith in Allah, there was nothing in common between the refined princes of Andalusia and the crude nomads of the desert who hastened to Spain under the orders of Yusuf ibn Tashfin in the name of a holy war and halted the Christian *Reconquista* in the memorable battle of Zallaqa (1086). In a short time, the Almoravids annexed Andalusia, eliminating the *Reyes de Taifas*.

But the turbulence of the Berbers quickly threw the Almoravid state into disarray, and its ultimate ruin was caused by the emergence of a new Moslem dynasty, it too composed of Berbers, hailing from Morocco's upper Atlantic coast. This dynasty sprang from a religious movement that repudiated the orthodox law schools and preached a return to the dogma of the absolute unity of God; for this reason it was called the *al-muwahhid*, "the one who professes the unity of God," which gave rise to our name for the dynasty, the Almohads. The movement was inspired by Ibn Tumart, who in 1121 proclaimed himself *mahdi* ("the one guided by God"), the sole interpreter of the law and tradition, drawing great strength from the fact that he preached and wrote in Berber. With the declaration of the holy war, Ibn Tumart initiated the conquest of the Maghreb, completed after his death (1130) by his disciple Abd al-Mumin. This latter was without doubt the greatest of all Berber military leaders; in 1160, he extended his dominions as far as Sirte, Libya, while in 1145 he

had embarked on the conquest of Andalusia. A fearless leader, he was also a wise administrator of his own conquests, which represented the only great Islamic empire ever formed in the west; the administration was centralized and the entire territory subjected to taxation. Abd al-Mumin assumed the title of caliph, setting himself up as a rival of the caliphs of Baghdad and Cairo, and managed to get a firm grip on his fellow Moslems, who were endlessly restless and desirous mainly of an excuse for a *jihad*. Since Abd al-Mumin compelled these populations to accept the hereditary prerogatives of his descendants, the next century or so was to see them wield supreme temporal and spiritual power over the immense territory making up all the Berber states and a good part of Spain. The Christians suffered a memorable defeat at Alarcos in 1196 at the hands of the third Almohad caliph, Yaqub al-Mansur (1194–98).

With the same rapidity it had arisen — and perhaps because of this — the Almohad dynasty began to collapse in the first half of the thirteenth century. The first blow against its prestige came from the victory won by the Christian forces at Las Navas De Tolosas (1212); Cordova itself broke away from Islam in 1236. In only a few years, numerous revolts flared up among the governors of other Almohad provinces, leading to the division of the empire into four states. In Ifriqiya (Tunisia), it was the Hafsid Arabs who proclaimed themselves independent, taking advantage of their distance from the central power, by now situated de facto in Seville. The Abd al-Wadits took over in Algeria, setting themselves up at Tlemcen (1235–1554). In Morocco, it was the Merinid nomads who got the upper hand, in the end establishing themselves at Fez (1269–1464); the Merinids attempted to maintain ties with Spain (1275–1344) and to reunite the Barbary states, but failed in both instances. In Spain, the Al-

Rabat (Morocco): The Mosque of Hassan, erected by the Almohad Caliph al-Mansur, apparently to mark the victory over the Christians at Alarcos in 1196. It was never completed. Its *pisé* walls, opening out by means of fourteen doorways into the immense prayer hall, form an enormous rectangle, 600 by 465 feet. At the center of the court on the north is a cistern, on an axis with the minaret. The court may have been surrounded by porticoes, extensions of the naves of the oratory; this is suggested by the bareness of the minaret's base, which the architects allegedly meant to cover with porticoes.

ANYTHING CAN I FORGET

Anything can I forget, but for the morning on the river when they were cramped in the galleys, like cadavers in the tomb.
 While the crowd covered the banks, watching those pearls float on the foam.
 All veils were fallen, no more was any chaste woman veiled, and the very faces were torn, like torn robes.
 Came then the moment of adieu, rose then cries of women and men from one to another the last goodbye.
 Sailed then the ships that bore them, on a wave of weeping, like camels driven on by the camel driver's cry.
 So many tears fell into the water, so many broken hearts those galleys bore away.

IBN AL-LABBANA
(d. 1113, of Denia, Spain)

Seville (Spain): The Tower of the Giralda, so called because of the weathervane crowning the statue of the Madonna at the top of the tower. The tower was originally the minaret of a mosque built in 1171 by the Almohad sovereign Abu Yaqub on the site of a minaret of the ninth century. The mosque was almost completely destroyed in the course of the construction of the Christian cathedral.

Following page:
Fez (Morocco): The court of the *madrassa* of al-Attarin ("the perfumers' quarter"), built in 1323. This is one of the most elegant and complete examples of the Mauresque style.

mohads were replaced by the Nasrids of Granada (1236–1492), who, subjected to an ever greater pressure from the *Reconquista*, ended by becoming vassals of the kings of Spain, until they were wiped out by the Catholic rulers, Ferdinand and Isabella. In the sixteenth century, all Africa, with the exception of Morocco, entered into the orbit of the Ottoman Empire.

The Moslem far west enjoyed an intense cultural life. Its center was Spain, where there was a particularly effective fusion between Islamic East and Christian West, a sort of symbiosis: the legacy of an intellectual movement born in the East was elaborated with originality in a climate of far-reaching intellectual freedom. In Spain, the way was paved for the transmission of Greek and Arabic thinking into Europe by such Andalusians as Ibn Bajja (died 1138) and Ibn Rushd (known to the West as Averroes, who won the admiration of Dante) — two thinkers who worked out a philosophy of the Aristotelian tradition that exerted an influence on medieval Scholasticism. Thanks to Jewish and Latin translations done in Spain, the West received an entire cabinet of knowledge, some forgotten, some new, with many different disciplines represented — scientific, medical, botanical, pharmacological, and agricultural. Particularly renowned is the treatise on ocular pathology by Ibn Zuhr (Avenzoar, died in 1162) and the *Guide to the Perplexed* of the Jew Musa ibn-Maimum (known to the West as Moses Maimonides, who died in 1208); the latter, a pupil of Averroes, was a physician as well as a philosopher. If on the whole the poetry calls to mind that of the classical Arabic variety, there is no lack of originality, especially in some of the rhymed strophic compositions that make extensive use of the colloquial and neo-Latin tongues, compositions that perhaps inspired troubador poetry. Excelling in prose was Ibn Jubair, with his travel accounts, while standing absolutely alone in all Moslem historiography was Ibn Khaldun (1332–1406), born of an Andalusian family at Tunis and a great sociologist as well as historian.

Islamic Maghreb remained fundamentally Sunnite and ended by rejecting heresies, whether that of the Kharijites — who isolated themselves in Mzab, Algeria — or that of the Almohads. It was a rather rigid type of Islam, but also capable of giving expression to a robust, popular religiosity of its own, which found support, as in the Seljuk world, in a sort of mysticism that developed a particular type of "saint worship," the *marabuts* (a distortion of *muribat*, "the ribat man"), which referred to combatants for the faith; the tombs of these latter became the object of great veneration, and subsequently there grew up around them *zawiyas*, or centers for the spreading and preservation of the faith, a development characteristic of western Islam.

Islamic art of the far west, also called Hispano–Mauresque in reference to the term *Moros* given in Spain to the Moslem invaders from Africa, was the original fruit of a crossbreeding of artistic traditions of eastern Islam, imported by the Umayyads, with those of the Moslem Berbers, on a terrain of ancient Roman culture veined with Visigothic elements. The inclusion of Andalusia, first in the Almoravid state and then in the Almohad empire, helped to spread this style throughout the Maghreb. The architectural lines were basically severe and essential, with a marked taste for compositions with clear volumes. Characteristic are the roofs of green glazed tile. The decorations are of sculptured stone and baked brick. Wide-scale use was made of molded plaster, especially for interiors, but also for the facades of the courts. In the mature Mauresque style, a particularly extensive use was made of faience mosaics, in white, brown, ochre, green, violet, and light blue, both for interiors, where they formed a high molding, and for the exteriors' panels. The decorative motifs are primarily of abstract, geometric arabesques, in addition, of course, to the usual bands of inscriptions. The *muqarnas*, imported from the east, was used widely, often creating, especially in later works, a strange impression of the interior of a geological cave. The horseshoe arch pointed at its keystone is the type most frequently used in the mosques, but rounded arches were also pressed into service, as well as still other forms worked out previously. Characteristic, too, was the use of the capital, which traces its form to the conventionalization of a composite Roman model.

The Reyes de Taifas

Among the most powerful of the *Reyes de Taifas*, the kings of the factions, were the Abbadids of Seville (1042–91), who decided to set up in their Alcazar an exceptionally brilliant court, in imitation of that of Cordova, in which men of letters and poets employed an elegant language embellished by the sweetness of Andalusian life. Since the culture of these small emirates, all indications are, was essentially secular, chiefly inspired by the religious skepticism of the classics, it is highly probable that their art was based on the same criteria; far too few traces of it still remain, however, to enable us to confirm this supposition. Worthy of mention in this connection is the small oratory of the Aljaferia in Saragossa, a palace that Emir Abu Jafar al-Muktadir (1046–81) had built. Outstanding in this structure is its decoration, inspired by that of Cordova but complicated by floral, geometric, and epigraphic motifs anticipating what was later to be known as the Hispano-Mauresque style. The walls of the simple square hall, once covered by an octagonal dome resting on corner niches, are virtually without interruption of any kind, so that the whole turns out rather heavy.

The struggles between the various *Reyes de Taifas* did lead to the development of an outstanding military architecture. The fortresses that served as the residences of the emirs themselves were modeled on those of the caliphs; they exploited the relief of the terrain and were reinforced by buttresses, oblong or semicircular towers, and barbicans. In the fortresses of this era, for reasons of economy, the freestone usually employed for doorways was replaced by *pisé*, a mortar of mud, clay, and gravel poured into forms, a practice that was also to be followed in the Maghreb, where it was typical of the indigenous architecture.

The Almoravids

The most impressive structures of these stern defenders of the faith were, needless to say, fortresses and mosques. These latter in particular provide us with an idea of the evolution of the Hispano-Mauresque style. Under the Almoravids, in fact, ties were strengthened between Spain and the Berber world — the one, as Marçais has put it, "a region rich in tradition and culture," the other, "rich in forces of combatants." The result was an exchange of artists and architectural models as well as of contingents for the holy war.

Still preserved in Spain are a number of mosques erected by the first Almoravids, but much more significant are the Algerian ones of the same period, the great mosques of Algiers, Nedroma, and Tlemcen. Their design, simple and severe, includes numerous naves perpendicular to the *qibla* wall, divided by pillars supporting rounded arches. In the Algiers mosque as in that at Tlemcen, we may note an intentional imitation of the Great Mosque of Cordova, with the presence, in Algiers, of two tiers of polylobed arches crossing in their full width the eleven naves of the oratory, and at Tlemcen, by the position of the middle nave and the *mihrab*, framed by epigraphic and polylobed friezes. At Tlemcen, as earlier at Cordova, a ribbed dome appeared, as well as a grilled window, which makes it possible to date at least this part of the mosque to 1135–36, the time of Sultan Ali ibn Yusur. Another dome at Tlemcen was built with *muqarnas*, which makes the mosque extremely interesting in that it alternates elements of Andalusian origin with others of eastern inspiration (Iranian, in this instance), and marks therefore an important stage in the evolution of the Hispano-Mauresque style.

A large part of the fortresses and defensive citadels built by the Almoravids have disappeared, but still to be found in northern Morocco are the outer walls of the citadel of Amargu (twelfth century) in unsquared stone, with a polygonal design, reinforced by round towers furnished

with a door preceded by a barbican. The same kind of stone was once again used in the oldest parts of the walls of Taza, in conformance with the usage of the Berbers (as in the structures of the Qala of Beni Hammad, at Ashir, etc.), and in the fortresses of Tasgimut (twelfth century), where it was already being used with *Pisé* in the Andalusian manner, which was also widely used by the Almohads.

The Almohads

During their century or so of power, the Almohads carried on building activity with intensity, including alongside the erection of religious edifices of great prestige, such as the great mosques of Marrakesh, Seville, and Rabat — the three capitals of the dynasty — numerous military structures and public works, such as hospitals, baths, and water conduits. Compared to the admittedly sober architecture of the Almoravids, that of the Almohads appears severe in its lines and downright poor in decoration, reduced as it is to only a few architectural elements or schematic floral adornments. In spite of the appearance of a number of motifs typical of the eastern Maghreb (such as *muqarnas* or enameled ceramic lining), the matrix of its patterns, whether in design or decoration, remains Hispano-Mauresque. In fact, due to the political unification brought about by the Almohads of all western Islam, their syncretic style — derived from the Almoravids, in turn derived from the Umayyads of Spain — spread in a uniform manner from the frontiers of Castille to the coasts of Libya and was destined to last long after the end of the Almohad dynasty.

While the most important religious and secular edifices arose in the three capitals, many minor centers as well — such as Taza, Tinmal, Fez, Meknes, Gibraltar, or Badajoz — still have reminders of the military and public works of the Almohad period. The oldest of these works — the mosques of Taza and Tinmal — appear to have been contemporaneous with the *mahdi* Ibn Tumart, whose tomb in his native village of Tinmal,

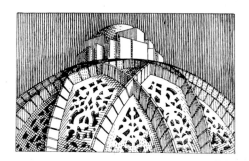

Tlemcen (Algeria): Drawing of the ribbed dome above the mihrab, *an Almoravid work executed under Sultan Ali ibn Yusuf.*

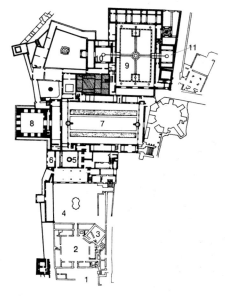

Granada (Spain): Plan of the Alhambra.

1 *Entrance court*
2 *First court*
3 *Mosque*
4 *Machuca court*
5 *Cuarto Dorado court*
6 *Cuarto Dorado*
7 *Court of the Myrtles (or the Alberca)*
8 *Torre de Comares and the Hall of Ambassadors*
9 *Court of the Lions*
10 *Hall of the Sisters*
11 *Hall of the Abenceragis*

quickly became a center of popular veneration. Although repeatedly rebuilt in the centuries that followed, these mosques clearly reveal substantial affinities with the great Almoravid mosques of Fez and Algiers, both based on that of Cordova. In other words, they are made up of a prayer hall with naves perpendicular to the *qibla* wall, with crossbeams supported by pillars and covered, in correspondence with the *mihrab*, by a truncated pyramid roof (at Taza) or by domes (at Tinmal). Also making its appearance in this latter mosque was a court bordered by two galleries, these being an extension of the oratory naves. Credit must go to Caliph Abd al-Mumin for having built the first "booksellers mosque," the Qutubiyya, at Marrakesh, in 1140, which was immediately abandoned because of its poor orientation and rebuilt several decades later (1195) in the same vicinity, but with an orientation that was even worse! This does not prevent the Qutubiyya, says Marçais, "from being considered one of the summits of Moslem architecture, due to the harmony of its design . . . the lovely views offered by its naves, the purity of its arcades' lines, the sobriety yet amplitude of its decorations, and the sovereign elegance of its minaret."

Contemporary to the second "booksellers mosque" was the construction, although never completed, of the mosque of Hassan at Rabat (1196–97). According to the chronicler Ibn Abi Zur, it was erected (with its minaret) by Caliph Abu Yusuf Yaqub al-Mansur on the occasion of his victory at Alarcos, Spain (1196), at the same time that he founded the city of Rabat (Ribat al-Fatah, "fortress of victory"), which he is believed to have surrounded with walls provided with monumental gates. The Great Mosque of Rabat has a rather enigmatic design, although inspired by ideals of symmetry, and has posed great problems for architects who have attempted to reconstruct it on paper. It was conceived in colossal dimensions — which is perhaps why it remained unfinished, like its minaret — probably to meet the needs of the numerous holy war participants who gathered in Rabat. The most important innovation of the sanctuary itself (a pillared hall with twenty-one naves at right angles with the *qibla*, and three parallel to it, as with the T-design familiar to North Africa) is represented by two rectangular courts interrupting the transverse spans, the function of which is not easy to perceive. It seems likely that they were intended to contribute to the illumination of the mammoth hall. Some twenty-five years earlier, the same grandiose criteria probably inspired the conception of the Great Mosque of Seville, demolished later to make room for the Christian cathedral; but the lovely minaret, begun in 1184, was transformed into the cathedral's bell tower, known as *La Giralda*.

The mosque of the Qasba of Marrakesh, built by Yaqub al-Mansur in 1196, has a design as strange as that of Rabat's mosque, although perhaps it was altered in later times. Its open spaces, represented by four small supplementary courts, arranged in pairs at the sides of the middle court, occupy the bulk of its entire area. The prayer hall, in the form of a T and with three domes on the transept, is made up of eleven naves at right angles to the *qibla* and two naves parallel to it. The minaret, situated at the northeast corner of the facade, does not have the large proportions of those mentioned above, although it is quite elegant and harmonious and has lovely faience decorations. All the Almohad minarets, as a matter of fact, while revealing analogies with those of the eastern Maghreb (Qairawan, Sfax, and Qala of Beni Hammad), reveal their derivation from the Umayyad minaret of Cordova. They were modeled on a watchtower, maintaining its square design and shaft, often with several tiers. They are crowned by a small lantern, or small structure, also square, covered by a smooth or ribbed dome (as at the Qutubiyya). The top of the tower, like that of the lantern, has crenellated battlements. The exteriors of the minarets are usually decorated with windows, cornices of small lobed arches, festoons, interlaced lozenges, and panels.

We know very little of the secular architecture of the Almohads, but in keeping with their spirit of religious austerity, it was aimed primarily at the erection of pious works such as *madrassas* or hospitals. The most numerous works of the Almohads, which we can mention only in passing, were those of a military nature, which they built throughout their empire. In addition to the extreme simplicity of their designs, the most characteristic trait of all the Almohad structures was the sobriety of their decorations. In reality, Almohad decoration, reserved for the framing of the *mihrab*, the dome, and minarets, was absolutely devoid of naturalistic motifs, with preference given to the schematized floral motifs — such as the Almoravid palm leaf reduced to a suggested profile — or to the use of architectural motifs — such as the polylobed, festooned, or canopy-style arch, perhaps derived from a combination of the pointed arch with *muqarnases*, already widespread in Tunisia. Bricks, freestone, and enameled ceramic were preferred for the minarets and monumental doors, stucco for the *mihrabs* and the lining of domes.

Granada (Spain): The Alhambra's Court of the Lions, built at the time of Muhammad V, second half of the fourteenth century.

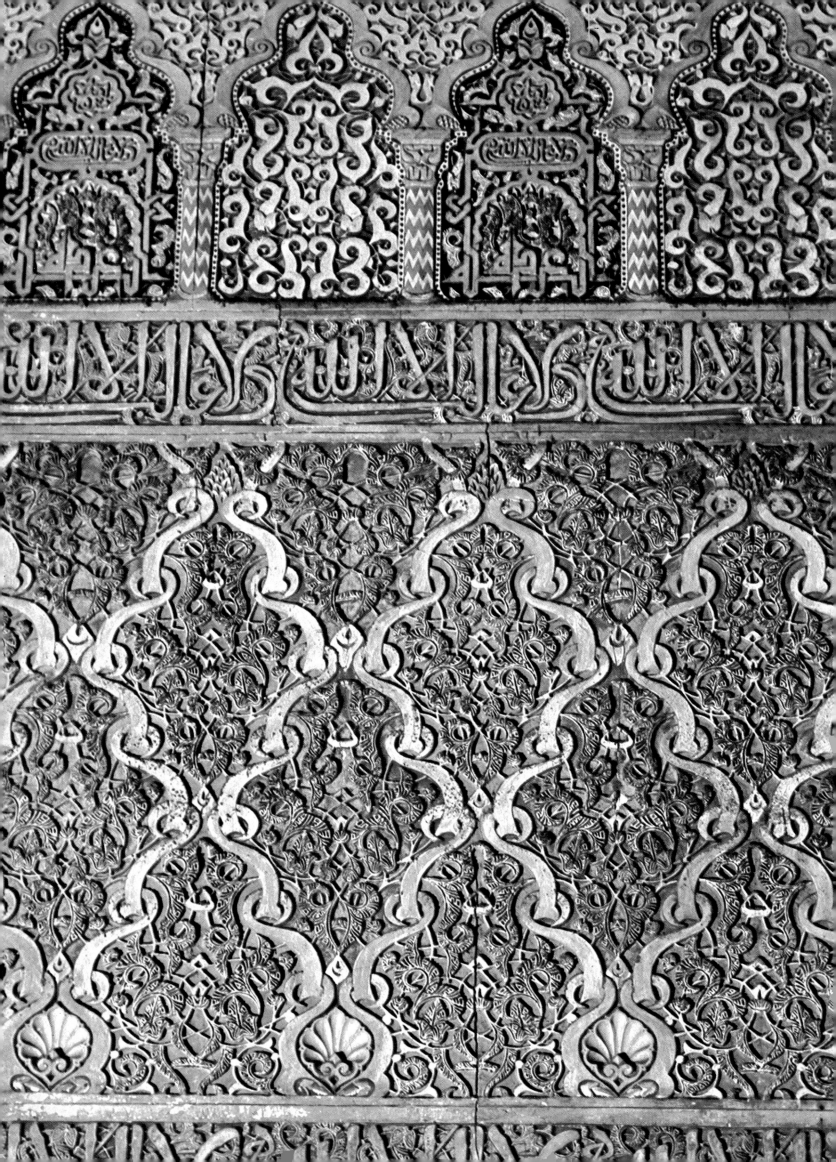

Granada (Spain): Close-up of a part of the sumptuous stucco decoration of the Alhambra.

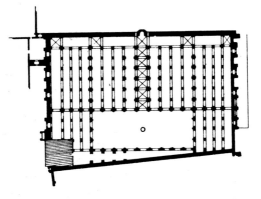

Marrakesh (Morocco): Plan of the Qutubiyya Mosque. This edifice has seventeen naves perpendicular to the qibla *wall; it employs the T design typical of the mosques of the Maghreb.*

Spain and the Maghreb: Thirteenth to Sixteenth Centuries

Of the various dynasties that began to divide up the Almohad empire in the first half of the thirteenth century, the most powerful from both military and organizational standpoints, and hence the most wealthy, was that of the Merinids, who set themselves up in Fez, where they built their new palace. Called Fas al-jadid, "new Fez," the city had a surrounding wall and later a Great Mosque (1276). It was with the Merinids, even more than with the Nasrids of Granada, that the apogee of the Hispano-Mauresque style was to be attained. Disdaining the decorative severity of the Almohads, the style was to lead to the triumph — and then to the decadence — of the Spanish and Maghrebian architecture that had been developing in the three preceding centuries. The dynasties of the Hafsids of Tunis and the Abd al-Wadits of Tlemcen, meanwhile, failed to equal the power of the Merinids, although in their structures they followed the same taste, often attaining their own unusual results.

Great builders, the Merinids erected a large number of mosques in addition to that at Fez, in other cities of the Maghreb such as Taza, Oujda, and Tlemcen. In the vicinity of this last-named, even while they were besieging it, the Merinids built the city-encampment of al-Mansura ("the victorious") with surrounding walls and gateway, as well as a monumental mosque virtually identical in its rigorously geometric design to that of Hassan at Rabat. The designs of the other mosques are rather simple, as were those of the *madrassas* that the Merinids also erected in such numbers, anxious as they were to spread the study of theology and law. The square court already seen at al-Mansura was to remain characteristic of the Merinid mosques, which also have prayer halls with naves that reach into the court and end in the back with a transept parallel to the *qibla* wall. The *madrassas* — except for the Bu Inaniyya of Fez, which harks back to the two Seljuk *iwans* at the sides of the court — are for the most part formed of a large central court, with a small basin surrounded by galleries and rooms for students, while a vast hall set aside for teaching and community prayer opens in the back.

The decoration of these edifices, in contrast with the simplicity of their designs, is truly sumptuous. The *madrassas* of al-Sarrij (1321) and al-Attarin (1323) of Fez, in addition to the small oratory of Sidi bel-Hassan (1296) at Tlemcen, may be considered as among the masterworks of the Mauresque style in the Maghreb. The decorations almost entirely cover the edifice's inner and outer walls alike and are for the most part of stucco, either engraved or painted. Cut into slabs and decorated with exceptionally low reliefs, stone is used only for the panels of the great doorways. Marble is used only in the cylindrical shafts of columns and capitals. Brick is used against a background of plaster and is in turn painted a dark red. Polychrome faience inlays form geometric interlacings at the top of the minarets or line the inner moldings of edifices or at times the shafts of columns or capitals. The ceilings are for the most part of wood, with lovely carved friezes divided by thin strips; in Spain, they were given the name *artesonados*. The windows have plaster grilles, with bits of colored glass inserted into them. The doors were lined with engraved, pierced bronze.

While religious edifices prevail in the areas dominated by the Berbers, the Nasrids who ruled Andalusia from their base in Granada placed great emphasis on their secular structures. Most expressive of this concern, in every way, are the palaces that comprise the Alhambra; these were erected successively by Yusuf I (1333–54) and by his son Muhammad V (1354–91) on a hill looking down over Granada. Their design, curiously irregular, perhaps owes something to North African models (such as the Qala of Beni Hammad). The Alhambra is made up of three separate units each joined around a central court. The two major complexes end in the Myrtle Court (*Patio de los Arrayanes*) and in the Court of Lions (*Patio de los Leones*). Also apparently to be ascribed to Yusuf I, in addition to the walls surrounding the palace, including numerous doors and defensive towers, are the salons surrounding the Myrtle Court (which is also called the Court of the Alberca, after the large rectangular basin, or *birka*, occupying its middle). The salons are the Cuarto Dorado and the splendid Hall of the Ambassadors, included in the Torre de Comares, and lastly the oratory and the baths. Believed to date from the period of Muhammad V are the structures surrounding the Court of Lions, which include the harem, a *rawda* (cemetery), and the audience halls, including the famous Hall of the Two Sisters, perhaps the most beautiful of the entire palace. Beginning in 1526, the Christian kings of Spain, especially Charles V, initiated the construction of another palace, never finished, and a chapel south of the Alberca courtyard.

In contrast with the sober austerity of the walls' exterior, the Alhambra owes its fame to the exceptional decorative opulence of its interiors. Not a few people, in fact, consider this the most perfect example of Islamic architecture, because of the balanced fusion between the simple design of its various buildings and the ornamental fancy at play inside. All the salons and courts, surrounded by arcades, are lined for the most part with plaster, sculptured, molded, chiseled, and painted in various shades of blue, red, and green, often with gold added, all producing a brilliant effect. The decorative motifs included a great variety of floral patterns, combined with arabesques and highly elaborate epigraphic friezes, arranged within panels, cartouches, or moldings. The ceilings often dissolve into intricate "beehive" *muqarnas*, or are formed by exquisitely wrought metal plates, divided by strips of wood. Functioning as a basic decorative element are the arches, usually of the horseshoe variety, broken at the keystone, with the interior curve formed by *muqarnases* or even brought out in rounded relief, the edges fine-toothed. At times, such as in the Lion Court, the arches appear to overlap one another, in that they form part, along with the columns supporting them, of two closely related patterns. Although no truly original element is to be found at the Alhambra, it must be admitted that its architects, and especially its decorators, succeeded in developing certain long-used forms to such a point that they endowed them with the appearance of unreality that was the ultimate aspiration of Islamic architecture.

The Mudejar Style

The term "Mudejar" (stemming from the Arabic, *dajana*, which has the double meaning of "settling somewhere" and of "submitting") has been used to indicate the work of the Moslem artists who, although the Christian reconquest of Andalusia had made them *vassalos moros*, were prepared to put their Moorish-Islamic aesthetic traditions at the service of the Christians. This art survived the fall of Granada by some three hundred years, although its original spirit, having lost its nourishment of Moslem ideals, began dissipating in both time and space long before that. The true Mudejar style — the continuation of Hispano-Mauresque art — is properly speaking a court art. The most significant monument in this style is the Alcazar of Seville, which was mainly erected under Peter the Cruel around 1364 (before, note, the fall of Granada). Although rebuilt in the centuries that followed (and all but ruined by clumsy restoration work in 1857), the Alcazar retains much of its original splendor. A number of Latin quotations from the Gospel of St. John and from a Psalm, alongside others in Kufic, celebrating the glory of Don Pedro confirm the composite nature of this Mudejar work. As in the Alhambra, the reception halls are arranged around a great central court, the Patio de las Doncellas ("The Court of the Maidens"), which was perhaps entirely redone by Charles V in the sixteenth century, in keeping with the Italian taste then in vogue.

Another typical Mudejar monument is found at Toledo, the synagogue that later became the Catholic Church of Santa Maria la Blanca. Probably originally established by a Jewish minister of Alfonso VIII (1158–1214), it was almost entirely rebuilt at the end of the thirteenth century because of a fire in 1250 that damaged it. The edifice was altered again in the

Toledo (Spain): Puerta del Sol (1375–99), an example of Mudejar art.

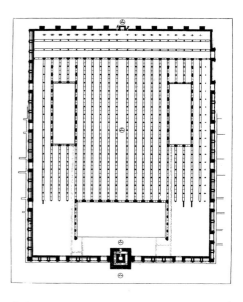

Rabat (Morocco): Plan of the Hassan Mosque. This mosque was of a rather unusual type, not only because of its colossal dimensions but also because of its two internal courts that break up the rhythm of the naves.

Toledo (Spain): The Church of Santa Maria la Blanca, formerly a synagogue, an example of Mudejar art. The edifice was founded under Alfonso VIII (1158–1214), but rebuilt after 1250. It has a wide-hall design and is divided into five naves and nine aisles, with horseshoe arches. The ornamentation along the naves above the walls connecting the arches calls to mind that of the Almohad mosques of North Africa.

centuries that followed; yet it still retains its original design, with a wide hall divided into five naves and nine spans, with four rows of heavy octagonal piers supporting massive horseshoe arches with sharply elevated peaks. The extremely sober decorations depend almost exclusively on capitals with floral motifs in high relief, and on friezes with geometric and floral interlacings on the walls above the arches, which vividly call to mind the Almohad mosques of Tinmal and Marrakesh, both built more than fifty years earlier. Also belonging to the Mudejar art of Toledo is a military structure, the *Puerta del Sol,* a great gateway that was erected in its present form by the city's bishop, Don Pedro Tenorio (1375–99); its design is based on the bastion towers of the twelfth century that jut out from a wall almost perfectly perpendicular to it.

In North Africa, meanwhile, after the decadence of the Merinids, the art and architecture moved into a period of inactivity. There was some resumption of building with the Sharifian dynasties of the Sadians and the Alawids, but by the end of the fifteenth century, the art of Islam's far west had become wearily repetitive. The most worthwhile achievements, although frequently falling more under the heading of folk art, are to be found in the architecture of the Sahara, such as that of the Ibadis of Mzab (Algeria) or in that of Black Islam. But if the zenith of Islamic architecture had been passed in this region, there were other quarters in the Moslem world — Safavid Iran for one, Ottoman Turkey for another — where high points were still to be attained. In any case, we have seen sufficient architecture and works of art produced by Islamic culture that qualify as among the great monuments of all civilization.

Seville (Spain): The Alcazar, a Mudejar work. Erected under Peter the Cruel about 1364, it was remodeled over the years, particularly under Charles V, whose coat of arms, is to be seen throughout the palace.

Qairawan (Tunisia): Drawing of the Bab Lalla Rihana, the fine doorway added to the Great Mosque of the Hafsid sovereigns in 1294.

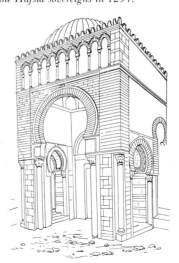

APPENDICES

The Islamic World as Seen by the West

The story of the relations between the Western and Islamic worlds is far too complex to recount here; we can only glance at a few aspects. For consider that the interactions go back almost to the beginning of Islamism — the Moslems had conquered most of Spain by 711 — and encompass a quite dazzling variety of forms. Just to single out one type, think of what is suggested by the various British "exotics" who have long related to the Islamic world — from Lady Hester Stanhope through Sir Richard Burton and Charles Montagu Doughty to T. E. Lawrence and Wilfred Thesiger. Even when we narrow the subject to the discovery and appreciation of Islamic monuments, the questions that arise differ considerably from those involved where the West has confronted other foreign cultures. For unlike these others' remains, and with some exceptions, the monuments of Islam did not await excavators to be seen and appreciated. Indeed, most structures have remained in active use throughout the centuries, and well within the range of Western vision. No, the problem has not been one of visual perception but of mental awareness, a matter of excavating through layers of Western prejudices. The free, unrestrained approach by Westerners to the art and archaeology of the Moslems has been deterred by several factors, two of the most powerful being a deep-seated, if not always conscious, anti-Islamic tradition in the West and the humanistic myth of the superiority of the so-called Greek miracle. The result is that the study of Islamic art and archaeology has been a fairly recent development; not until the opening decades of our own century has it been conducted on a truly scholarly-scientific basis. It is this aspect that we shall focus on here.

It is true, of course, that the excellent artistic and craft works of the countries of Islam were well-known and appreciated by the West in the Middle Ages: it is sufficient to think of the many objects preserved in the treasuries of European churches. Such admiration did not diminish in the highly refined Renaissance, even when Moslem art — at least in some fields and from several regions — was already well into, or at least entering, its decline. The Renaissance with its concomitant, the Reformation, represented a period of great intellectual ferment. To its east, Europe had to cope with a new political situation, the one determined by the appearance of the powerful Ottoman Empire — the second time, in fact, that the presence of organized Islam posed a menace. And it was in this framework that Europeans' interests began to broaden; a need was felt for more abundant information, with a greater emphasis being given to the civilizations of the East.

Thus, it was with the aim of confuting the "Muhammadan fraud" that a Latin version of the *Koran* was published in Basel, Switzerland, in 1543, edited by the learned Orientalist, Theodor Buchmann, known as "Bibliander." He worked with a version that had been translated at the beginning of the twelfth century by Robert of Chester for Peter the Venerable, Abbot of Cluny. This was followed shortly afterward, in 1547, by an Italian version, the first in a modern European language, printed by Andrea Arrivabene in Venice. It was in this same city, between 1518 and 1530, that the first printed edition of the *Koran* in Arabic characters was published — and apparently destroyed on orders from Pope Paul III. Not until the end of the seventeenth century was the first critical version in Latin brought out, the work of Lucchese Lodovico Marraci, published in three volumes in Padua between 1691 and 1698; it was the result of more than forty years of study and, significantly, was titled, *Refutatio Alcorani*. In case anyone thought the matter of prejudice was being exaggerated at the outset, such details point up the anti-Islamic tradition that permeated Western culture.

Meanwhile, the seventeenth century was also the era of those we might call "the fathers" of the archaeological recognition of the Islamic world. Among them were sage travelers such as the Roman Pietro della Valle (1586–1652), the first to note the cuneiform script. Despite the limitations of his training as a man of the Counter-Reformation, which often caused him to fall into traps in religious matters, Della Valle's *Lettere familiari* provide a vivid, charming, and even accurate picture of the countries and peoples with whom he came into contact — principally Turkey, Persia, and India. Another representative of these early travelers was the Frenchman, Jean Chardin; he went to the Levant, it is true, to broaden his knowledge, but at the same time, good merchant that he was, "*pour travailler à l'établissement de ma fortune*," as he puts it in the opening of his *Voyages en Perse*, published in 1683.

Antoine Galland's translation of the *Arabian Nights* into French, published between 1704 and 1717, opened the century of revelation of the East, introducing into the brilliant European society of the time a taste for turkerie, chinoiserie, and such exotic forms. In the second half of the eighteenth century, this fashion affected even architectural design, although one can hardly expect to find much fidelity, let alone of an erudite kind, in the capricious creations of the rococo period. For the most part, in fact, garden pavilions were the chief productions.

Another type of Moslem antiquity that was among the earliest to be studied in the West was the epigraphy. In 1790, the Sicilian Rosario Gregorio brought out what might be described as an anthology of the Arabic inscriptions of Sicily in his *Rerum Arbicarum quae ad Historiam Siculam spectant ampla collectio.* This was an ambitious, if immature, attempt at what was to be achieved, with consummate mastery, between 1875 and 1885 by the great historian of the Moslems in Sicily, Michele Amari. The first serious epigraphic work, however, was that of the Frenchman Reinaud, *Descriptions des monuments musulmans du Cabinet de M. le Duc de Blacas,* printed in Paris in 1828. For the first time, a book put before the public an entire collection of precious objects of Moslem art, and with a profound knowledge of the subject. But the work that in a certain sense represents the cornerstone of Moslem archaeology is the *Description de l'Egypte,* published between 1809 and 1828, the result of the systematic archaeological explorations carried out in Egypt during the Napoleonic expedition of 1798. (Its best-known find, typically, was from pre-Islamic Egypt — the Rosetta Stone.)

It was under the prodding of the new spirit of romanticism that the first works dedicated expressly to Moslem architecture or an entire region of the Islamic world began to appear, such as that of James Murphy, in 1815, devoted to Spain, *Arabian Antiquities of Spain.* The crisis of the Ottoman Empire, meanwhile, and Europeans' colonial exploitation of the territories of Islam opened the way to a whole series of works devoted to the recognition of the monuments of the East. During the nineteenth century, in the West, familiarity with Asia was to become increasingly extensive, but the time had still not arrived for a general or thorough understanding, even though the eighteenth-century "enlightenment" seemed to have exposed a number of systematic prejudices in the Western tradition. In the wake of the *Description de l'Egypte,* a series of large-scale works on Moslem architecture and other works began to appear in Europe, but the materials were to remain primarily an object of philological and antiquarian investigation.

Only gradually did Islamic culture take its place in the broader framework of European cultural appreciation. Alois Riegl (1858–1905), an art historian of the Viennese school, although not an Orientalist, produced a mild response by opposing the reigning philology and positivism and by combating the hierarchic distinctions in the history of art between "major" and "minor" arts. But Riegl's work paved the way for a more independent attitude toward the artistic output of Islam hitherto considered second-rate or decadent. And one can legitimately begin to speak of the history of Islamic art with the beginning of this century and the appearance of the works of Friedrich Sarre (1865–1945). With his broad range of interests and great knowledge, Sarre undertook the task of investigation and stylistic classification that had heretofore essentially been neglected.

Another outstanding personality in the field was Ernst Herzfeld (1879–1948). It is to Sarre and Herzfeld that we owe that consummate work on the investigation of Mesopotamia, *Archaeologische Reise im Euphrat- und Tigris-Gebiet* (Berlin, 1911–20, 4 Volumes). This work (to which Van Bercham also contributed) constitutes the first volume of their *Forschungen zur islamischen Kunst* ("Researches on Islamic Art"). We also owe to these two men, Sarre and Herzfeld, the archaeological excavations that were perhaps the most important in any Moslem locality, those of Samarra, the temporary capital of the Abbasids; this pioneer work made it possible to establish some of the solid points fundamental to our knowledge of the material culture of classical Islam. The opening years of the twentieth century also began to unveil the richness of Umayyad architecture, which was to come into ever sharper focus between the two world wars. Here, too, we should single out the British scholar, Keppel A. C. Creswell, whose prodigious labors and books on Islamic architecture, particularly in Egypt, are one of the monuments of modern scholarship. In another area, the origins of Islamic art, we might mention a work of fundamental interest, although it came out (in 1966) posthumously and incomplete: *Introduzione allo studio dell'archeologia islamica: Le Origini e il periodo omayyade,* an exceptional work on the history of art, by Ugo Monneret De Villard (1881–1954).

Today, of course, the subject of Islamic art and architecture is being approached from many fronts: the distinguishing among the individual artistic provinces of Islam involves the basics of classification; the publication of materials conserved in museums — ceramics, metalwork, ivories, miniatures, glasswork, textiles; architectural monuments are increasingly being discovered and described in remote or previously ignored places; and finally, archaeological excavations, although limited, are revealing still more of the ancient Islamic past. Fundamental to those goals are the works of such as Pope, Diez, and Godard in Iranian architecture; Marçais and Terrasse for the countries of Islam's west; Gabriel for the Turkish monuments; Herzfeld and Sauvaget for Syria during the Ayyubid and Mamluk periods. Another rich artistic province is Central Asia, the profile of which is becoming clearer thanks to the activity of a whole group of Soviet specialists, including Denike, Rempel, and Pugachenkova.

So much for the contributions of Western scholarship. But what of the roles and attitudes of the indigenous peoples and Moslem intellectuals with regard to the art of their past? India, which boasts one of the oldest active antiquity services of Asia — founded in 1861 — is rich in its Islamic architectural patrimony, although only a small part of this is known or written about in the various series published by the Archaeological

Survey of India. Meanwhile, Egypt is justly proud of its Department of Conservation of the Monuments of Arabic Art; dating back to 1881, it is one of the oldest institutions in the world set up specifically to preserve Islamic monuments. And there is no lack of Turkish, Iranian, Arab, or Pakistani scholars and specialists on Moslem art, although they are still closely tied to European models, not only technically but often ideologically as well. Some countries such as Turkey actively promote the study of their Islamic monuments. But elsewhere there is frequently a tendency, in practice if not in theory, to pay more attention to the pre-Islamic past, almost as if it were not "modern" to study Islamic culture. It is perhaps not far-fetched to see in this tendency the long-term effects of the colonialism of the "superior civilizations." But the newly found *esprit* among the nations and peoples that comprise the world of Islam should soon be reflected in the pride and study of their own monumental heritage.

Chronological Chart
of the Islamic World

DATES	ISLAMIC DYNASTIES & CAPITALS	EVENTS IN ISLAMIC WORLD	WORLD ARCHITECTURE
622		Hegira of Prophet Muhammad	532–63: Ayia Sophia at Constantinople
632–661	The Four Orthodox Caliphs Capital at Mecca	Period of rapid conquest: 635, Syria and Iraq; 638–40, Persia; 641, Egypt	625–75: Mamallapuram Temples, India
661–750	Umayyad Caliphs Capital at Damascus	669 (–800): Caliphs appoint governors of North Africa; 710–12, conquest of Spain; 711, conquest of Pakistan	685–705: Dome of the Rock, Jerusalem 706–715: Umayyad Mosque at Damascus
750–1258	Abbasid Caliphs Capital moved to Baghdad (762); then to Samarra (836)	786: Harun al-Rashid	785–987: Great Mosque at Cordova
756–1031	Umayyad Caliphate rules Spain from Cordova		
800–909	Aghlabid Dynasty in Ifriqiya (Tunisia), Algiers, Sicily		c. 825: Barabudur Temple, Java
819–1005	Samanid Dynasty in Transoxiana and Khurasan; principal centers, Nishapur and Samarkand		
868–904	Tulunid Dynasty in Egypt Capital at Cairo		876–79: Ibn Tulin Mosque at Cairo
909–1171	Fatimid Dynasty	Based in Ifriqiya to 972; rule Sicily to 1071; rule Egypt from 969 to 1171	914: First Cluny Abbey Church, France 950: Pagoda of Daigo-ji, Kyoto
932–1056	Buid Dynasty in Persia and Iraq		967: Banteay Srei, Cambodia
972–1148	Zirid Dynasty rule Ifriqiya		990–1012: al-Hakim Mosque at Cairo
977–1186	Ghaznavid Dynasty in Afghanistan, Khurasan, N.E. India Capital at Ghazni		
992–1211	Qarakhanid Dynasty in Transoxiana and E. Turkestan		

DATES	ISLAMIC DYNASTIES & CAPITALS	EVENTS IN ISLAMIC WORLD	WORLD ARCHITECTURE
1010–1086	*Reyes de Taifas* in Spain		1017–37: St. Sophia, Kiev (first Russian stone church)
1038–1194	Seljuks of Iran Capital at Rayy and Isfahan		1052–65: Westminster Abbey, London
1056–1147	Almoravid Dynasty in North Africa and Spain	1071: Defeat of Byzantines at Manzikert	1063–94: San Marco in Venice
1077–1327	Seljuks of Rum in Turkey		1113–50: Angkor Wat, Cambodia
1100–1215	Ghorid Dynasty in Afghanistan and Hindustan		Many Gothic cathedrals being built throughout Europe
1102–1408	Artuchid Dynasty in Upper Mesopotamia		
1127–1262	Zenghid Dynasty in Mesopotamia and Syria		
1130–1250	Almohad Dynasty in North Africa and Spain (1269)		1163: Notre Dame, Paris, begun
1169–1250	Ayyubid Dynasty in Egypt and Syria (1271)		1174: Campanile (Leaning Tower), Pisa
1196–1269	Merinid and Wattasid Dynasties in Morocco		1194–1260: Chartres Cathedral, France c. 1200: The Bayon, Cambodia
1206–1555	Sultanates of Delhi ruling northern India Mamluks (1206–1290) Khalji (1290–1320) Tughlaq (1320–1414) Sayyid (1414–1451) Lodi (1451–1526) Suri (1526–1555)	1206–27: Genghis Khan leads Mongols into Islamic world	1200: Begin Quwwat al-Islamd Mosque and Qutb Minar in Delhi
1228–1534	Hafsid Dynasty in Tunisia and E. Algeria		
1230–1492	Nasrid Dynasty in Spain Capital at Granada		1246–58: La Sainte Chapelle, Paris
1250–1517	Mamluks in Egypt Bahrits (1250–1382) Burjites (1382–1517)		
1256–1353	Ilkhanid Dynasty in Iran Capitals at Tabriz and Sultaniya		
1271–1516	Mamluks (of Egypt) rule Syria		1296–1434: Florence Cathedral
1300–1924	Ottoman Turks Capitals at Bursa, Edirne, and Istanbul		
1314–1393	Muzaffarid Dynasty in Iran and Kirman		
1336–1432	Jalairid Dynasty in Iraq, Kurdistan, and Azerbaijan		1333–91: Alhambra, Granada
1370–1500	Timurid Dynasty in Iran Capitals at Samarkand and Herat	1370–1404: Tamerlane's rule	
1380–1468	Turkomans Qara Qoyunla in Azerbaijan and Iraq Capital at Tabriz	1453: Conquest of Constantinople	1394–1413: Ulu Cami at Bursa
1428–1599	Shaibanid Dynasty in Iran and Transoxiana	1492: Granada falls to Ferdinand and Isabella of Castille	1420–34: Dome of Florence Cathedral 1440: Pitti Palace, Florence 1485–1523: Jami Masjid, Champanir
1502–1736	Safavid Dynasty in Iran Capitals at Tabriz, Qasvin and Isfahan	1520–66: Suleiman the Magnificent, Ottoman ruler	1547–61: Dome of St. Peter's, Rome 1550–56: Mosque of Suleiman the Magnificent, Istanbul
1517–1805	Ottoman Turks gain control of Egypt and Syria		
1526–1858	Mogul Dynasty in India Capitals at Delhi, Fathepur Sikri, and Lahore	1556–1605: Akbar, Mogul ruler of India	1550: Villa Rotonda of Palladio, Vicenza 1565: Humayun's Mausoleum, Delhi

Recommended Reading

The numbers of books about the architecture and art of the Islamic world have been fast increasing with the renewed appreciation of Islamic culture in many areas. This list is merely a selection of titles that complement various aspects of this volume. They have also been chosen on the basis of their accessibility, in terms of price, recent printings, and their attempts to communicate with the general public.

Arberry, Arthur: *Aspects of Islamic Civilization*. (Univ. of Michigan, 1957)

Arnold, Thomas: *Painting in Islam*. (Dover, 1928)

Aslanapa, O.: *Turkish Art and Architecture*. (London, 1971)

Bargebuhr, Frederick: *The Alhambra: A Cycle of Studies on the Eleventh Century in Moorish Spain*. (DeGruyter, 1968)

Brown, Percy: *Indian Architecture: Islamic Period*. (Vol. 2) (Int. Publ. Serv., 1968)

The Cambridge History of Islam: edited by Holt, Lambton, and Lewis. (2 Vols.) (Univ. of Cambridge, 1970)

Corbett, S.: "Sinan, Architect in Chief to Suleyman the Magnificent" in *Architectural Review*, Vol. 113, May 1953.

Creswell, Keppel A. C.: *A Bibliography of the Architecture, Arts and Crafts of Islam to 1960*. (Oxford Univ., 1961)

> *Early Muslim Architecture: I — Umayyads A.D. 622–750*. (Oxford Univ., 1959, 2nd edition)
>
> *Early Muslim Architecture: II — Abbasids*. (Oxford Univ., 1940)
>
> *Muslim Architecture of Egypt I: Ikhshids and Fatimids*. (Oxford Univ., 1952)
>
> *Muslim Architecture in Egypt II: Ayyubids and Early Mamluks*. (Oxford Univ., 1960)
>
> *A Short Account of Early Muslim Architecture*. (London, 1958)

Dimand, M. S.: *A Handbook of Mohammedan Decorative Arts* (New York, 1958, 3rd edition)

Du Ry, Carel J.: *The Art of Islam*. (Abrams, 1971)

Ettinghausen, Richard: *Arab Painting*. (London, 1962)

Frothingham, Alice W.: *Catalogue of Hispano-Moresque Pottery in the Collection of the Hispanic Society*. (New York, 1936)

> *Lustreware of Spain*. (New York, 1951)

Garlake, Peter: *Early Islamic Architecture of the East African Coast*. (Oxford Univ., 1966)

Guillaume, Alfred: *Islam*. (Penguin, 1954)

Hill, Derek, and Oleg Grabar: *Islamic Architecture and Its Decoration, A.D. 800–1500*. (Univ. of Chicago, 1965)

Hitti, Philip K.: *Islam and the West: A Historical-Cultural Survey*. (Van Nostrand-Reinhard, 1962)

Hoag, John D.: *Western Islamic Architecture*. (Braziller, 1963)

Jairazbhoy, R.: *An Outline of Islamic Architecture*. (Asia, 1971)

Jeffrey, Arthur, ed.: *A Reader on Islam: Passages from Standard Arabic Writings*. (Humanities Press)

The Koran: trans. by R. Bell (Edinburgh, 1937–39)

Kühnel, Ernst: *Islamic Art and Architecture*, trans. by Katherine Watson. (Cornell Univ., 1966)

> *Minor Arts of Islam*, trans. by Katherine Watson. (Cornell Univ., 1971)

Kuran, Aplullah: *The Mosque in Early Ottoman Architecture*. (Univ. of Chicago, 1968)

Landau, Rom: *Morocco*. (Putnam, 1967)

Lane, A.: *Early Islamic Pottery*. (London, 1937)

> *Later Islamic Pottery*. (London, 1960)

Lane-Poole, Stanley: *Studies in a Mosque*. (Verry, 1966)

Lewis, B.: *The Arabs in History*. (Hutchinsons, 1968)

Otto-Dorn, Katherine: *The Art of Islam*. (Crown, 1967)

Pope, Arthur: *Persian Architecture*. (Braziller, 1965)

Rice, David Talbot: *Islamic Art*. (Praeger, 1965)

Rice, Tamara Talbot: *The Seljuks*. (London, 1961)

Unsal, Beccet: *Turkish Islamic Architecture*. (Transatlantic, 1959)

Vogt-Göknil, Ulya: *Living Architecture: Ottoman*. (Grosset & Dunlap, 1966)

Vohwahsen, Andreas: *Living Architecture: Islamic Indian*. (Grosset & Dunlap, 1970)

Von Grunebaum, G. E.: *Classical Islam*, trans. by Katherine Watson. (Aldine, 1970)

Wilber, Donald: *Architecture of Islamic Iran: The Ilkhanid Period*. (Princeton Univ., 1955)

Recommended Viewing

Nothing brings the Islamic world into sharper focus than a visit to at least some of the monuments and centres of the Moslem culture — a possibility that lies well within the reach of many people today. The next best thing is a visit to a museum with a collection of Islamic art or artifacts.

There are fine collections in the following museums:

GREAT BRITAIN
  The Ashmolean Museum, Oxford
  The British Museum, London
  The Victoria and Albert Museum, London

U.S.A.
  The Metropolitan Museum of Art, New York City, New York
  The Museum of Fine Arts, Boston, Massachusetts
  The Freer Gallery of Art, Washington, D.C.
  The Walters Art Gallery, Baltimore, Maryland
  Cleveland Museum of Art, Cleveland, Ohio

In addition, there are many other collections throughout the United States — all are open, within certain restrictions, to the general public; they offer people a chance to start or to renew an acquaintance with some aspects of the great Islamic culture.

For specialized collections (indicated by their respective names), the following are outstanding:
  The Textile Museum, Washington, D.C.
  The Glass Museum, Corning, New York
  The Museum of the Hispanic Society, New York City, New York

Other fine collections are:
  Illinois: Chicago Art Institute
  Massachusetts: Cambridge: Fogg Art Museum, Harvard University
  Michigan: Detroit Institute of Art
  Missouri: Kansas City: William Rockhill Nelson Gallery of Art
  Ohio: Cincinnati Museum of Art
  Washington: Seattle Art Museum
  Canada: Toronto: The Royal Ontario Museum

Acknowledgments

The plans and drawings have been reworked by Giuliano and G. Battista Minelli, using those in the following works:
C. E. Arseven, *L'Art Turc* (Istanbul, 1939); O. Aslanapa, *Turkish Art and Architecture* (London, 1971); H. Brentjes, *Die Araben* (Wien, 1971); O. Brown, *Indian Architecture — Islamic Period* (3rd ed.) (Bombay, 1942); K. A. C. Creswell, *Early Muslim Architecture, I — Umayyads* (Oxford, 1932); K. A. C. Creswell, *Early Muslim Architure, II — Abbasids* (Oxford, 1940); K. A. C. Creswell, *The Muslim Architecture of Egypt, I* (Oxford, 1952); E. Diez, *Die Kunst der Islamischen Völker* (2nd ed.) (Potsdam, 1928); *Dizionario Enciclopedico di Architettura e Urbanistica* (Rome, 1969); H. G. Franz, *Hinduistische und Islamische Kunst Indiens* (Leipzig); A. Gabriel, *Les Anciennes mosquées de l'Iran,* in *Athar-e Iran* (1936); A. Gabriel, *Une Capitale Turque, Brousse, Bursa* (Paris, 1958); H. Glück, *Die Bader Constantinopels* (Wien, 1921); A. Godard, *L'art de l'Iran* (Paris, 1962); G. Goodmin, *A History of Ottoman Architecture* (London, 1971); E. J. Grube, *The World of Islam* (Feltham, 1966); C. Gurlit, *Orientalisches Archiv, I* (Berlin, 1967); R. W. Hamilton, *Khirbet al-Mafjar: An Arabian Mansion in the Jordan Valley* (London, 1959); E. Herzfeld, *Geschichte der Stadt Samarra* (Berlin, 1948); E. Kühnel, *Die Kunst del Islam* (Stuttgart, 1962); V. A. Lavrov, *Grados-troitel'naja Kulture Srednej Azii* (Moscow, 1950); G. Marçais, *L'Architecture Musulmane d'Occident* (Paris, 1955); U. Monneret de Villard, *Arte Cristiana e Musulmana del Vicino Oriente,* in "Le Civilta dell'Oriente," IV (Rome, 1962); A. U. Pope and Ph. Ackerman, *A Survey of Persian Art, I–IV* (London, 1938–39); G. Pugachenkova, *Iskustvo turkmenistana* (Moscow, 1967); G. Pugachenkova, *Samarkand-Boukhara* (Moscow, 1968); D. Schlumberger, *Les fouilles der Qasr el-Heir el-Gharbi* (Syria, 1939); B. Ünsal, *Turkish Islamic Architecture* (London, 1959); D. N. Wilber, *The Architecture of Islamic Iran* (Princeton, 1955); H. Wilde, *Brussa eine Entwickelungsstadt Türkischer Architektur in Kleinasien unter den ersten Osmanen* (Berlin, 1909).

Index

For their collaboration in obtaining photographs, we wish to thank especially:
Arborio Mella, Milan; Borromeo, Milan; Darbois, Paris; Michaud, Neuilly-sur-Seine; Ory,
Paris; Powell, Rome; *Réalités*, Paris; Roger-Viollet, Paris; Tomsich, Rome.

The literary and other texts translated in the margins are based on versions taken from
the following works, with the kind permission of the translators and publishers:
A. Bausani, *Le letterature del Pakistan e la letteratura afgana* (Sansoni-Accademia,
Florence–Milan, 1968); A. Bombaci, *La letteratura turca* (Sansoni-Accademia, Florence–
Milan, 1969); *Corano*, introduced, translated, and commented on by A. Bausani (Sansoni,
Florence, 1955); F. Gabrieli, *La letteratura araba* (Sansoni-Accademia, Florence–Milan,
1967); F. Gabrieli, *Storici arabi delle crociate* (Einaudi, Turin, 1957); A. Pagliaro and A.
Bausani, *La letterature persiana* (Sansoni-Accademia, Florence–Milan, 1968); U. Rizzitano,
Letteratura araba (Vallardi, Milan, 1969); G. Scarcia, *Letteratura turche* (Vallardi, Milan,
1969); G. Scarcia, *Letteratura persiana* (Vallardi, Milan, 1969).